3 0000 001 041 916

D1776900

# WITHDRAWN

**DATE DUE**

| FEB 17 1997 | | | |
|---|---|---|---|
| MAR | | | |
| APR 0 | | | |
| | | | |
| | | | |
| | | | |
| | | | |
| | | | |
| | | | |
| | | | |
| | | | |
| | | | |
| | | | |
| | | | |
| | | | |
| | | | |
| | | | |

# ADVANCES IN STRATEGIC MANAGEMENT

*Volume 11* • 1995   (Part A)

INTEGRAL STRATEGY:   CONCEPTS AND DYNAMICS

Proceedings of the Integral Strategy Collegium
Graduate School of Business, Indiana University
September 16-18, 1992

# ADVANCES IN STRATEGIC MANAGEMENT

INTEGRAL STRATEGY: CONCEPTS AND DYNAMICS

*Series Editors:*   PAUL SHRIVASTAVA
Department of Management
Bucknell University

ANNE S. HUFF
College of Commerce and
  Business Administration
University of Illinois

JANE E. DUTTON
School of Business Administration
The University of Michigan

*Volume Editor:*   HANS B. THORELLI
Graduate School of Business
Indiana University

VOLUME 11 • 1995 (Part A)

 JAI PRESS INC.

Greenwich, Connecticut                    London, England

Copyright © 1995 by JAI PRESS INC.
55 Old Post Road No. 2
Greenwich, Connecticut 06836

JAI PRESS LTD.
The Courtyard
28 High Street
Hampton Hill
Middlesex TW12 1PD
England

All rights reserved. No part of this publication may be reproduced, stored on a retrieval system, or transmitted in any form or by any means, electronic, mechanical, photocopying, filming, recording, or otherwise, without prior permission in writing from the publisher.

ISBN: 1-55938-957-5 (Set)
ISBN: 1-55938-958-3 (Part A)

Manufactured in the United States of America

# CONTENTS

## VOLUME A

| | |
|---|---|
| LIST OF SPEAKERS, PANELISTS, AND CHAIRS | xiii |
| FOREWORD<br>*E. W. Kelley* | xvii |
| PREFACE | xix |
| INTEGRAL STRATEGY: AN INTRODUCTORY SYNTHESIS<br>*Hans B. Thorelli* | 1 |

### I. REFLECTIONS ON THE HISTORY OF STRATEGY

| | |
|---|---|
| STRATEGY HISTORY:<br>THROUGH DIFFERENT MIRRORS<br>*Edward H. Bowman* | 25 |
| TWENTY YEARS OF STRATEGY THEORY AND<br>PRACTICE: WHAT HAVE WE LEARNED?: A RESPONSE<br>*Fred G. Steingraber* | 47 |
| DISCUSSION<br>*E. W. Kelley, Chair* | 55 |

### II. GLOBALIZATION AND THE LOCATION OF ADVANTAGE

| | |
|---|---|
| GLOBAL COMPETITION AND THE<br>LOCALIZATION OF COMPETITIVE ADVANTAGE<br>*Michael E. Porter and Rebecca E. Wayland* | 63 |
| DISCUSSION<br>*James K. Baker, Chair* | 107 |

## III. THE GLOBALIZATION OF AMERICAN TELEPHONE AND TELEGRAPH

THE GLOBALIZATION OF AMERICAN
TELEPHONE AND TELEGRAPH
   *Randall L. Tobias*     115

DISCUSSION
   *Richard D. Wood, Chair*     125

## IV. INTEGRATION OF A GLOBAL ENTERPRISE: THE SIME DARBY EXPERIENCE

ORGANIZING FOR INTEGRAL STRATEGY
FORMULATION AND IMPLEMENTATION:
SIME DARBY OF MALAYSIA
   *Tunku Ahmad Yahaya*     135

DISCUSSION
   *James A. Henderson, Chair*     143

AN INTERVIEW WITH TUNKU
TAN SRI DATO' SERI AHMAD YAHAYA
   *Hans B. Thorelli*     147

SIME DARBY BERHAD: A DESCRIPTION     155

## V. DYNAMICS OF INTEGRAL STRATEGY

BUILDING SUPERIOR CAPABILITIES FOR
SERVING CHANGING MARKETS
   *George S. Day*     163

ACHIEVING CONTINUOUS IMPROVEMENT IN
BUSINESS STRATEGIES: RESPONSE TO GEORGE DAY
   *Everett Shorey*     187

DISCUSSION
   *Kathryn Britney, Chair*     195

## IV. INTEGRAL STRATEGY AND CORPORATE CULTURE

CROSS-FUNCTIONAL TEAMS:
THE DRIVING FORCE TO CHANGE
   *Robert J. Hershock*     205

PRODUCTIVITY, QUALITY, AND CUSTOMER
SATISFACTION AS STRATEGIC SUCCESS
INDICATORS AT FIRM AND NATIONAL LEVELS
    *Claes Fornell*      217

DISCUSSION
    *Allen Paison, Chair*      231

# CONTENTS

## VOLUME B

| | |
|---|---|
| LIST OF SPEAKERS, PANELISTS, AND CHAIRS | xiii |
| FOREWORD<br>    E. W. Kelley | xvii |
| PREFACE | xix |

### I. INTERCOMPANY RELATIONS AND INTEGRAL STRATEGY

| | |
|---|---|
| THE ROLE OF INTERCOMPANY COOPERATION IN INTEGRATED STRATEGY: STRATEGIC ALLIANCES AND PARTNERING ARRANGEMENTS<br>    Kathryn Rudie Harrigan | 5 |
| INTERCOMPANY AND INTRACOMPANY COOPERATION IN INTEGRATED STRATEGY: RESPONSE TO KATHRYN RUDIE HARRIGAN<br>    Gerald D. Sentell | 21 |
| DISCUSSION<br>    Charles L. Bowerman, Chair | 25 |

### II. INTEGRATED STRATEGY AT GENERAL MOTORS?

| | |
|---|---|
| GENERAL MOTORS CORPORATION: AN ORGANIZATION IN TRANSITION<br>    Maryann Keller | 35 |
| INTEGRAL STRATEGY, THE AUTO INDUSTRY, AND GENERAL MOTORS<br>    David J. Andrea | 47 |
| DISCUSSION<br>    Hans B. Thorelli, Chair | 59 |

## III. INTEGRAL STRATEGY: BOON OR BANE FOR CONSULTANCY?

ANY ROOM FOR CONSULTANTS
IN THE BUILDING OF INTEGRAL STRATEGY?
    William S. Ferry     79

THE CHANGING ROLE FOR CONSULTANTS AT CIGNA
    W. Sanford Miller, Jr.     89

STRATEGIC DECISION-MAKING AND
TOP MANAGEMENT CONSULTANCY IN
EUROPE IN LIGHT OF THE NEW "EC 92" REALITIES
    Bo Arpi     93

DISCUSSION
    R. Kerry Clark, Chair     105

## IV. PANEL: IMPLICATIONS FOR MANAGEMENT EDUCATION AND DEVELOPMENT

INTEGRATING MANAGEMENT AND
MANAGEMENT EDUCATION
    Stephen C. Burnett     113

THE CUSTOMER: A RECENT GRADUATE
STUDENT'S PERSPECTIVE
    Derica W. Rice     121

PROFESSIONAL EDUCATION:
AN INTERDISCIPLINARY APPROACH
    Herbert W. Desch, Jr.     125

RECENT INTERDISCIPLINARY EVOLUTION
IN INDIANA UNIVERSITY'S MBA PROGRAM
    Jack R. Wentworth     129

DISCUSSION
    Jack R. Wentworth, Chair     133

## V. STRATEGY FUTURES

STRATEGY FUTURES: WHAT'S LEFT TO WORRY ABOUT?
    Dan Schendel     143

PANEL: RESPONSE TO DAN SCHENDEL
    S. Tamer Cavusgil, Conny Jägsander, and Charles Kitz     189

DISCUSSION
   *B. Heckroodt, Chair* ............................................. 195

## VI. POSTSCRIPTS

THE ECOLOGY OF ORGANIZATIONS
   *Hans B. Thorelli* ................................................ 201

NETWORKS: BETWEEN MARKETS AND HIERARCHIES
   *Hans B. Thorelli* ................................................ 229

THANK YOU ........................................................... 249

APPENDIX A: INTEGRAL STRATEGY: A MANIFEST ........................... 251

APPENDIX B: LIST OF PARTICIPANTS .................................... 253

# List of Speakers, Panelists, and Chairs
(Titles and Affiliations as of September 1992)

| | |
|---|---|
| David J. Andrea | Office for the Study of Automotive Transportation<br>University of Michigan |
| Bo Arpi | President<br>Arpi + Gibson/International S.A., Brussels |
| James K. Baker | Chairman of the Board and CEO<br>Arvin Industries |
| Charles L. Bowerman | Executive Vice President and CIO<br>Phillips Petroleum Company |
| Edward H. Bowman | Reginald H. Jones Center<br>Wharton School, University of Pennsylvania |
| Kathryn Britney | Vice President, Corporate Planning<br>Metropolitan Life Insurance Company |
| Stephen C. Burnett | Kellogg School<br>Northwestern University |
| S. Tamer Cavusgil | International Business Centers<br>Michigan State University |
| R. Kerry Clark | Vice President & General Manager, Laundry Products<br>Procter & Gamble Company |
| George S. Day | Huntsman Center for Global Competition & Innovation, Wharton School<br>University of Pennsylvania |

## LIST OF SPEAKERS, PANELISTS, AND CHAIRS

*Herbert W. Desch, Jr.*  Managing Partner
Arthur Andersen & Company

*William S. Ferry*  Vice President, Consumer Industries
Business and Policy Group
SRI International

*Claes Fornell*  Donald C. Cook Professor of Business
Administration
University of Michigan

*Kathryn Rudie Harrigan*  Graduate School of Business
Columbia University

*B. Heckroodt*  Managing Director
Transtrade Limited, Johannesburg

*James A. Henderson*  President and C.O.O.
Cummins Engine

*Robert J. Hershock*  Group Vice President, Abrasive
Technologies Group
3M Company

*Conny Jägsander*  Vice President
Bohlin & Strömberg AB, Stockholm

*Maryann N. Keller*  Managing Director
Furman Selz, Inc.

*E. W. Kelley*  Managing General Partner
Kelley and Partners, Ltd.

*Charles Kitz*  Director, Corporate and Public Policy
Planning
Chrysler Corporation

*W. Sanford Miller, Jr.*  Chief Marketing Officer
CIGNA Corporation

*Michael E. Porter*  C. Roland Christensen Professor of
Business Administration
Harvard Business School

# LIST OF SPEAKERS, PANELISTS, AND CHAIRS

| | |
|---|---|
| *Derica W. Rice* | Manager in Finance, Medical Devices & Diagnostics Division<br>Eli Lilly & Company |
| *Dan Schendel* | Krannert Graduate School of Management<br>Purdue University |
| *Gerald D. Sentell* | President<br>Tennessee Associates International, Inc. |
| *Everett Shorey* | Vice president<br>Arthur D. Little, Inc. |
| *Fred G. Steingraber* | Chairman of the Board and CEO<br>A.T. Kearney |
| *Hans B. Thorelli* | E. W. Kelley Professor of Business Administration<br>Indiana University |
| *Randall L. Tobias* | Vice Chairman of the Board<br>AT&T |
| *Jack R. Wentworth* | Graduate School of Business<br>Indiana University |
| *Richard D. Wood* | Chairman of the Board<br>Eli Lilly & Company |
| *Tunku Ahmad Yahaya* | Group Chief Executive<br>Sime Darby Berhad, Kuala Lumpur |

# FOREWORD

The key challenge of managers is to achieve a match between the capabilities of their organizations and the opportunities of the marketplace. This is basic to optimal attainment of objectives. The crucial factor in this perennial game of wits is strategy.

These sentences opened my foreword to the volume *Strategy + Structure = Performance*, edited by Hans B. Thorelli in 1976. Systematic thinking about strategy was relatively new at the time. Shortly thereafter strategic planning as a kind of interdisciplinary function moved into the business world with a vengeance, from Strategic Business Units at the operating level to the bullpens of strategy at corporate headquarters. The trouble was that strategic planning only too easily degenerated into a formal ritual performed at regular intervals. Due to bureaucratization, planning of strategy too often became disconnected from the *management* of strategy, which, of course, is a continuous process, and one calling for the integration of strategic planning and its implementation. At least we learned the lesson that while professional planners may have their place, ultimate responsibility for any planning effort must be taken by those who are to implement the plans.

The 1976 volume represented the proceedings of a conference on Structure-Strategy-Performance relationships arranged by the E. W. Kelley Chair under the auspices of the Graduate School of Business at Indiana University. To practitioners and scholars alike, the strategic imperative of our opening lines remains as urgent now as ever before. The increasing complexity of today's business environment has induced a degree of specialization among managers as well as academics where the benefits of division of labor are constantly being threatened by the costs of suboptimization in both theory and practice of strategic management. In recognition of the need for an integrated approach to strategy among executives and a synthesis of the considerable work on the subject by scholars of diverse backgrounds in the last 15 years, the E. W. Kelley Chair at the Indiana University Graduate School of Business again arranged a strategy conference in 1992.

The Integral Strategy Collegium was based on an holistic view of strategy as a subject (see the *Manifest* in Appendix A). It was also founded on a conviction that this was the appropriate time to bring men and women of thought and action together, attempting to strike integrative bridges between practice and theory. The present volume, being the record of the colloquium, provides a measure of our success in this regard. Professor Thorelli, again initiator and general chairman of the proceedings, joins me in a profound note of thanks to all featured contributors as well as all other participants. In this collegium every member was indeed part of the program. Most papers have been revised on the basis of our informal discussions.

We are grateful to Dr. Gerald L. Bepko, Vice President of Indiana University and Chancellor of the Indiana University-Purdue University campus in Indianapolis, for opening the collegium and for his remarks on the need of integral strategy in university governance. Special thanks are due to the executives who took time off to chair individual sessions, including Messrs. James K. Baker, Chairman of the Board and CEO of Arvin Industries; R. Kerry Clark, Vice President and General Manager of Laundry Products, Procter & Gamble; James A. Henderson, President and COO of Cummins Engine; Fred G. Steingraber, Chairman of the Board and CEO of A. T. Kearney Consultants; and Richard D. Wood, Chairman of the Board, Eli Lilly Company, at the time, as well as the then Dean Jack Wentworth of the School of Business for his unstinting support.

*E. W. Kelley*
Managing General Partner
Kelley & Partners, Ltd.

Chairman
Consolidated Products, Inc.
and Other Companies

# PREFACE

The idea behind the Integral Strategy Collegium was the perceived need for more *integrative* approaches in both theory and practice to the formulation and implementation of business strategy. The theme is developed in the *Manifest* in Appendix A. The strategy in organizing the colloquium was itself integrative, in that a cadre of experienced executives, acclaimed academics and trusted consultants was represented both in the official program and among participants at large. In fact, we placed particular emphasis on making all participants take active roles in the program. This is evidenced not only by the abstracts of discussions after the introductory presentation, but also by the fact that most authors incorporated ideas from these discussions in the final versions of their papers presented.

As background to collegium discussions the formal presentations examined the historical role, present practice as well as theory, and future implications in the strategy area. We have tried to achieve a degree of integration of the various papers and discussions from the viewpoint of the overall theme, in two different ways. The record of each collegium session is preceded by a note from the Editor. Further, the introductory essay, *Integral Strategy: An Introductory Synthesis*, sets the stage for this volume and attempts both to summarize and integrate collegium proceedings. The two *Postscripts* by the Editor, together with the *Manifest*, furnish the overall theme underlying the initial integrative summary.

The discussions following the formal presentations and panels are necessarily reported in condensed form. As noted, many points raised in the debates were later incorporated by the authors of the papers. Nevertheless, we hope to have distilled the essence of these proceedings. To assist readers interested in special subjects, we have made liberal use of *italics* to highlight topics and points raised. Readers should note that the contributions reflect the thinking and challenges of the speakers in September 1992.

This volume would not be possible without the dedication and commitment of the authors. We gratefully acknowledge the thoughtful *original papers* presented by distinguished executives and scholars, by panelists and respondents. Proceedings were also enriched by a number of chairpersons and panelists who agreed to serve in these roles on an impromptu basis. Special thanks go to the 60 additional participants who did so much to enrich our open discussions.

An affair such as this collegium demands a great deal of organizing and administrative input. Personal thanks are extended to Dr. Sarah V. Thorelli for her ideas in the planning effort, and to Mrs. Ruth Teh who served both as executive and editorial assistant. It was a pleasure to work with two talented MBAs, Mark Schloegel and Dale Richardson, whose administrative and editorial contributions were essential.

Finally, on behalf of the School of Business, and as general chair of the colloquium, I wish to extend our sincere appreciation to E. W. Kelley for his personal interest in as well as financial sponsorship of the Integral Strategy Collegium.

*Hans B. Thorelli*
Distinguished Professor of Business
Administration Emeritus
(Former E. W. Kelley Professor)

# INTEGRAL STRATEGY: AN INTRODUCTORY SYNTHESIS

Hans B. Thorelli

Concept of Strategy ............................................... 2
Hierarchy of Objectives and Strategies ............................ 4
Objectives, Vision, Mission ....................................... 4
Leadership ........................................................ 5
Corporate Culture ................................................. 5
Strategy as Process ............................................... 6
Organization Structure ............................................ 7
Information Technology and Organization ........................... 8
Competitive Advantage ............................................. 9
Cooperative Advantage: networks, Strategic Alliances, and so forth ... 10
Consulting and Educational Implications .......................... 11
Future of Integral Strategy ....................................... 14
   Why integral strategy?; Strategy change with speed; Changing organization structures; Coordination of the MNC; The value added chain and scope decisions; Accounting for strategic management; The tentalizing toolbox of strategic management; Research technology; Research aims and the practice of integral strategy

The purpose of this introduction is to provide an integrative perspective of the contributions to this volume and of the Integral Strategy Collegium on which the volume is based. The need for integral strategy is developed in the collegium Manifest (Appendix A). The need was also recognized in the predecessor symposium of 1975 and in the subsequent book, *Strategy + Structure = Performance*, cited in the notes.

The concept of strategy is certainly a multifaceted one, as amply demonstrated by speakers and discussants at the collegium. There is a risk, however, that a reader exploring this volume in staccato fashion may get a fragmented impression. This paper is an attempt to forestall such an impression.

## CONCEPT OF STRATEGY

One initial difficulty is that there is no real consensus of what is meant by the word strategy. For purposes of this essay we shall apply the concept embodied in the organizational ecology paradigm presented in the last article. In this contextual view, the organization is surrounded by various layers of environment. The significance of any one layer is determined by its relevance to the fulfillment of actual or potential objectives of the organization. When the term strategy is used, it typically refers to the [*intentional*] *interaction of the organization and its environment, utilizing the* [*perceived*] *competitive and/or cooperative advantage of the organization.* It is crucial to note that no simple environmental determinism is at work here. We are dealing with *environmental probabilism*. In any given context a number of more or less efficacious strategies are feasible. As the future is never fully known, the strategist eager to follow environmental signals may well pick a much less than optimal strategy. Further, rather than kowtow to the environment the organization may deliberately pursue a strategy as *change agent*, that is, "resetting the environmental parameters." Moreover, decisionmakers in the environment, customers, suppliers, competitors and governments, play the key roles here (Porter).* They are pursuing their own strategies, which may match but may well be on a collision course with the strategy of our focal organization.

At the level of detail, we refer to strategy as *intentional*, as it implies aiming at the attainment of one or more objectives. We say "utilizing" *advantage*; however, one important strategic objective is often the maintenance or (re-) building of advantage. Indeed, in the "futures" paper, strategy is primarily concerned with advantage (Schendel).[1] The advantage is that perceived by the organization; however, the organization may have misperceived its relative advantage. In this era of networking we self-evidently include *cooperative* as well as competitive advantage.

---

*Here and in the following, last names within parentheses refer to collegium session.

As the collegium proceeded, the notion of *integral* strategy became increasingly crystallized. A crucial ingredient is *synergy*, that is, the mutually reenforcing effect resulting from the integration of functional or other "partial" or subordinate strategies. This concept goes considerably beyond the "mix" concept typically used, for example, in marketing textbooks. Without the synergy element any mix of functional strategies is likely to be suboptimal and lack internal consistency. Hence integral strategy is more than merely interfunctional and interdisciplinary. Integral strategy also implies the *fusion of the content and process elements of strategy*, as opposed to the bifurcation of these elements frequently found in academic writings as well as in practice.

Should the going get rough in its current environment, or better opportunities beckon, the organization may simply change its *scope*, that is, any one or any combination of the five key variables that define the concept of a business (or any other) organization, namely:

*Product* (or service) offered
*Functions* performed in the value added chain
*Clientele*
*Territory*
*Time* (and timing)

In other words, chameleon-like the organization may trade in its old environment for a new one. It should be clear that *choice* and *change* are crucial to strategy formulation. Note that scope is Janus-faced: It defines not only the concept of the business, but also the environment where it chooses to operate. Note, too, that in shaping company strategy, in-depth analysis of scope greatly facilitates the identification of synergistic opportunities, as well as directions of growth.

The borders between the organization and the environment, always a gray area, are becoming increasingly fluid. Thus, we may speak of interorganizational strategy (Harrigan), or *network strategy* (overall strategy of an organization of organizations). As most organizations are themselves agglomerations of subunits, such as overseas subsidiaries, strategic business units (SBU), functional departments, and so forth, it follows that intra-organizational strategy between headquarters and subunits, and between subunits, is of major importance (Day, Shorey, Sentell). So are strategies pursued by subunits interacting with their environments. Actually, the integral strategy imperative often is especially relevant in the *intra-organizational* context.

## HIERARCHY OF OBJECTIVES AND STRATEGIES

Herbert A. Simon has drawn our attention to levels of strategy in another important sense, that is, *the hierarchy of objectives and strategies*. The underlying assumption is that a strategy represents the key means to reach an objective. Assuming further that objectives exist at all levels from the chief executive to the mail clerk or the worker on the factory floor, it follows that a more or less interlocking hierarchy of objectives from top to bottom obtains. To the hierarchy of objectives corresponds a hierarchy of strategies. Indeed, as one goes from the objective at level 1 (the top), the strategy to reach the level 1 objective becomes the objective of level 2, and so on.

Note that the notion of hierarchy of objectives takes on full validity only in the case of integral strategy. If strategies at different levels are "out of sync" there is no guarantee that the overall strategy of the organization will actually be implemented as planned. How many "degrees of freedom" any given level can or should have in designing its strategy to reenforce the overall strategy (and vice versa) is a major point of debate (Hershock, Tobias, Yahaya).

## OBJECTIVES, VISION, MISSION

Objectives are ultimately subjective and intentional. As strategy presumes objectives, strategy, too, is *intentional*. The question arises, how do we ensure that the subordinate strategies chosen are oriented toward meeting overall objectives. Three overlapping concepts from the contemporary discussion provide recipes here: vision (or mission), motivation, and company culture. Vision has been variously described as an image of the future (M. L. King: "I have a dream."), as a source of inspiration and motivation. The formulation and dissemination of vision to make sure it becomes *shared* by all is often said to be the key role of leadership. J.C. Penney, going blind at 90, is stated to have said in addressing an audience, "I apologize, I don't see very well—but I *do* have vision." However, the role of the concept is not free from controversy; incoming IBM Chairman Louis V. Gerstner, Jr. stated at an analyst conference on July 17, 1993 that "what I'd like to say to all of you is that the last thing IBM needs right now is vision." (Gerstner half a year later came out with some clearly visionary statements.) About a year earlier, President Bush volunteered he was not very adept at "that vision thing." That even visions need to adapt to changing times—and be in tune with the times—is illustrated by a comparison of the performance in the last half of the eighties of GM, IBM, and Sears on one hand and General Electric, ABB, Wal-Mart and Microsoft on the other. All these companies had articulated visions.

Without for a moment denying that an inspiring vision (or "dream") may have a crucial role to play, we prefer the idea of *mission* as less emotionally charged. Mission has three major components: company philosophy, business concept (scope), and objectives. The philosophy embraces such values as attitude towards risk-taking, growth, innovation, networking, diversification, outsourcing, empowerment, and so forth, and, importantly, ethical standards.

Scope was discussed above. Objectives to a fair degree are derivatives of philosophy and scope, short-term being more specific than long-term. Philosophy and scope are also vital in setting parameters for strategy choice and implementation.

Tobias vividly accounts for AT&T's changing philosophy toward engagements abroad, Yahaya for the Sime Darby philosophy about cooperation with MNCs based in industrialized countries, and Hershock sets forth 3M's philosophy regarding empowerment, motivation and cross-functional cooperation in the innovation process. Sharing mission is no less important than sharing vision when it comes to employee motivation.

## LEADERSHIP

Without getting into the endless discussion of whether all leaders have certain traits in common, and, if so, whether these characteristics are in-born, may be acquired, or contextually stimulated, it seems safe to say that leadership in general is changing in the direction of greater egalitarianism (with the notable exception of compensation). Autocrat and controller approaches are gradually giving way in favor of leader roles as mentors and facilitators, with a growing emphasis on selection, motivation, and development of associates, and increasing their involvement and participation in decisionmaking. Leaders who set examples as role models, sources of inspiration, and creators of a company culture of "orderly informality" are gaining increasing recognition. Academic deans, in particular, like to characterize their leadership role as "servants of the faculty."

## CORPORATE CULTURE

Every organization and every society has its own culture. "Culture" is a catch-all term, including the philosophy, vision, style of leadership and decisionmaking, formal and informal rules of behavior of organization members (such as the dress-code at IBM in the heyday of Big Blue), outlook toward cooperation with other organizations (the Not-Invented-Here syndrome vs. the 100-plus cooperative arrangements of Philips N.V.), and so on. Indeed, it is high fashion among management writers to ascribe any otherwise inexplicable phenomenon as an effect of organizational culture.

While cause-effect relationships involving culture are often quite difficult to document, there can be little doubt that the local culture has a pervasive influence on organizations and societies. This is especially evident in times of culture shift. At the societal level the freshest illustrations are the problems experienced by Russia and its current and former satellites in achieving some kind of transition from totalitarianism to economic and political democracy.

At the level of the individual firm, the restraining influence of an established culture at a time when a culture shift was clearly needed by the operating environment was amply demonstrated by our session on General Motors Corporation.[2] Glacial trends in corporate society at large may also leave their mark on the culture of individual companies.

Claes Fornell points to the truly awesome shift in performance measurement from an emphasis on quantity (productivity), via quality (as perceived by quality professionals), towards "ultimate quality," i.e., quality as perceived by the customer. A somewhat parallel shift in corporate ideology is the tenet calling for the flattening of hierarchy in order to favor the "empowerment" of individuals and groups at the level of action (Hershock). Philosophically, some observers might refer to this as moving toward "industrial democracy."

## STRATEGY AS PROCESS

At least a quarter of a century ago it was widely recognized that the process elements of strategy may be just as important as the content (Bowman). The Strategic Planning movement of the seventies realized that "strategy never ends," and put great faith in designing formal machinery for periodic reviews, and reformulating of overall strategy. An unfortunate side effect was a dichotomous separation of strategy content and process, when for maximum impact they should be viewed simply as parts of an integral concept (Schendel). Presently, we see at least two important trends at work here. First, an increasing awareness that properly conceived strategic planning must be a *continuous* activity in today's dynamic (in many industries, turbulent) environment, and second, that strategic planning, to eliminate an "implementation gap," must involve those employees expected to execute the plans (Steingraber).

Everett Shorey points to strategy as an *on-going learning process*, necessitating the greater involvement of managers at all levels, especially those who do not spontaneously devote their best energies to the continuous shaping and reshaping of strategy. In many organizations managers do not look upon greater involvement in this process as a form of empowerment, but as a kind of annoying breakaway from short-term implementation duties. In such cases top management has a real challenge on its hands, the challenge of motivating these colleagues, and to bring out their creativity. Above all, top management needs to convince them that their ideas do count, and that what is proposed is nothing less than giving them a voice in setting the parameters of their own future.

One of the key benefits of treating strategy as a continuous process is that it draws the attention to *continuous improvement* in all activities—*kaizen*, as the Japanese refer to it. This also helps satisfy the need for *time compression*, which is becoming steadily more pronounced. Indeed, many strategic opportunities are becoming increasingly time-specific—a fact reflected in the poignant phrase "strategic windows," used as early as 1979 by Derek Abell. We are now talking about the importance of *timing*. In the electronics industry, cutting the time from conception of a new product to its market introduction from, say, twelve months to six months, can provide a decisive competitive advantage. Indeed, the dynamics of even mature industries, for example, automobiles, are becoming more intense every year, as emphasized by both Maryann Keller and David Andrea in the GM session.

## ORGANIZATION STRUCTURE

Still staying with the organization itself, the collegium offered much insight about *structure*. Perhaps the emphasis on flexible structures was the single most important notion here; we might well speak of the *kaleidoscopic organization*. Prompted ultimately by the demands for integral strategy in an increasingly dynamic environment, the modern business organization presents a different face for different purposes. Thus we find the cross-functional innovation teams of 3M (Hershock), the platform teams of Chrysler (Kitz), the "fusion teams" of Black & Decker, and the Querdenkers ("cross-functionalists") of Daimler-Benz. Matrix organization, as practiced by ABB, by way of further example, at one time emphasizes local empowerment and at another, central or regional integration. A new emphasis on *process management* (Steingraber, Sentell, Shorey) is another integrative structural device.

Organization structure ultimately should serve no other purpose than formulating and implementing marketplace strategy. In this sense structure *is* strategy. In practice, however, it has generally been true that the two coincide only when the organization is *new* (Tobias). As soon as structure is in place vested interests and resistance to change typically set in (Keller and Andrea). The 1980s emphasis on restructuring, downsizing and turnaround management may be viewed as belated efforts to synchronize internal structure and strategy with marketplace reality. The emerging philosophy of kaleidoscopic transformation would seem to meet the need of strategic choice and change.

A kaleidoscope approach to organizational design may well be a station on the road toward the oft-touted *learning organization*. The constantly shifting organization places greatly enhanced demands on employee flexibility and skills. Training and retraining will be the order of the day for individuals subject to these demands, to technological change and to perennially changing sources of information and expertise. For employees as well as the organization it is becoming increasingly true that "learning is a life-long process." (The question is, Will we live long enough?) Naturally, human resource management must take the ability to learn into consideration in promotion and compensation plans. Properly conceived, such plans will have significant motivational effects (Session 11).

## INFORMATION TECHNOLOGY AND ORGANIZATION

The learning organization, the greater involvement in strategic design of managers at all levels, and the empowerment of integrative teams of various kinds—all topics discussed in the collegium—bring up issues of information acquisition (Day, Fornell) and organization. Although the interaction of info technology and organization was not a specific topic, some reflections seem in order. The new groupware (e.g., Lotus Notes) is likely to become a true bonanza for integrative teams composed of members in different physical locations. Groupware in many instances has also turned out to be a powerful creativity stimulant even among group members meeting in the same room. To a varying extent, similar positive effects may be expected from Local Area Networks (LAN), as well as Wide Area Networks (WAN) hooking up entire networks of organizations. In the early days of computers it was usually claimed that they would enable organizations to exercise more centralized planning and control than ever before. (To some observers, this raised images of Big Brother and/or invasion of privacy.) Without denying this possibility, it seemed to me then as now much more important that innovations of the type just mentioned make decentralization and delegation much more practicable than in the past. The same thing is true of such developments as relational (kaleidoscopic!) databases. Emerging multimedia technology is likely to make interpersonal interaction more intense, but may not otherwise have great impact on organizational parameters. Perhaps we may say that computer links more often than not will reduce the dominance of hierarchical aspects of organizations. Beyond this observation it would seem that info-tech is substantially organization-neutral; its overall potential is that of facilitating more effective information flow, exchange and analysis.

The greater challenge is probably the growth in the number of "bits" of information floating around freely like the "junk" in space. In the mind of this observer, the problem is still not one of "information overload." It is rather one of *information anarchy*. Notwithstanding the important efforts of corporate MIS builders, A.C. Nielsen, and Information Resources, the overall challenge of organizing available data in more meaningful ways does not seem to have diminished in importance over the years. Thus far, the information superhighway seems to be single-lane in both directions. From the viewpoint of the individual consumer, a good case can be made that information in the marketplace is more fragmented and disorganized than ever before.[3] We do indeed have quite a way to go before one is really justified in talking about the Information Age!

In some respects, it seems that info-tech and multimedia communications may have greater short-term payoff potential in education than in business (Desch)—provided, of course, that the educational community is willing to embrace the challenge (Grant in Session 10 discussion).

## COMPETITIVE ADVANTAGE

Turning our attention now to external strategy, we immediately face the issue of *competitive advantage*, a central ingredient of Porter's presentation. What the organization will consider as its prime source(s) of advantage must be part of its mission definition—whether the mission is well articulated or merely implicit. In any given case, the sources of advantage may be highly focused as evidenced by Sime Darby's reliance on its superior knowledge about several Pacific Rim country markets, and its attendant ability to secure local financing (Yahaya), or more broadly based, as in the case of AT&T with Bell Labs symbolizing technological prowess, great financial resources, and management skills (Tobias). Both of these otherwise dramatically different cases add credence to Porter's thesis about the importance of a "home base" in even the most global operations. One is led to conclude that *advantage is like a stock of capital* which is continuously consumed in a competitive environment, dynamically maintained or added to (Day). As the environment changes, advantage may even have to be transformed. The GM case in the two decades before 1992 evidences the perils of managerial misperception of first the transitory nature of competitive advantage, and second of how to rebuild it.

## COOPERATIVE ADVANTAGE: NETWORKS, AND STRATEGIC ALLIANCES

Networks, strategic alliances, and joint ventures may be viewed as macro-organizations (Harrigan and Thorelli networking article). An important initial observation is that networks, like firms, are also in competition with outside firms or other networks (Harrigan). A corollary is that at the network level—as well as at the level of participating firms—competitive advantage is essential for long-term survival. Clearly, members have to share their respective competitive advantages to a fair extent. At the network level it seems that advantage is usually the result of *synergy*, that is, the network can achieve something that individual member firms would have difficulty achieving on their own. The development of the Power PC microprocessor by the network IBM-Apple-Motorola appears to be a good example. Even if IBM or Motorola conceivably could have developed this processor on their own, it would certainly have taken a much longer time. And *timing* is of the essence these dynamic days: The Power PC arrived in the nick of time to be a likely serious competitor to Intel's Pentium. A related synergistic effect of the alliance is these three erstwhile hotly competitive companies together have an influence on the marketplace that in effect establishes a *standard* competing with that of Intel. For long-term survival a network of whatever kind must be a win-win proposition for all participants, although from time to time one member may gain more from the cooperation than another.

While most industrial economists have recognized the crucial role of *trust* among network members,[4] they have tended to give short shrift to the inter*personal* relations among the boundary spanners representing members. Network maintenance is an obvious task for middle management, presumably countervailing its often predicted demise. The relative stability of a network is contingent on minimizing the turnover of key liaison people (Harrigan). As in practice, this has been observed in runs of this author's International Operations Simulation/Mark 2000 (INTOPIA). In the middle of an extended simulation run, teams reorganize (at a minimum involving "musical chairs" rotation of executives). Frequently, however, teams will ask for an exemption of a member who represents it in one or more networks. They fear that a trustful relationship built up over an extended period might be endangered by possible misunderstandings and personality conflicts. Of course, that does not mean that top management from time to time should not ascertain that a solid win-win relationship is not degenerating into some kind of social club.

Companies may create networks for any number of reasons (Thorelli on networking). Two reasons have lately emerged as particularly significant: *outsourcing* ("vertical disintegration") and *learning*. In many companies, the 1980s were a decade of restructuring and "downsizing," and this "fashion" seems to continue in the nineties. Beyond simply tightening the belt in tough times, the strategy at work here emanated from a renewed urge to emphasize core competencies (Day). This could be done by selling off unprofitable lines of business. Typically, however, the movement went further, as firms were in effect repositioning themselves in the value added chain from mine to consumer. The outsourcing of components and delivery as well as distribution systems has become increasingly common. This has given rise to new niche-oriented markets at many links of the chain, leading some observers to talk about "the modular corporation." To survive these modules must fit into networks. The electronics industry is replete with examples. This dynamic industry also furnishes examples of networks being used in a seemingly opposite direction, that is, for entry into new businesses. Toshiba has been especially skilled at making use of its alliances with GE, IBM, Motorola, and Siemens to perfect technologies for new markets. Note in passing that many almost seamless networks have reduced transactions costs (in the Oliver Williamson sense) to such an extent as to make vertical integration look almost old-fashioned.

The second major force behind network formation is the urgency of learning referred to in our reflections on organization structure. The area of R&D and production technology is generally referred to here, and Toyota and Toshiba are mentioned as illustrating what many feel is an intrinsic talent of Japanese management to use networks with Western firms as some kind of sponges of information. The view taken here is that Western firms fairly often (in part for language reasons) have failed to grasp fully the opportunities that networks offer them as lodes of purely technical information. As the AT&T and Sime Darby examples demonstrate, Westerners have often resorted to joint ventures and strategic alliances to learn about local marketing, accounting, and human resources areas in expanding to unfamiliar cultures. Thus "technology transfer" is very much broader than "technical transfer;" it is actually more akin to *intercultural transfer*.

In the almost unbridled enthusiasm for networking in academic as well as management circles in the last few years or so, the point seems to have gotten lost that not all networks are for the good. Not all networks are necessarily "win-win" propositions even for participants; in fact a dominant partner may well make a junior one increasingly dependent on him. Worse, if the network—like an old-fashioned cartel—is used mainly as a device to create collective monopoly power, it will hurt not only outside competitors, but even more importantly, consumers and the public interest as well.[5] Harrigan found that most strategic alliances are relatively short-lived—three to five years seems to be fairly typical. At least in the instances just cited a limited lease on life may well be a good thing!

## CONSULTING AND EDUCATIONAL IMPLICATIONS

In the collegium, as in current management literature, several participants stressed the importance of the *learning organization*, especially in turbulent times (e.g., Steingraber, Yahaya, Day, Miller, Burnett, Desch). Any effort to implement this concept faces some king-size problems. The organization needs to know what it needs to learn about. It also needs an understanding of how to make sense out of incomplete and often inconsistent data, and how to handle the problem that current data (and bodies of knowledge) quickly become obsolete in the constantly changing environment of strategic planning—both at the corporate and subordinate levels. Technology—in the "technical" as well as the intellectual sense—evolves rapidly in all functional areas. At the same time, information technology and such developments as cross-functional teams at subordinate levels and macroenvironmental forces surrounding the executive office provide high-pressure inducements toward integral strategy approaches (Kitz, Cavusgil).

Several ideas on how to cope with the challenge of learning were advanced. A company may intentionally hire *outsiders* as CEOs or as part of the executive office in an extended sense. Recent examples include IBM, Kodak, Lilly, CIGNA (Miller). In some respects, this is tantamount to building a set of internal consultants into the organization. At least in the CEO case, this procedure will frequently force a dramatic change in corporate culture, a change conducive to fresh strategic thinking. Naturally, it also involves taking some deliberate risk, as not all leadership is generic. Some leaders may have talents suitable only in a given ecological context, or type of context ("downsizers," "turnaround artists"). But then, in most cases, merely continuing on the old track would be taking even larger risks.[6]

It is clear, however, that "refreshment" of the upper cadre of managers in and of itself is not sufficient for a company seriously bent on becoming a learning organization. Such an organization also calls for continuous effort of executive development at all levels of the firm (Desch). Most important here, we must assume, is a culture where senior executives set examples of personal development beneficial to the organization, as well as to themselves as management professionals. Beyond this, we find an almost bewildering flora of organized executive development programs. The most broad-ranging would typically be university-sponsored, general (or functionally oriented) executive programs and seminars. Increasingly, universities as well as free-standing institutions of executive education will produce tailor-made programs for individual companies or groups of firms. Currently, the area of hottest growth is probably company in-house programs. The only inherent risk in company-run programs is that they may be too tied in with the internal culture and with the "politically correct" view of the external environment. A rich sprinkling of outside inputs is probably good advice.

Whatever the type of program, Ameritech is setting a timely example by making managers responsible for leading their own employees through a similar exercise. This helps motivate the manager who was sent to the initial program, and increases the impact of executive development activities on both company culture and strategic planning and implementation.

The unique contribution of *consultants* traditionally has been that they may bring a fresh perspective to company problems (Bowman, Arpi, Jägsander). Of late, such talent has been brought to bear notably on the definition and creation of core competencies, the transformation (e.g., turnarounds) of businesses, and the deployment of strategies into several levels of the organization (Ferry). On the latter score, there still seems to be a significant difference between American and European consulting, in that Europeans are more often called upon to take an active part in the *implementation* of strategy, in addition to their classic advisory part. The use of small, specialist firms seems to be growing, for example, in the area of competitive intelligence. At least in Europe there is also a major trend among client firms to *view consulting as a healthy, normal phenomenon*, rather than as an antidote to acute or impending crises (Arpi, Jägsander). In such long-term relationships, prevailing on consultants in effect becomes a part of the client's networking strategy.

An extension of consultants being hired in part to assist in the implementation of their ideas into less fanciful areas of business activity is the burgeoning practice of hiring outside people for *specific, temporary assignments*. Currently, the hiring of "temps" is by no means confined to typists and other routine personnel but increasingly includes knowledge workers of all kinds as well.

Deliberately, the collegium emphasized the crying need for integral strategy. But clearly we cannot afford to be without professional specialists at junior and middle management levels. Even here, however, we see in retrospect that in the prime of American-style MBA programs we greatly overemphasized functional specialization (and even narrow-minding *functional cultures*, as in marketing and finance), at the expense of the ability to integrate and to think "upstream" (Burnett, Rice). Incidentally, this weakness applies not only to MBA programs but also to other professional schools of interest, such as engineering and accounting. Not wishing to be led too far astray, leaders of such specialist-oriented programs might well ask for a guide as to what integral strategy means in practical terms. The emerging answer from the collegium was unambiguous: Emphasize strategy based on market orientation in general, and customer orientation in particular (Burnett, Day, Fornell).

## FUTURE OF INTEGRAL STRATEGY

The last two sessions of the collegium were devoted to likely implications of recent experience of strategic management to practice, research and education in the future. Against the background of this record it would indeed be presumptuous to attempt any full-fledged forecast here. Rather, the objective is to reemphasize some points believed to be of special importance and in the process add a few personal reflections.

### Why Integral Strategy?

Several speakers emphasized the political, technological, economic, and social *turbulence* to be expected throughout the foreseeable future. Paradoxically, in the marketplace this turbulence will manifest itself in terms of both more intense competition and more intense cooperation. In this environment of change integral strategy with a definite overall direction is likely to be a critical source of advantage. (For other reasons in favor of integral strategy, see the *Manifest*.) If market orientation is the direction adopted, top executives might bear in mind that recent studies indicate that their ideas of what such an orientation implies often differ dramatically from those of their own customers. It is also critical to keep in mind that in current usage of the term, it refers to market (or customer) orientation of the business as a whole and *all of its functions*—the market is too important to be a preserve of the marketing people!

## Strategy Change with Speed

Every company has a core offering (be it electric motors, cars, or restaurant meals) which we may look upon as "hardware." Another part of the offering is "software," comprising such matters as pre- and post-sales service, warranties, customer information, speedy and friendly handling of complaints, credit terms, delivery, spare parts, applications engineering advice, etc. It is crystal clear that software aspects are rapidly gaining in importance relative to hardware. This is true whether the hardware is a product or a service (e.g., an insurance policy). Whether we are speaking of hardware or software, the pressure is growing for greater *speed*. Speed can be increased by integral product development teams, by superior management information systems (MIS), as well as consumer information systems (CIS), and in many instances by networking (e.g., in R&D and in synchronized distribution systems). Total Quality Management (TQM) may also play a role here. These and other modes of time compression need further management analysis and, certainly, more research. Speed will be a major source of competitive advantage, notwithstanding the growing impression that being the "first mover" is not always advantageous in an era when time required to copy a competitive initiative is manifestly shrinking.

A challenge from both practitioner and researcher points of view is the search for appropriate mixes of competition and cooperation in different ecological settings. Of course, this issue is also of concern to public policy makers with regard to antitrust law as well as regulated industries.

## Changing Organization Structures

Flatter organization structures react faster than complex hierarchies. So do integral, self-empowered teams. Quite apart from the questionable logic of "industrial democracy," delegation and integration will become increasingly prevalent in order to compress time. In pace-setting organizations there will be more involvement in strategic management at all levels simply due to the realization that enhanced understanding and motivation will increase speed and quality of implementation. These statements are probably true, "other circumstances equal." Research is needed concerning the determinants at play.

## Coordination of the MNC

The multinational corporation of the future will have at its disposal an essentially global/financial market, though for reasons of minimizing total cash needs and taxation, the finance function may tend to be centralized. Experience indicates that accounting for a subsidiary in country A may often be done cheaper—sometimes even be of higher quality—in country B. Production of one product may be done in countries CDE and of another in DFG. Marketing of both products may be done in countries C, D, I, J and K. Raw materials may be sourced in countries L and M, and components made in N, O, P, depending on the advantages at hand. Political risk, local trade and labor policies, infrastructure and, especially in end markets, cultural factors play a major role here in addition to short-term cost and profitability concerns. In addition other issues of integral internal strategy remain, such as intra-company transfer policy, service payments from one unit to another, competition among subsidiaries in third markets, etc. The MNC also faces the intercultural dimension of the standardization ("low cost") versus differentiation strategy issue. All these crucial matters of integral strategy in the MNC need a great deal more of scholarly attention at both the theory and practice levels. This also applies to the individual entry-mode decision, whether the entry contemplated is an input or output market.

## The Value Added Chain and Scope Decisions

Our reflections on the MNC bring up the conceptually exciting value added (VA) chain concept, and the closely related scope decision of the individual company. At least half a century old, the VA notion has only recently been taken seriously in the strategy literature (e.g., Porter). It needs a great deal more of work (even at the definitional level) to become more than an interesting idea. On the other hand, the scope decision, which in effect expresses the company's position in the VA chain, is a good deal more concise. It must be noted, however, that scope decisions are not made once for all times, but are subject to change with every movement a company makes along any one of the handful of dimensions of scope previously enumerated. Heavyweight issues closely related are make-buy, networking and nichemanship strategies; all affect company scope. Exciting as it is, this entire area is as yet comparatively underdeveloped.

## Accounting For Strategic Management

Traditional accounting systems tend to be of marginal value in strategic management; they were constructed for other purposes. Typically, an entire supplementary system would be needed to serve strategists. A first major step is the introduction of activity-based costing (ABC), which focuses on processes and tasks employees perform, rather than on such classic categories as salaries, fringes, supplies, and so forth.

For strategic purposes a different philosophy of what constitutes investments and expenses is also needed. From a strategic point of view, setting up a captive sales organization in another country would largely be considered an investment, for example. Further, serious attempts should be made to find quantitative equivalents in evaluating intangible assets (brand equity, patents, skills of particularly valuable employees, etc.). Costs in intersubsidiary transactions should also be evaluated, including such costs as managerial time. Decades ago, the editor was involved in a study which showed that transactions between some General Electric subsidiaries were actually more costly than analogous sales to outside customers, due to interminable internal bargaining and requests for preferential treatment.

Accounting systems should also be developed that explicitly take into consideration the multi-faceted goal structures of modern corporations, such as customer satisfaction (Fornell), cost of increasing current market share by one point, and so on.

## The Tantalizing Toolbox of Strategic Management

As pointed out in both the Bowman and Schendel papers there is presently quite a box of tools developed to assist strategic analysis. The list of these tools includes such items as the product life cycle, the experience curve, the growth-share matrix, the PIMS program, Total Quality Management, the value added chain, and transactions cost analysis. Both Bowman and Schendel (and Fornell with regard to TQM) express skepticism and/or caution with regard to many or most of these and similar tools or "fads." Certainly, their validity and, hence applicability, tends to be situation-specific—that is, ecologically conditioned. Nevertheless, there is no denying that most of these tools have been and still are used to *stimulate creative thinking about strategic issues.* In the cases of the value added chain and transactions cost analysis clearer operational definitions and much more empirical research is required. Most of the other tools need contingency-theory oriented research to establish under what empirical conditions (if any) they are applicable.

## Research Technology

Several speakers and participants expressed the need for a richer set of research methodology than that currently fashionable in American strategy-oriented academic literature. The strategy field is still young enough to call for exploratory, in-depth, qualitatively oriented (and yet theory or hypothesis-based) research. Under this view an important mission of statistically based, natural-science oriented research is to do the follow-up necessary to establish (or reject) the validity of the more preliminary inquiries. This writer would add another arrow to the quiver of research techniques, that is, strategy simulations. We are thinking here of highly sophisticated management games, in which participants—be they executives or MBA students—are facing typical strategic issues in a laboratory situation.[7] In this manner, behavioral and economic variables will interact in at least a quasirealistic way. Such simulations, as well as so-called expert systems (based on the particular skills of one or several employees), naturally also have a major role to play in personnel training and executive development.

Research ultimately aimed at benefiting business will typically have to be done *in* business. Until, say, ten years ago American business was by far more open and willing to share data and experiences with academic researchers than business anywhere else in the world. In recent years, however, this type of cooperation has been less willingly offered, perhaps due to the frequency of requests from academia. Meanwhile, the willingness to be examined has grown markedly in Europe, and to some extent even in Japan (especially if the researcher happens to be Japanese!). To maintain the momentum of strategy research in this country executives and academics face a joint challenge of restoring the traditional research friendly atmosphere for mutual benefit.

## Research Aims and the Practice of Integral Strategy

Enough has been said in collegium papers and discussions and in this essay about the need for further research on specific topics in the strategy area. What should be the ultimate, integral aims? Two interrelated, overarching themes come to mind. The first is a general theory of structure-strategy-performance relationships, from which strategy practitioners can directly derive actionable conclusions appropriate to any given ecological configuration. The second is a new theory of the firm integrating behavioral as well as economic aspects.

What, then, are some of the challenges for strategizing executives for the duration of the nineties? The adoption of a true market orientation (Day)[8] might well be a top priority, at least from an integral strategy perspective. Competitive benchmarking and the building of competitive advantage, as well as cooperative advantage via networking, form important parts of such an orientation. But being competitor-driven should not be an end in itself. The key to successful strategy is, and remains, *customer orientation of all parts of the organization.* To be on target here calls for sophisticated measurement of a battery of indicators of consumer (customer) satisfaction (Fornell), rather than loose perceptions on the part of executives (or their spouses) of what constitutes such satisfaction. A customer-driven strategy is built on the realization that the customer is the final arbiter of what constitutes *quality* (rather than ISO or some conventional TQM guru).

A second avenue in the direction of integral strategy is the implementation of *speed, creativity* and *agility* in the organization. Speed and creativity have already been discussed, notably in the context of integral teams for product innovation. Such teams are likely to have other applications, for example, in the development and strategic interpretation of consumer satisfaction indicators. Incidentally, in this context *internal* customer satisfaction should not be neglected. Experience indicates that agility tends to be a distinct competitive advantage of small firms. This is especially the case in the exploitation of small, often temporary market segments inviting what may be called a "nichemanship" strategy. By various instruments of delegation and the use of integral teams for continuous competitor and customer sensing, however, some large companies have already demonstrated that small business need not have a monopoly on flexibility.

A third approach to integral strategy is to employ a *process* perspective in strategic thinking as applied to company organization (Sentell, Steingraber). This is actually at the heart of "reengineering," whose practitioners have recognized its integrative nature.

*International operations* still constitutes a weak spot in the strategic thinking of American business (Cavusgil). A majority of executives from the United States think of operations abroad as "foreign" business, and, similarly, of "foreign" competitors in the U.S. market. Opinion surveys of executives in this country indicate that only a minority believe that the understanding of global business is an essential characteristic of future managers. In Europe more than 80 percent of executives interviewed replied in the affirmative, and the corresponding figure in Japan was literally 100 percent. To start with, we need to think of NAFTA as one domestic market, where the United States is but the largest region, a region almost as diverse in cultures as NAFTA in its entirety. Taking a cue from Percy Barnevik of ABB and several other keen observers (including a number of American executives) successful strategists in the future will "think globally, and act locally."

## NOTES

1. Here and in the following, last names within parentheses refer to collegium sessions.
2. Interestingly, famous consultant Ram Charan is quoted as saying that "Where it is most effective, executive education is being used as a lever for cultural change."
3. Hans B. Thorelli and Sarah V. Thorelli, *Consumer Information Systems and Consumer Policy* (Cambridge, MA: Ballinger Publishing Co., 1977).
4. It is only natural that the importance of *trust* is increasing in an age when its prevalence clearly is declining. At the same time what Oliver Williamson labels *opportunism* is running hogwild in Wall Street, financial services, savings and loan associations—not to speak of executive compensation.
5. Hans B. Thorelli and James M. Patterson, "Longer Live the Sherman Act!" *The Antitrust Bulletin* 35 (Fall 1990): 537-574.

6. See, for instance, the Starbuck-Hedberg paper on the traumatic final years of the Swedish Facit Corporation as an independent unit in the predecessor *SSP* volume, Hans B. Thorelli, ed., *Strategy + Structure = Performance: The Strategic Planning Imperative* (Bloomington, IN: Indiana University Press, 1977). Facit, a world-renowned maker of manual and electrical calculators, went through three sets of top managers in short order, all believing that the emerging electronic calculators represented but a passing fad.

7. For a state-of-the art simulation of this type, see H. B. Thorelli, J.-C. Lopez and R. L. Graves, *International Operations Simulation/Mark 2000 [INTOPIA] Executive Guide* and H.B. Thorelli and J.-C. Lopez, *International Operations Simulation/Mark 2000 [INTOPIA] Compendium for the Administrator* (both at Englewood Cliffs, NJ: Prentice-Hall, 1994).

8. For detail see, for example, George S. Day, *Market Driven Strategy: Processes for Creating Value* (New York: Free Press-Macmillan, 1990).

I  REFLECTIONS ON THE HISTORY OF STRATEGY

# EDITOR'S NOTE

The Integral Strategy Collegium focused on current strategy issues, the need for integrated approaches, and future implications. Before tangling with the issues of the day and the challenges of tomorrow, it seemed wise to review how we got to where we are in strategy theory and practice. What is to be learned from the last quarter of a century of strategy development? To our delight, Edward Bowman accepted this assignment. In fruitful accomplishment of the task, Bowman weaves the contributions rendered by academics, consultants and executives into an integrated pattern and an integral view of strategy. That his provided a successful opening is reflected by the frequent references to it in subsequent deliberations.

In following up on Bowman, Fred Steingraber pointed out that the key problem often is not strategy but its execution. The growing importance of line relative to staff in strategy formulation is a hopeful sign in overcoming *implementation gap*. As key means of reaching the ideal of integral strategy, he stressed process management as inherently cross-functional, and the decentralization of major aspects of planning to "where the action is." We need "an integration breakthrough that refocuses on the customer (internal as well as external)."

After digesting Bowman and Steingraber and the discussion summary following their remarks, the reader in a hurry to get from the prelude of today to the prologue of tomorrow may wish to take an advance peek at Dan Schendel's view of Strategy Futures, that after a retrospect presents a somewhat different perspective of the future.

# STRATEGY HISTORY: THROUGH DIFFERENT MIRRORS

Edward H. Bowman

## INTRODUCTION

To really understand an important topic one should know something of its history, especially if there is some curiosity about current transitions. In the field of strategy, this can show some cumulative learning, as well as bring perspective to occasional utopias. This paper then attempts to set out the history of strategy over the past three decades. Because some issues or approaches speak more to a particular reader than others, we offer several different, though linked, mirrors of strategy. Richard Rorty describes philosophy as the mirror of reality and criticizes this mirror as inadequate. He is especially critical of its emphasis on truth rather than on meaning—on the "contrast between contemplation and action, between representing the world and coping with it." Through the looking glass we will also see reality, and how it has changed, but imperfectly. With the reader's forbearance we will list the mirrors briefly here, and then expand on them over the course of the paper. They are the generic types of academics, consultants' stages of strategic planning and practice, the changing emphasis on arguments in the strategy process, General Electric's visible chief executives, the literature of strategy writers and research streams in strategy journals, and finally, philosophy and strategy gestalt.

Our choice, as it must be for anyone who writes history, is whether to take historical time stage-by-stage with a rather complete description of each stage. Or on the contrary, to acknowledge the multiple streams which flow through each stage and describe these in sequence. Our choice is the latter which takes these separate streams or mirrors as a way to see the history unfold, with some possibility of seeing across each stage.

A study of strategy (Bowman 1974) can distinguish among practice, methodology, and theory. Practice for academics is captured in cases and histories. Methodology is elaborated in planning systems, an uneven link of theory and practice, which has been the bulwark of much consulting practice. Theory comes primarily from economics and/or behavioral sciences. Practice and theory are not always well connected, and the way we talk and the way we act are often at variance (March 1980).

Professional historians have a major intellectual argument among themselves (Gertrude Himmelfarb), between a focus on major players (the "old history"), or a focus on major forces (the "new history"). The Annalistes in France led by Fernand Braudel (*The Wheels of Commerce, Civilization and Capitalism, 15th-18th Century*) have introduced the new history which seems to be the dominant mode today. Our history of strategy will not be drawn entirely to either side. It will deal with major players such as Chandler and Porter for the academics, Gluck and Zakon for the consultants, and GM's Sloan and GE's Welch for the industrialists. But, we cannot ignore the major changes in our society following the post World War II recovery, growth and the trouble from foreign competition, and the advent of the Japanese.

When we deal with the history of theory we should bear in mind its major intended roles to describe, explain, predict, and control. These are progressively more difficult tasks to accomplish. To describe is often improved by rich institutional detail, what anthropologists call "thick description." To explain requires a clear definition of factors and variables, and a strong sense of cause/effect. To predict is often hampered by noise overwhelming signal, exogenous happenings, and adversaries (the key to game theory). Control is dependent on frequently ambiguous instruments. One could argue that it is necessary to progress through these four stages sequentially and yet academics and consultants often start with the last phase, control, ignoring their inability to handle well the previous three. This is perhaps facilitated by what March (1987) calls the "functionality of illusion." He argues that it is better to assume you understand in order to act, rather than to assume you do not understand and are precluded from acting. Either assumption may be in error, and he wagers the first (Type I Error) is less costly than the second (Type II Error).

## GENERIC TYPES OF ACADEMICS

Our history of strategy, as found in the academy, seems to have moved across three types of academics in the three decades. While all still exist and thrive today, their relative importance, their day in the sun, has changed. First came the institutionalists in the middle 1960s. Though they varied in their approaches they were able to describe the strategy issues of the firm from inside-out. They could supply rich descriptions of these issues. They offered cases, and histories, and planning systems. They have kin in economics as described by John Kenneth Galbraith (*Economics in Perspective*), and in organization studies as admired by Charles Perrow (*Complex Organizations*). Because of their approach they were able to investigate a broad sweep of problems, people, and issues. Their "methodology" did not limit them to a narrow slice of reality. And they were comfortable with both prescription, as well as field studies. They would be sympathetic with T. S. Eliot's Prufrock: "Oh do not ask 'What is it?' let us go and make our visit."

Secondly came the economists in the late 1970s, spilling over into the 1980s. Industrial organization economics was the background on which they drew to analyze the problems of the firm, but especially the industries in which they existed. Issues of industry market concentration, barriers to entry, cost and price structures, economies of scale, investment choices, vertical integration, profitability rates, and growth patterns were explored. A newer version of economists more lately interested in strategy have been the game theorists, who argue that the primary issues are those that surface in the competitive environment with industrial adversaries.

Thirdly came the behavioral scientists in the 1980s, spilling over into the 1990s. These have been the organization psychologists, the political scientists, the sociologists, and the population ecologists. They have dealt with a broader spectrum; from the firm, to the industry, to the population of industries. They focus not on the optimization and equilibrium of the economist, but the functioning and survival of the organization, and the behavior of its people. Cooperative networks as distinct from competitive markets start to inform this analysis. Von Hippel's, *The Sources of Innovation*, illustrates this networking along the value chain, where innovations move between suppliers, and manufacturers, and users.

It is argued that the relative impact of these three groups, institutionalists, economists, and behavioralists has followed a historical progression. They are all present today in the academy working on issues of strategy and they all cope, though imperfectly, with the two central questions of strategy: first, Why are some firms more successful than others? (a question of the type "what is"), and secondly, How can we make this firm more successful? (a question of the type "how to"). Both Herbert Simon (*The Sciences of the Artificial*) and Donald Schon (*The Reflective Practitioner*) have taken the academic community to task for being more interested in and more comfortable with the "what is" question, and less so with the professional questions, "how to" (Bowman 1990). They feel that the education of professionals in our universities suffers from this bias.

Before looking explicitly at the way strategy thinking has changed in America, it is useful to look at how America has changed over the past three decades. The idea will at least be offered that some of these changes have influenced what the strategy issues of importance are and how we think about strategy.

In the 1960s there was a continuation of the post World War II recovery and prosperity. The U.S. was flowering, and it was a growth decade for business. In order to enhance this growth many businesses moved toward diversification, and it was the age of the conglomerate. Much academic research in this period focused on growth, expansion, acquisition, diversification, and corporate control of the conglomerate enterprise. ITT under Harold Geneen could be offered as the exemplar of his decade.

In the 1970s stagflation, a combination of stagnation and inflation, was evident. A malaise in the land was articulated by the President of the United States. There were increasing problems abroad, and the cold war seemed everywhere. The American business community looked to a style of hunkering down, and a move away from diversification toward corporate focusing was evident. A comfortable "positioning" in the corporation's dominant industry was called for. Much academic research in this period, and spilling over into the next, focused on industry analysis, competitive behavior, strategic groups, and corporate performance. The petroleum industry which had major upheavals in this decade, and had tried diversification, now thought better of it.

In the 1980s there was strongly increased foreign competition. The national budget deficits, the foreign trade imbalances, mainly from Japan, caused a rethinking in American industry. Corporate restructuring toward the end of the decade became the dominant mode, with detractors decrying "the hollowing of the American Corporation." Sometimes this restructuring was abetted by the U.S. Government, with American Telephone & Telegraph being a salient example—business portfolios changed, organizations and people were rearranged, and often the capital structure changed, as with RJR Nabisco. Much academic research in this period focused on aspects of this restructuring or derivative issues, such as leveraged buyouts, divestments of divisions, organization downsizing, and top management teams.

Finally, the 1990s are ushered in with dramatic changes in the international environment. The cold war expires, Eastern Europe awakens, Japan pauses, and the Common Market forms. Attending all these is great uncertainty. Multiple Scenario analysis is called for, but so is a dramatic increase in networking. IBM, a jewel in the crown of American industry, is now extending its networks and alliances around the world, including in Silicon Valley.

Academic research in this period deals with multinational alliances, corporate ventures, technology change, and continuing restructuring.

All these changes over the three or four decades have changed the face of the strategy issues. With a change in issues we have in a natural way a change in practice, a change in the (theoretical) literature, and a change in consulting needs and opportunities.

## CONSULTANTS AND INDUSTRY PRACTICE

Fred Gluck of McKinsey (now its CEO) and partners S. P. Kaufman and A. S. Walleck wrote an interesting treatment of the progressing history of strategy (*HBR* 1980). Their argument implies that the stage-wise progression is one of relative sophistication and effectiveness as well. First came financial planning (1950s and earlier), then Long Range Planning (1960s), then Strategic Planning (1970s), and then Strategic Management (1980s). One assumes that these stages also map the consulting practice of McKinsey and other major consultants. Our recent interviews with a dozen strategy consultants for this paper support this view.

Financial Planning largely focused on budgets for one and two years. The data and variables were all reduced to financial measures. These were largely projections from the past into the future as computed by the financial executives of the firm.

Long range planning in the 1960s focused essentially on the inside functions of the firm. The task was to arrange that each of these functions, marketing, production, finance, human resources were all coordinated with preparations made for future growth, whether new products, or new facilities, or new resources, or new people. Staffs were employed and trained to develop these long range plans at both the corporate level, and the individual unit or division level.

Strategic Planning in the 1970s (and 1980s) focused largely on the outside players. Here customers and competitors were the major focus, and the organization of the firm was rearranged in strategic business units (SBUs) to map these customers and competitors. To borrow a literary metaphor from *The New Yorker* ("Briefly Noted" 1987), the look was through the window (Walt Whitman), rather than in the mirror (Emily Dickinson).

Strategic Management (1980s) was Fred Gluck's last stage and dealt with all the necessary implementation steps to assure the strategy worked. The appropriate line executives had to be involved, incentives established, information systems designed, and programs articulated. Strategic Management can connote other changes as well—away from a calendar driven system, e.g., "It's September so the strategic plan must be due," and toward an analysis that can be continuous and line-executive centered.

Another leading consultant we interviewed, Alan Zakon, CEO of the Boston Consulting Group (BCG) for a decade and now a Managing Director of Bankers Trust, offered a rather similar view of the history of strategy in response to our direct questioning:

**Phase 1.** McKinsey "profit centers" (SBUs)...a huge buildup of post World War II opportunities...focus on internal issues, such as how to manage (at a) distance (the profit centers)

**Phase 2.** Profitability comes from advantages (BCG 1970)...the management of advantage (i.e., compared to competition). It was the age of strategy (1970 and 1980s)...Advantage: what is it, how to get it, how to manage it...the use of data...The use of analysis.

**Phase 3.** "Behavioral Strategy" (as opposed to structural), that is, work with the clients, such as salesmen (but it's more strategy creation, not implementation)...will it work...will the clients really buy it. [Here Alan Zakon stopped, but when pressed for a fourth stage, if there is one:]

**Phase 4.** It might be *corporate* strategy (as opposed to business strategy)...Should the company keep the money (re: dividends)...should the company diversify (for growth)...yes or no, "Finance" may say no, but "behavioral" says yes.

Tools of Strategy

A history of strategy would be incomplete without mentioning the more visible "tools of strategy," and it is perhaps appropriate to include them along with the consultants' commentary. These are in large part the result of consultants' work (though triggered in some cases by academics). Our list will include items not strictly "tools," and others not strictly "strategy." They are best placed as a group somewhere in the middle of my three decades of history, from the late sixties to the early eighties—"the age of strategy," as Alan Zakon labeled it. These tools of strategy include the ten listed here:

1. *Learning curves (late sixties)* showing the relationship between unit costs and cumulative production. These ideas introduced in World War II to understand aircraft production economics were popularized by Bruce Henderson at BCG as a way to frame market leadership and pricing problems.
2. *The growth-share matrix (late sixties)* showing for each unit of the corporation where it placed in the two dimensional picture of its industry growth and its relative market share compared to the leading

competitors. BCG's emphasis here was on where the resources of the corporation might/should be moved between divisions.

3. *Strategic Business Units (SBUs)* (*1970*) were framed as stand alone businesses that could be managed and judged on a profit and loss basis. Product markets were focused and the specific competitors (and customers) could be identified. Strategic plans for such units could be understood by the top management of the company. McKinsey working with GE developed these ideas.

4. *The Industry Attractiveness-Business Strength Matrix* (*early seventies*) also coming from the GE-McKinsey work facilitated placing each of the corporation's SBUs in a framework permitting corporate analysis. Special attention was given here to which units were "keepers" and which were not.

5. *PIMS* (*Profit Impact of Marketing Strategies*) (*mid-seventies*) also developing out of GE, and then set up as a separate group by the Strategic Planning Institute (SPI). Many companies participated in supplying a large data base, with the SBU the level of analysis. Scores of variables of business, industry, and performance measures were organized to permit statistical analysis of important relationships.

6. *Life Cycle Analysis* (*1970s*). The premise of this work was that strategy issues and approaches might be best understood in the context of the particular phase or stage of an industry's or product's life cycle. Arthur D. Little was a strong advocate of this approach.

7. *Scenario Analysis* (*1970s*) popularized by Royal Dutch Shell as a means of coping with multiple variables uncertainty, their possible combinations, and alternative strategies.

8. *Five Forces* (*1980*), a central theme of Michael Porter's seminal book, for purposes here, will be treated as a strategy tool. Industry competitive analysis is facilitated by the careful identification of the forces at work—suppliers, competitors, customers, substitutes, and potential entrants. Consultants were ready to use these ideas, and as with the other tools could use them repeatedly.

9. *Net Present Value* (*NPV*), *Discounted Cash Flow* (*DCF*) *and Market/Book* (*M/B*) (*early eighties*). While derivative from finance theory, several consulting firms such as Marakon and Strategic Planning Associates used such financial tools to throw light on the value of individual business units within the corporation. This again facilitated questions of resource allocation, and determination of the "keepers."

10. *Value Chain* (*middle eighties*) featured in Porter's (1985) book, bringing attention to where in the economic chain competitive advantage might be critical, and where important synergies might exist across different businesses, that is, economies of scope.

I have no doubt that these strategic tools have been of use to both consultants and industrial practitioners through our stages of history—even though both now indicate that their use has dropped. They do bring to mind some Japanese poetry (Issa 1763-1827):

> The man pulling radishes
> pointed the way
> with a radish.

### Journals of Record

In an effort to understand the developing history of strategy over the past three decades, we not only interviewed a dozen consultants; we also made a rather complete survey of strategy articles in two "journals of record," *Fortune* magazine (thanks to Bertha Chan) and the *Harvard Business Review* (thanks to Jim Stephenson). Our survey of these journals through the 30 years was to get some sense of industry practice.

The first impression one gets from these surveys is the great diversity of practice and problems across all three decades, and some caution in making declarative statements about predominant issues. However, with this caution a few things do seem to stand out.

The 1960s were documented in the journals as occupied with diversification and growth; organization change; and top management control, especially financial. The 1970s brought out issues of social performance, mergers and acquisitions, global expansion and integration, and detailed plans and planning. The 1980s have offered the strategy issues of technology management, employee empowerment, global alliances, restructuring, Boards of Directors and Shareholder value, quality and speed, and fewer planners.

The above sketch of changing industrial issues and practices comes after an attempt to be more systematic with coding and counting which largely failed. The industrial issues which were revealed from our survey of the two journals of record have also been mapped in part by academic research.

## ARGUMENTS IN THE STRATEGY PROCESS

Almost 20 years ago (Bowman 1974), a review of the strategy literature and practice and its epistemology resulted in the following two figures. Figure 1 describes the various ways, or lenses, for looking at strategy, and all had their own advocates in the academy. Figure 2 describes in more detail one of the ways, a planning or decision process lens.

Our argument was and is that all of these approaches have value, and that the concurrent use of all offers the chance that our response to strategy issues

|  | Less Formal | More Formal |
|---|---|---|
| Practice | Cases | History |
| Methodology | Analytical Approach | Management Science |
| Theory | Behavioral | Economics |

*Figure 1.* Lenses for looking at strategy.

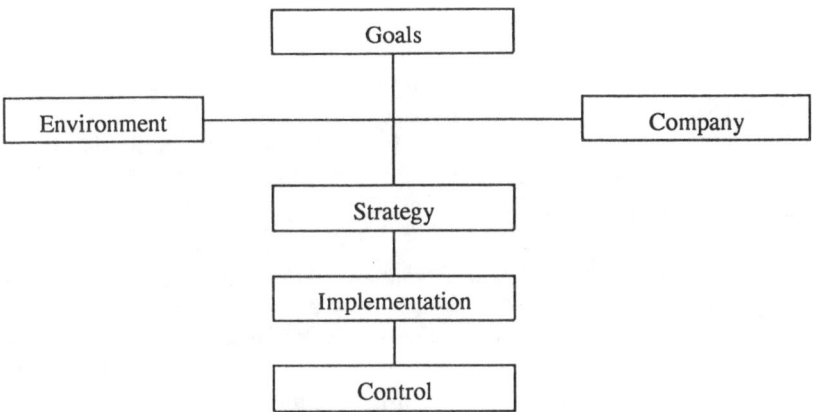

*Figure 2.* A planning or decision process lens.

can be robust. But our use of the second graph for the Analytical Approach serves our main argument for history and its changing emphases.

We argued that considering the *Goals* of the firm (e.g., growth, profit, risk and social) the strategy task was to put together the *Environment*, the industry and its threats and opportunities and anticipated changes, with the *Company*, its strengths and weaknesses as unfolded from its historical path, into a sensible *Strategy*. This *Strategy* would include (Ansoff 1965) choices of product/market domain, competitive advantage, synergy, growth direction, and vertical integration alternatives. (We would now also include the multiple characterizations of strategy as issues of plan, position, pattern, and perspective (Mintzberg, *California Management Review*).) Finally, the literature review includes aspects of *Implementation*, such as people, organization structure, incentives, information systems, programs, budgets, and provision for strategic *Control*.

This revisiting of an early review is for the purpose of reinforcing the major point of this paper, and we now come to the heart of the matter. While all of the steps or arguments in this strategy process continue to be relevant today for our analysis *the relative emphasis given to each has, in our judgment, shifted over the three decades.*

- Circa 1965, *Strategy* was the emphasis with the particulars of interest.
- Circa 1975, *Environment* was the emphasis, with industry analysis at its center.
- Circa 1985, *Implementation* was the emphasis, with people being the focus.
- Circa 1995, *Company* is now the emphasis with its core competence of central concern.

Again, all of these are of course given consideration in an analysis of strategy of the firm, but a subtle change in emphasis or focus has been apparent in the literature, in consulting, and in practice. Our interviews with the dozen consultants has reinforced our perception of this shifting emphasis. Several academic statements speak to this last and current stage (sometimes my dating of stages is slightly askew):

- Robert Hayes (*HBR* 1985), "In short, the logic here is: Do not develop plans and then seek capabilities; instead build capabilities and then encourage the development of plans for exploiting them. Do not try to develop optimal strategies on the assumption of a static environment; instead seek continuous improvement in a dynamic environment."
- Richard Rumelt (1987) talks about "isolating mechanisms"—factors that retard imitation of core competencies. "Given an innovation expected to be socially efficient, and absent appropriation challenges, entrepreneurship will not be justified unless there are impediments to the immediate *ex post* imitative dissipation of entrepreneurial rents. I call such impediments *isolating mechanisms*..."
- Herbert Simon (*JEP* 1991) "Modern industrial societies are better understood, not as market economies, but as organization economies." (J. R. Williams 1992)
- Giovanni Dosi (Harvard Seminar 1992) argues, that "most of the firms' activities concern games against nature (uncertainties within the organization), with respect to which, strategic interactions induce only relatively minor fluctuations...(rather than) their primary activity involves playing complicated and devious games with each other."
- Prahalad and Hamel (*HBR* 1990) argue, "In the 1990s they (top executives) will be judged on their ability to identify, cultivate, and

exploit core competencies that makes growth possible—indeed, they'll have to rethink the concept of the corporation itself."

The interviews with a dozen consultants are rich with illustrative support for the changing emphasis in strategic analysis. Where we must select from the dozens of pages of notes, a section of one interview is given here to establish the flavor of the response from these consultants:

> In the 1960s and early 1970s in the U.S. companies were thinking, What business should we be in? How do we look at our businesses? How do we find out what businesses we should be in? That was the period where the concepts of portfolio analysis were fresh. They were addressing questions that people didn't really know how to solve. It gave a perspective that clients didn't have.
>
> In other industries the question was, How do we get our costs in line? and How do we become competitive? These issues overlapped the question of how do we increase our share place. The 1980s were really the hey day of cost reduction and big growth in shareholder value.
>
> A lot of the major industries have been through the How do we survive? and are now coming out and saying, "How do we prosper? We are going to do it (with) the businesses we are in. Our portfolio is basically set. We own these assets, what are we going to do with our assets?"
>
> Another thing that we've seen a lot of is, How do I think more creatively about the assets that I have? What is an asset? Is it a physical asset, a core competency, my people, my market position, my customers? How can I use these assets? And how can I find people with complementary assets that we can work together?

To repeat, there has been an historic shift in emphasis over the three decades from Strategy, to Environment, to Implementation, to Company. This shift is especially noticeable in the academic literature and industrial consulting; the chances are therefore reasonable that it is also true in industrial practice.

One company very visible to students of strategy in its chief executive officers and in its strategy thinking has been General Electric. I believe GE supports the previous argument. In the 1960s, Fred Borsch made the visible move to SBUs in conjunction with McKinsey, permitting a focus on each unit's strategy and performance. The strategy of the competitive unit could be presented by its managers and understood by top management. Reginald Jones in the 1970s built a very strong and well documented, strategic planning practice for competitive analysis. The organization shifted into "sectors" in order to permit the continuing attention to competitive strategy throughout the company. Important resource commitment choices could be made between key strategic units. Jack Welch in the 1980s worked at a simplification of both the strategy ("Be number one or two in an industry") and the strategy process, with a special emphasis on the executive group to be inclusive in strategy consideration through organization "workouts." The "boundaryless" organization could be advocated and sought. If our previous argument for the shifting emphasis in strategic analysis from the 1960s to the 1990s is correct, then our estimate is that the 1990s are bringing to GE a renewed interest in the core competence of the firm, with focus on capabilities reinforcement.

## STRATEGY BOOKS AS LEADERS AND FOLLOWERS

The literature of strategy, upon which the business schools are dependent, has tracked the history(ies) described above, sometimes leading and sometimes following. Our discussion of the changing styles of academic involvement in strategy has somewhat anticipated our treatment of the literature, but not entirely.

The 1960s were the start of the modern era in strategy and their authors' impact is still felt. Alfred Chandler, Igor Ansoff, and Kenneth Andrews were all institutionalists in one way or another. They all provided a look at strategy from the inside-out. They offered an abundant and worldly view of the firm coping with the issues of strategy.

Chandler's *Strategy and Structure* was the exemplar strategy history book focusing on the developing history of four major American corporations, DuPont, General Motors, Standard Oil of New Jersey, and Sears Roebuck. The book derives from an investigation of these unfolding histories the ideas of strategy and structure. As the firms grew, expanded geographically and diversified, they were virtually forced to change their organization structures (and processes) to cope with these changes. The decentralized, divisionalized operating corporation, with centralized control, as designed by GM's Alfred Sloan came into being.

The Ansoff book, *Corporate Strategy*, laid out a systematic series of analyses that would allow the corporation to determine what its strategy would be, and how to take the important next steps. Major considerations were product market domain, competitive advantage, synergy, growth direction, and make-or-buy choices. Growth and diversification were virtually assumed in this treatment of strategic planning.

Kenneth Andrews was the co-author of *Business Policy: Text and Cases* who wrote the text material (later rewritten in a separate book). This book allowed the reader to work through the major questions in strategy formulation and strategy implementation. Cases were amply supplied to facilitate group discussion of these questions. Andrews argued that though he was not interested in theory per se, he was providing "an everyman's theory" for corporate strategy. All three of these books emphasized corporate strategy in all its particulars.

While a bit late in the 1970s the switch in corporate strategy literature was substantial. The leading book in this era, anticipated by earlier articles, was

Michael Porter's *Competitive Strategy*. This book relied strongly and explicitly on industrial organization economics. Though of many parts, the book's major emphasis was on the competitive actors in the corporation's industry: "the five forces." These forces for consideration and analysis were suppliers, competitors, possible substitutes, potential entrants, and customers. Around these forces were arranged the factors that would be present in various life cycle stages of a corporation's existence and how to think about them.

Another important book in the 1970s (1980s extended) was the Miles and Snow book, *Organizational Strategy, Structure, and Processes*, which was more systematically empirically based, and included aspects of the (previous) institutionalists and of the (future) behavioralists. It dealt with a number of industry studies and showed how generic strategies of the firm came about and how influential such generic strategies seemed to be in all aspects of a coordinated strategy. Their discovered generic strategies were (a) the Prospector, (b) the Analyzer (between a and c), (c) the Defender, and (d) the Reactor. The first three were all viable approaches to positioning within most industries, and the most interesting book extension of these constructs was the tobacco companies study, following the Surgeon General's report as described by Miles and Cameron in *Coffin Nails and Corporate Strategies*.

A book a bit earlier than Porter's but fitting into this period was Oliver Williamson's *Markets and Hierarchies*. The treatment here was the efficacy of the divisionalized structure (the M-form) for managerial control and the appropriate boundaries of the firm. The boundaries of the firm are involved with the make-or-buy decisions, and are influenced by the nature of the assets and the markets involved.

The major treatment in all of these 1970s books (1980 stretched) is the industry environment in which the company is embedded. As the 1960s looked to the strategy of the firm as central in a relatively benign environment, the 1970s (and 1980s) looked in a major way outside the firm at the competitive environment.

The 1980s brought a new literature looking at the implementation issues and problems of the corporation's strategies. Hax and Majluf's *Strategic Management: An Integrative Perspective* offered an extended treatment of the planning steps necessary for strategy. Rappaport's financial treatment of strategy issues, *Creating Shareholder Value: The New Standard for Business Performance*, offered a value added or value based approach to strategy with a continuing look to the stock market for guidance and calibration. Itami's book, *Mobilizing Invisible Assets*, asked the reader to look at the more intangible aspects of the firm's nature, especially its people commitments, in order to capture the advantage of these assets. Teece's book, *The Competitive Challenge: Strategies for Innovation and Renewal*, supplied an intellectual breadth addressed to the issues of strategic management by several leading authors of the day.

The 1990s are still in a stage of exploration but they look different than the previous three decades. The major books perhaps still have to be written, but they will include discussions of flexibility, global alliances and networks, technology, skills and learning. Nelson and Winter's book, *An Evolutionary Theory of Economic Change*, and Piore and Sable's *The Second Industrial Divide* might be offered as early harbingers of some of these ideas. Neither are about corporate strategy per se; yet both speak to its important issues. The first deals with skills within the firm, and how they are searched for, changed, and selected. The second deals with the alliances the firm can build up (regions of Northern Italy are used as example) to supplement its own skills. Core competence, learning, change, and flexibility come through these two books.

It is interesting and perhaps unusual in a field that all of these books from the three or four decades are relevant and pertinent to today's problems. They are dated, but not out-of-date. At least to this stage, strategy and its history have taken advantage of intellectual pluralism.

An addendum to the discussion of strategy literature can be the interesting and subtle shift in performance measures that people have talked about: authors, executives, and consultants. In the 1960s, growth was the measure and concern of top management. In the 1970s ROE (return on equity) and other measures of profitability were at the forefront. In the 1980s, market value divided by the book value, (market/book or Tobin's Q) was the emphasis. Value added and the market for corporate control (sometimes unfriendly) were the ideas at stake. One possible extension into the 1990s for performance measures are real options values. These options (embedded in part in the firm's value) are platforms of limited cost which may subsequently be greatly expanded, or alternatively abandoned (Hurry, Miller and Bowman 1992). Examples are (Kogut 1992) core technology, joint ventures, country platforms, and flexible manufacturing systems. Japanese companies owe some of their success to the explicit use of this options mentality (Hurry, Miller and Bowman).

## STRATEGY RESEARCH AS HISTORY

Research efforts have mapped the decade stages of the more general literature but with more variation. Rorty makes the argument that philosophy is a mirror of reality, and a not very good one. In the same spirit, research is offered here as a mirror of reality, though also an imperfect one. Only two examples are offered for each stage, and the volume of possibilities increases yearly.

Institutionalists:   Strategy/Choice

Bower's book on the resource allocation process showed how a large firm functioned at three levels of management for generation, reinforcement, and choice of projects to fit within and develop the strategy of the firm.

Rumelt's book on the efficacy of diversification used the Fortune 500 companies to show how some kinds of diversification (related) were more effective than others, and how the organization structure of these companies were influenced by these moves.

### Economists: Environment/Industry

Porter and Spence offered a scenario study of capacity expansion in an industry under conditions of uncertainty of demand, prices, and technology. Based on assumptions of rational expectations and equilibrium (standard fare in economic analysis), the several companies in this oligopoly and their choices could be approximated based on their characteristics.

Armour and Teece showed how the petroleum companies changed their organization structure over several decades and how the divisionalized-decentralized (M-form) companies for a while gained a competitive advantage for a differential profit.

### Behavioralists: Implementation/Executives

Frederickson and Mitchell investigated the efficacy of comprehensiveness in strategic planning under different conditions of industry turbulence. Their use of scenarios for executive questionnaires was instructive for other researchers.

Hirsch's comparative study of institutional strategy in the phonographic records and pharmaceutical industries showed how important the government and critical gatekeepers can be in the implementation of strategy throughout a whole industry. He argues average profits differ by a factor of three largely due to these factors.

### Institutional Behavioral Economists: Company/Competence

Cohen and Levinthal's study of the absorptive capacity effects of R&D spending offers a new look at learning in the critical fields of technology as supporting the competence of the firm.

Hurry, Miller and Bowman's comparative study of Japanese and U.S. high technology venture capital investments showed that the later looked at such investments as projects to be rewarded with relatively short term profits; the former looked at them as options to be extended later (where favorable) into new technology opportunities.

## PHILOSOPHICAL VIEWS

A final way to capture the history of strategy is to look at some possible gestalt shifts which one sees, at least in some quarters. A double distinction will be made, permitting a standard four-fold table.

Rational versus Natural (almost an ideological division in the academy)

- Rational, assumes a logical, informed, goal directed positioning (Porter, Hax and Majluf).
- Natural, assumes learned procedures, and historical, path-dependent unfolding (Mintzberg, March).

Figure versus Ground (a distinction borrowed from psychology and the arts)

- Figure, treats the big key obvious decisions for commitment (Ghemawat).
- Ground, treats the many pervasive subtle facets for incremental improvement (Itami).

## The 2 X 2 Table

Figure 3 is a representation of our double distinction, including Rational, Natural, Figure and Ground concepts.

- Commitment requires major irreversible moves for major issues based on a thorough analysis of the strategy situation. It is the major intellectual position for the rational actor, where the few important issues are identified for substantial analysis. Ghemawat offers several examples in detail.
- Garbage can model of organization choice connotes a series of four flows, problems, solutions, actors, and occasions which come together haphazardly. March offers a number of examples but an extended discussion is offered of university presidents and the world they face.
- Options are limited commitments which can later be expanded or abandoned. These are "real options" as distinct from, but drawing on, the literature of financial instruments options. Kogut describes these as platforms offering limited commitment, early positioning, and future flexibility. The net can be spread widely.
- Crafting connotes a series of small steps which are learned from the executive's own experience and from others. Management is a craft, and trial and error learning is encouraged as described by Aaron Wildavsky in *Searching for Safety*.

Michael Piore points out "...the relationship between the individual and the external reality is not direct. It is mediated by a set of cognitive structures. The role of these structures is to give *coherence* to experience. Without them, the experience is simply a jumble which has no shape or meaning." The ideas described here—rational, natural, figure, ground—are cognitive structures which have a powerful interpretive effect for their holders.

|  | Rational | Natural |
|---|---|---|
| Figure | Commitment ––––––––– Ghemawat | Garbage Cans ––––––––– March |
| Ground | Options ––––––––– Kogut | Crafting ––––––––– Mintzberg |

***Figure 3.*** A representation of philosophical views.

As March (and Argyris) argue, the way we talk and the way we act are not always congruent. The tie to history of this probe into philosophical gestalt is that it seems that the way we talk is moving to the left of the chart, and lower (options). And the way we act is moving to the right of the chart, but also lower (crafting). Both devote less emphasis to figure, and more to ground. A stylized difference for strategic planning in the rational-figure versus the natural-ground polarities is the distinction which James Schlesinger, Cabinet Member in several administrations, made between Cooks Tour Planning and Lewis and Clark Planning. The former lays out all in advance: place, timing, mode; the latter packs the bags with gear based on very general suppositions and possibilities (such distinctions may affect the involvement and spirit of the crew).

An analogy might help. While our argument here for the concepts of figure versus ground (and rational versus natural) is addressed to issues of business policy, some of the major positions on "industrial policy" can also be usefully framed in this fashion. Where some advocate major decisions about particular industries (i.e., figure), others argue for improving the infrastructure: education, tax policy, research cooperation, etc. (i.e., ground).

## CONCLUSION

### What Have We Learned—The Propositions

- What happens in the world affects how we think about strategy (more than how we think about strategy affects what happens in the world).
- Strategy constructs have moved from institutionalists (little theory) to economists (hyperrationality theory) to behavioralists (bounded rationality theory). Hopefully, the next steps may combine the best of each.
- Strategy constructs are more widely diffused in the firm as result of both education and experience, and for this reason perhaps are more a

responsibility of the line executives and less of staff. A corollary could be that there is a movement from figure to ground.
- The field of strategy, as most fields, goes through a sequence of enthusiasms, with some cumulative learning (which should continue), and some strongly advocated utopias (inviting deconstruction).

Wisdom Sought—What Have We Not Learned

- We do not do very well putting together the rational and the natural, the economic and the behavioral. Academic departments of management should be especially good at this (Bowman 1991).
- Academics should learn again how to be institutionalists, to tell rich stories and not only theories and models. The narrative rather than the paradigmatic is sometimes called for (Bruner 1986).
- We are not very good at offering professional help. The link between theory (what is) and practice (how to) is not well made, (Simon; Schon) and executives are often disappointed with consultants. Rorty's criticism of focus on representation rather than coping applies here.
- We are only slowly learning to transfer best practices (in such a complex world); benchmarking hasn't really come to the field of strategy (DiMaggio and Powell's treatment of mimetic isomorphism needs to be extended).
- We haven't really learned how to think of strategy choices as options and platforms, one advantage of the Japanese (Bowman and Hurry 1993).
- Change, restructuring, and learning continue to be extremely difficult, and the old adage is still "to change a policy regime you have to change the people" (throw the rascals out), and "innovation still seems to come from outside the current industry players." (Peter Temin, MIT, and Dan Raff, Harvard, papers at the Wharton History Conference 1992).
- Governance and the roles of major investors and the Boards of Directors still have to be clarified for critical strategy issues, (Berle and Means redux).
- Social welfare, the health of the body politic, and externalities are virtually ignored by academic and industrial strategists (Shleifer and Summers).
- Our infatuation with the latest strategy idea, or at worst, the newest strategy fad, may shortchange the sensible study of history. While worldly people might be forgiven such preferences, the responsible academic should not.

## ACKNOWLEDGMENTS

For help and/or commentary on this project I would like to thank Wharton students Bertha Chan, Rita McGrath, Jim Stephenson, and Professors Connie Helfat, Dan

Levinthal, Harbir Singh, Mike Useem, and Hans Thorelli; as well as the many strategy consultants interviewed.

# REFERENCES

Andrews, K. R. (1971). *The Concept of Corporate Strategy*. Homewood, Il: Dow-Jones Irwin.
Ansoff, H. I. (1965). *Corporate Strategy: An Analytic Approach to Business Policy for Growth and Expansion*. New York: McGraw Hill Book Company.
Argyris, C. (1985). *Strategy, Change, and Defensive Routines*. Boston: Pitman Publishing Co.
Armour, H. O. & Teece, D. J. (1978). "Organization Structure and Economic Performance: A Test of the Multidivisional Hypothesis." *Bell Journal of Economics 9*:106-122.
Berle, A. A., & Means, G. C. (1932). *The Modern Corporation and Private Property*. New York: Medallion Co.
Bower, J. (1970). *Managing the Resource Allocation Process*. Boston: Harvard Business School, Division of Research.
Bowman, E. H. (1974). "Epistemology, Corporate Strategy, and Academe." *Sloan Management Review15*(2): 35-50.
Bowman, E. H. (1990). "Strategy Changes: Possible Worlds and Actual Minds." In *Perspectives on Strategic Management*, ed. J. W. Frederickson, 9-37. New York: Harper and Row.
Bowman, E. H. (1991). "Some Puzzles with Risk and the Strategy Canon." University of Minnesota Strategic Management Society Conference paper, October.
Bowman, J. & Hurry, D. (1993). "Strategy Through the Option Lens: An Integrated View of Resource Investments and the Incremental Choice Process." Paper 92-10, University of Pennsylvania.
Braudel, F. (1986). *The Wheels of Commerce: Civilization and Capitalism, 15th-18th Century*. Academy of Management Review, 18: 760-782.
"Briefly Noted." (1987). *The New Yorker*, October 5.
Bruner, J. (1986). *Actual Minds, Possible Worlds*. Cambridge, MA: Harvard University Press.
Chandler, A. D., Jr. (1962). *Strategy and Structure: Chapters in the History of American Enterprise*. Cambridge, MA: MIT Press.
Cohen, M. D. & March, J. G. (1974, 1986). *Leadership and Ambiguity*. Boston, MA: Harvard Business School Press.
Cohen, W. M. & Levinthal, D. (1990). "Absorptive Capacity: A New Perspective on Learning and Innovation. *Administrative Science Quarterly 35*:128-152.
DiMaggio, P. J. & Powell, W. W. (1983). "The Iron Cage Revisited: Institutional Isomorphism and Collective Rationality in Organization Fields." *American Sociological Review 48*:147-160.
Dosi, G. & Marengo, L. (1992). "Toward a Theory of Organizational Competence." Working Paper University of Rome.
Eliot, T. S. (1917). "The Love Song of J. Alfred Prufrock." In *Selected Poems*. NY: Harcourt Brace Jovanovich, (1988).
Frederickson, J. W. & Mitchell, T. R. (1984). "Strategic Decision Processes: Comprehensiveness and Performance in an Industry with an Unstable Environment." *Academy of Management Journal 27* (2): 399-423.
Galbraith, J. K. (1987). *Economics in Perspective: A Critical History*. Boston: Houghton Mifflin Company.
Ghemawat, P. (1991). *Commitment: The Dynamic of Strategy*. New York: Free Press.
Gluck, F. W., Kaufman, S. P., & Walleck, A. S. (1980). "Strategic Management for Competitive Advantage." *Harvard Business Review 58* (4): 154-161.

Hayes, R. H. (1985). "Strategic Planning—Forward in Reverse?" *Harvard Business Review* 85 (6): 111-119.
Hax, A. C. & Majluf, N. S. (1984). *Strategic Management: An Integrative Perspective*. Englewood Cliffs, NJ: Prentice-Hall.
Himmelfarb, G. (1987). *The New History and the Old*. Cambridge, MA: Harvard University Press, The Belnap Press.
Hirsch, P. M. (1975). "Organizational Effectiveness and the Institutional Environment." *Administrative Science Quarterly, 20*:327-344.
Hurry, D., Miller, A. T., & Bowman, E. H. (1992). "Calls on High Technology: Japanese Explorations of Venture Capital Investment in the United States." *Strategic Management Journal 13*:85-101.
Itami, H. & Roehl, T. W. (1987). *Mobilizing Invisible Assets*. Cambridge, MA: Harvard University Press.
Kogut, B. & Kulatilaka, N. (1992). "Options Thinking and Platform Investments: Investing in Opportunity." Reginald H. Jones Center Working Paper 92-07. University of Pennsylvania.
Learned, E. A., Christensen, C. R., Andrews, K.R., & Guth, W.D. (1965). *Business Policy: Texts and Cases*. Homewood, Il: Richard D. Irwin.
Levitt, B. & March, J. (1988). "Organization Learning." *Annual Review of Sociology 14*: 319-340.
March, J. G. (1980). "How We Talk and How We Act: Administrative Theory and Administrative Life." In M.D. Cohen and James G. March, (Eds.),*Leadership and Ambiguity*, pp. 273-90. Boston, MA: Harvard Business School Press.
March, J. G. & Shapira, Z. (1987). "Managerial Perspectives on Risk and Risk Taking." *Management Science 33* (11): 1404-1418.
Mintzberg, H. (1987). "Crafting Strategy." *Harvard Business Review 87* (4): 66-77.
Mintzberg, H. (1987). "The Strategy Concept I: Five Ps for Strategy." *California Management Review 28* (Fall): 11-24.
Miles, R. E. & Snow, C.C. (1978). *Organization, Strategy, Structure, and Processes*. New York: McGraw-Hill.
Miles, R. H., & Cameron, K. S. (1982). *Coffin Nails and Corporate Strategy*. Englewood Cliffs, NJ: Prentice Hall.
Nelson, R. R. & Winter, S. G. (1982). *An Evolutionary Theory of Economic Change*. Cambridge, MA: Harvard University Press, The Belnap Press.
Perrow, C. (1986). *Complex Organizations: A Critical Essay*. New York: Random House.
Piore, M. (1992). "The Social Embeddedness of Labor Markets and Cognitive Processes." Keynote Address, 9. European Association of Labor Economists, Warwick, England.
Piore, M. & Sabel, C.F. (1984). *The Second Industrial Divide: Possibilities for Prosperity*. New York: Basic Books.
Porter, M. E. (1980). *Competitive Strategy*. New York: Free Press.
Porter, M. E. (1985). *Competitive Advantage: Creating and Sustaining Superior Performance*. New York: Free Press.
Porter, M. E. & Spence, A. M. (1982. "The Capacity Expansion Process in a Growing Oligopoly: The Case of Corn Wet Milling." In J.J. McCall, (Ed.),*The Economics of Information and Uncertainty*, pp. 259-309. Chicago: University of Chicago Press.
Prahalad, C. K. & Hamel, G. (1990). "The Core Competence of the Corporation." *Harvard Business Review 68* (May-June): 79-91.
Rappaport, A. (1986). *Creating Shareholder Value: The New Standard for Business Performance*. New York: The Free Press.
Rorty, R. (1979). *Philosophy and the Mirror of Nature*. Princeton, NJ: Princeton University Press.
Rumelt, R. P. (1974). *Strategy, Structure, and Economic Performance*. Boston: Harvard Business School, Division of Research.

Rumelt, R. P. (1987). "Theory, Strategy, and Entrepreneurship." In D. Teece (Ed.), *The Competitive Challenge: Strategies for Industrial Innovation and Renewal*, pp. 137-58. Cambridge, MA: Ballinger.

Schlesinger, J. (1966). "Organization Structures and Planning." Rand Paper, P-3316 (25 Feb.).

Schon, D. A. (1983). *The Reflective Practitioner: How Professionals Think in Action*. New York: Basic Books.

Schleifer, A. & Summers, L. (1988). "Breach of Trust in Hostile Takeovers." In A. Auerbach (Ed.), *Corporate Takeovers: Causes and Consequences*, pp. 33-56. Chicago: University of Chicago Press.

Simon, H. A. (1969). *The Sciences of the Artificial*. Cambridge, MA: MIT Press.

Simon, H. A. (1991). "Organizations and Markets." *Journal of Economic Perspectives 5:* 25-43.

Teece, D. (Ed.), (1987). *The Competitive Challenge: Strategies for Industrial Innovation and Renewal*. Cambridge, MA: Ballinger.

Temin, P. & Raff, D. (1992). *The Wharton School History Conference Papers*, 30, April.

Von Hippel, E. (1988). *The Sources of Innovation*. Oxford: Oxford University Press.

Wildavsky, A. (1988). *Searching for Safety*. New Brunswick, NJ: Transactions Books.

Williams, J. R. (1994). "Strategy and the Search for Rents: The Evolution of Diversity Among Firms." In R. Rumelt, D. Schendel, and D. Teece, (Eds.), *Fundamental Research Issues in Strategy*. Boston: Harvard Business School Press.

Williamson, O. E. (1975). *Markets and Hierarchies: Analysis and Antitrust Implications*. New York: The Free Press.

# TWENTY YEARS OF STRATEGY THEORY AND PRACTICE: WHAT HAVE WE LEARNED?
## A RESPONSE

Fred Steingraber

### INTRODUCTION: HOLISTIC MANAGEMENT

My role tonight is as provocateur and respondent to Ned Bowman's remarks on the history of strategy. Following Ned, on the subject of strategy, is a little like trying to follow Henry Kissinger on geopolitical affairs. In fact, you shouldn't if you're smart. Even if you aren't smart, you shouldn't.

I found Ned Bowman's comments on the history of strategy enormously valuable and insightful. He puts the evolution and different approaches to strategy—and its theorists and many practitioners—in a coherent framework.

In the process, we once again have the opportunity to muse over that classic—and always fascinating—dichotomy between the theoretical and the practical, the rational and the intuitive. I always find this debate fascinating because it has taken on so many guises over the centuries.

Even today in the discussion of total quality management, for instance, we see that the theoretical and the practical are not always well connected. As Professor Bowman says, "The way we talk and the way we act are often at variance." Or as we say in discussing the chief executive's role in TQM, you have to walk the talk to make TQM succeed.

My role this evening is to briefly respond to Professor Bowman's comments and to stimulate your participation and observations. To do this, I would like to refer to both Professor Bowman's identification of things learned and wisdom we still must seek.

## WHAT WE HAVE LEARNED

Professor Bowman's first proposition is, to my mind, one of the most important pieces of wisdom of the last few decades. He points out that perhaps what happens in the world affects how we think about strategy—more than strategy affects what happens in the world.

This revolutionary thought should have had the impact of Copernicus's pronouncement that the earth revolves around the sun, rather than vice versa. Unfortunately, I think there are still some planners who believe in the vice versa—in their power to control the environment.

If I can leave you with only a single message in response to Professor Bowman's proposition, it is this: Today, strategy is not the issue; execution is. Just as there are many roads to Rome, so too there are many strategies that can lead to success. The challenge isn't in defining some new economic insight or model that will win. It is in effectively executing the known models or paradigms.

To reprise some of Ned's historic landscape, I would add that strategic planning and planners gained continuously in stature throughout the sixties and early seventies and probably reached their zenith in the mid to late seventies. Planning staffs became larger, more sophisticated. They often sat at the seat of power and had access to CEOs. Increasingly, they looked very prescient especially when our economies were only going up and there was little foreign competition.

In those decades of rapid growth, too much strategic planning was (and still is) based on extrapolationism. The inherent failure of planning and of most economic models is that they are static and based on fixed assumptions. They would have us believe that the future will be like the past and present, only more so.

In the now maligned decade of the eighties, strategic planners and executives alike became especially obsessed with financial value creation.

Success in the eighties meant maximizing shareholder value. Companies were dismembered and reconstituted through divestiture, acquisitions, LBOs and ESOPs. Public companies went private, private companies went public and many reverted back to their original forms. In short, we went from the seventies where big was beautiful and diversified and the whole was greater than the sum of the parts, to the end of the eighties where small was beautiful, less risky and the sum of the parts became more valuable than the whole.

But through all of this, top executives and planners alike failed to focus on real wealth creation through products and services, rather than on maximizing short-term financial value creation. They did not foresee how their failure to create wealth, combined with no-growth markets, would be exacerbated by the recession of the nineties and increased global competition.

Today planning no longer has its boardroom elitist status. The planners of the late seventies and eighties are more distant from the boardroom and are closer to the action today—and rightfully so. They are often assigned down within the business units. This was also one of Ned's propositions: that strategy constructs are widely diffused in the firm and now are more the responsibility of line and less of staff. He is absolutely correct.

Today strategic planners no longer can play "masters of the universe" as many tried in the sixties and seventies. They have lost their sense of control over the environment. The challenge today is less one of trying to perfectly predict outcomes, and more one of responding in a timely and effective way to changes in the underlying assumptions when we recognize them. It's better to be fast than right. Today planners are increasingly at the seat of action, worrying far more about micro models than macro models, worrying about what to do to improve the competitiveness of the enterprise.

As Ned implies, the learning curve has been steep for planners and executives alike and we have come a long way. But as Ned points out, there are still plenty of things we have not learned. These range from

- Managing the rational and natural, the economic and behavioral
- To linking theory and practice
- To incorporating benchmarking into strategy among others.

## WHAT WE HAVE NOT LEARNED

First of all, let me say I believe we are already in a new phase of the development or evolution of strategy and strategic planning, a phase that is attempting to address some of the items "we have not learned." Today we are focused much more on effective execution, on wealth creation and on winning.

Hans Thorelli, in fact, very appropriately set the stage with this collegium and his manifesto on integral strategy, which he refers to as a holistic concept. Integrated strategy or the integration of functions is truly a prerequisite to holistic management and is the challenge of the day or decade.

We at A.T. Kearney observe this interdisciplinary approach or interfunctional fit in companies that transcend mere functional excellence to reach what we refer to as Stage 4 in A.T. Kearney's Stages of Excellence. This is a diagnostic tool we use in combination with benchmarking and best practices. The stages concept shows how companies change in a predictable pattern of growth, from entrepreneurial in Stage 1, through budget-driven or bureaucratic in Stage 2, to functionally excellent in Stage 3.

But, to reach Stage 4, a company has to make an integration breakthrough that refocuses on the customer (internal as well as external). This can only be achieved when the company looks at its work as a series of business processes carried out by teams that cross functional lines. Stage 4 companies—and very few companies today have reached this stage—blur the functional organization structure. They refocus around the key business *processes*—the processes that are most important to their success. This may have to be done as we develop and engineer new products, or to achieve a total downstream and upstream seamless supply management chain. Or we may integrate functionally to support the delivery of core products and services with a broad range of peripheral service enhancements tied to meeting key customer goals.

The ultimate effect of this breakthrough is that the company more closely reaches a stage of holistic or integrated management.

There are many implications for strategy and strategic planners in this concept. Today's planners, no matter what their role or location within the organization, need to see the value of this in the approach to their work. And if there are traditional turf battles to be fought in the cause of integration, the planner should be in the thick of the battle—on the side of the forces of process over the forces of function and form.

I would like to briefly outline what I believe to be the three principal areas of debate and change now taking place in this phase of the evolution of strategy.

## AREAS OF DEBATE AND CHANGE

### Favor Execution Over Planning

Executives and planners alike are becoming more concerned about good execution than about good planning.

The key to winning is a strong focus on best practices of others and developing real strategic alliances with suppliers and customers. This is true no matter what business we are in.

The key to good execution is integration of the functions that I described earlier. This enables employees to work across department lines to concentrate on customers, service and quality for competitive advantage. The bridge between the internal and external is the emphasis on business processes. When employees are empowered to act to improve business processes (whether we're talking about new product development, logistics, or order processing), the result benefits the customer and disadvantages the competitor. The emphasis on reengineering our business processes means a de-emphasis on function and all that is attendant to that.

To add value, planners have to be closer to the customer in this interaction. The relocation of the planner to the division or business unit within many companies—while it may have seemed like banishment from the seat of power—is an invaluable opportunity to get close to the customer and to make a difference for the customer by adding value.

### Develop Responsive, Innovative Organizations

Successful organizations today are, to use Jack Welch's word, *borderless*. They are flatter, and are relearning how to be responsive and innovative. There's no time in today's organization for hierarchical decisionmaking.

Internally the key to a strong customer focus is empowerment. Employees must be empowered to create change, to improve quality on the spot and to respond to customer needs when they're on the front line. As Ray Smith of Bell Atlantic says, "We have to move from linear decisions to simultaneous decision-making capabilities. Power must become intrinsic in every job, not just the office of the CEO."

The economy and the dramatic changes in the global marketplace in the last decade leave us no choice in this matter. We have to re-engineer our companies.

Demand is flat. Mature economies are in a no-growth mode and we will continue to have fairly high unemployment, depressed consumer confidence and purchasing power.

The challenge is to work on innovation. As defined by Akio Morita of Sony, that means *working on both the denominator and numerator simultaneously*. The denominator means making continuous productivity improvements to maintain competitive parity. The numerator means introducing new products and services that add value and have higher margins. This means looking for ways to define new or additional peripheral products and services to the core offering, thereby adding value and avoiding having to compete on price alone.

### Turn Planners Into Activists

For strategic planning to contribute leadership in this phase of the continuing evolution of planning, planners must be close to the action and take more of an activist and less of an analyst role in helping to bring about change.

That means they should begin by intellectually engaging the organization in benchmarking and best practice comparisons. Stages of Excellence is a step beyond benchmarking and best practices per se. It provides an independent framework for improvement within stages and from one stage to the other.

It means planners must participate in defining the change process. They must help establish a vision for the corporation that inspires people to act. They must focus on helping leadership establish a few ambitious goals to drive the organization forward, then make sure that the operating plans and actions support the goals.

Moreover, planners should help companies articulate values that support their goals. In recent A.T. Kearney research, we found that the top-performing companies in the world emphasize the need for values more than procedures, policies or even systems. They emphasize the need for values because in an environment of constant change, geographic and cultural diversity, *values become the bonding agent*.

The real challenge today is to motivate people with average abilities to achieve above average results. We can't wait for educational reforms and improved skill and management training. The most important things to be communicated across the corporation are goals and values, whether they are related to quality, service, innovation, or empowerment. This is one of the biggest challenges for the chief executive today—and the chief executive needs help from the whole team, including the strategic planner.

Today the role of strategic management is to make a difference competitively at the operational level. That's what good execution is all about: To be value adding as part of the business process, and to help the company move through the stages of excellence.

## CONCLUSION

In conclusion, I would observe that the biggest challenge of the nineties is leadership, not management or even planning. Management deals with knowns. Leadership deals with unknowns. Leadership converts unknowns into knowns so they can be managed. Leadership's key task is to take risks.

- Without risk, there is no change.
- Without change, there will be no growth.
- Without growth, there is no value creation.

Each and every one of us, whether chief executive, manager or planner must become risk-takers, missionaries for change and better executers in the nineties. We must facilitate, energize, encourage empowerment and seek ways to improve the execution of strategy and change, and not preserve the status quo.

This is the new phase of strategic planning, which I believe we have already entered. I believe early in the next century we will have found a good deal of the wisdom necessary to address the challenges that Professor Bowman so correctly cites as "What we have not learned."

So, one era of strategic planning is over and another has begun. And by the time we believe we have mastered the challenges of the nineties, it will be time for Ned to reassess and remind us all of how wrong we are if we ever believe there is an end to this process.

# DISCUSSION

## E.W. Kelley, Chair

At least one participant took exception to Fred Steingraber's statements that it is more important to be fast than right. From the perspective of one executive, it was suggested, "It is much more important to be fast and right, because you can bet your company. You could be betting your whole future if you make the wrong decisions." (But too much contemplation may mean a lost opportunity? –*Ed. note*)

*Lester Balick* asked Fred Steingraber to clarify the role of planning: "Does the planning function need to continue to exist in industry with a position such as 'planning guru,' or should the role be incorporated into the company's leadership function?"

*Steingraber:*

The planning activity, or function as you referred to it, continues to exist, but it has been placed in a different location in many organizations. The chief executive and the key leaders of organizations now are far more involved in this process than they were back in the seventies, in my view. I think there was a tendency back in the seventies to "throw it over the wall," as they used to say in the engineering/manufacturing vernacular, and see what comes out. Today, however, there is a much greater emphasis on reducing disconnected planning efforts. There is also a more integrated focus on determining the few basic things that we need to do as an organization to win, to become number one or two.

*Robert Klemkosky* suggested that strategic planners often lack fundamental economics training and that they were naive regarding the concept of corporate governance issues in the 1980s. He asked for the speakers' opinions of these potential educational problems.

*Bowman:*

The short answer to your question is "yes." I believe that the people involved in strategic planning in firms should know a great deal more about economics. I also believe they should be versed in the *behavioral sciences*, especially those attempting to understand why people make decisions the way they do.

*Steingraber:*

I think all individuals that aspire to a position of leadership in business must have some economics background, whether you are a planner or whether you are a plant manager. I think it is invaluable.

Now, having said that, I think it would be very interesting—and I would love to see the University tackle it—to compare the backgrounds of leaders in U.S. industry versus leaders of Japanese industry and European industry. My limited research and anecdotal evidence suggests that there are potentially significant differences in the backgrounds that these people have. Further, it appears that the relative pay of executives in different functional areas seems to differ considerably from one culture to the other. This brings up the significance of issues in *reward systems* and *motivation*. Sometimes, I think we should ask ourselves if we have been doing everything that we should have in terms of preparing our leaders.

*Rajan Varadarajan* expressed concern about the emphasis on *benchmarking best practices and strategy*. He indicated that strategies can be secretive, manipulative, preemptive, and often take competitors with surprise. When that is the case, they can't be recognized up front (or discovered during benchmarking). Second, certain aspects of strategy often cannot be clearly articulated even by the firm. "Even if it can be articulated by someone in the firm it may be detrimental to the interest of the firm to do so." And finally, "too often strategy is retrospective rationalization...so, how can one go about benchmarking best practices and strategies?"

*Bowman:*

Your question is appropriate, but I think that the idea of learning from people that are doing at least some things better than you makes an awful lot of sense. Our intelligence in the complex world is highly limited, and we will only learn so many things from textbooks and academic training. Therefore, it makes sense to reach out and study what steps competitors are taking, what their analysis is, what their information sources are.

I would also agree with you in some sense that one firm could better explain to another how they do quality assurance, say, than how they do strategy. Sometimes the strategy process is ill-understood in the firm, and you may not get a good picture of the strategy process. However, I am offering a challenge rather than having all of the answers.

One example of potential benefits of benchmarking the process of restructuring has resulted from some recent research. One could ask the question, If we are going to be restructuring, can we discover the good stories and bad stories of restructuring before we move forward? Our study suggests that there is a negative correlation between being able to solve new product development problems and the amount of restructuring you are going through. This is the case for at least two reasons. The people who develop products have to do questionable things, borrow a little here, fix a little there, and they have to stick their neck out. People are just not willing to stick their neck out if the company is going through substantial downsizing. Second, in order to really make the new product development process work, you cannot do it all formally; you have to do a lot of it informally. Layoffs can break informal networks that people have learned to use.

*Ed:*

It was suggested that benchmarking is something that professional consultants do without even trying. That is, they develop best practices from what they observe in various industries, and they share their observations with different clients.

*Steingraber:*

I would like to make three points. I think the first thing we all have to remember, is that the *usefulness of benchmarking is* not understanding somebody's strategy as much as it is being able to emulate it or *to improve upon it.* In other words, knowledge of a best practice is not going to help you win if you cannot execute it better than the competitor. Second, today's leading companies are not out benchmarking against their competitors, they are benchmarking best practices *across industries.* For example, the transportation industry is looking at the manufacturing industry practices and the banking industry is looking at the manufacturing industry practices.

My third point is that a set of standards is beginning to emerge with regard to benchmarking. A code of ethics is in the process of being established. Meanwhile, we have adopted as a firm our own code of ethics, and we are willing to share that with anybody who is going to participate in benchmarking exercises. It is important that they know on what basis the information is being collected, on what basis other people may have access to the information, and if an individual is looking for exclusivity, and other special circumstances, and so on. The chances are that the information may be obtained, processed and protected in a way that is more neutral if a third party is involved.

*Hans Thorelli* closed the Session with a few observations about the nature of strategic planning:

I would just like to add two points that may be rather obvious, but perhaps so obvious that you didn't even think about them. The first point is that we have finally learned that strategic planning is not a one-time shot, a once-every-three-years shot, or a-once-every-five-years shot. Strategic planning must be a *continuous process,* heavily influenced by unforeseen events and opportunities that will inevitably occur—no matter what scenarios were developed in past plans.

The second, and slightly related point, has to do with *implementation gap*. Ned Bowman talked a lot about strategy planning, and I think that Fred's idea was to suggest that the key is not strategy itself. The key is implementation. Most of us, whether we are executives or academics or consultants, have experienced this question of implementation gap. Over two or three decades, we have also learned something about the reasons for implementation gap. Of course, the key reason was that in the beginning of this "strategy story" we thought that planners were the people who were going to do the planning. So we hired all kinds of experts and put them away in a bull pen and three months later they came out with the plan...and that was the last thing we heard of it. However, we have learned that people who are going to execute have to be part of the planning process. That has taken three decades to learn. It is a self-evident concept when you think about it, especially in Western countries, democratically organized, and therefore inherently biased in favor of participation, such as the United States. So participation in planning by the so-called "line people," is indispensable to the implementation and the success of the plan.

# II GLOBALIZATION AND THE LOCATION OF ADVANTAGE

# EDITOR'S NOTE

In the nineties it is certainly proper to begin with the topic of globalization of strategy in any attempt to inventory current trends and issues. The academic speaker of the day on this topic is Michael Porter. In his presentation he makes a vigorous claim that the growing internationalization of business notwithstanding, the local context of key elements of any strategic business unit constitute a vital source of competitive advantage. Relating to his celebrated strategic "diamond," Porter develops in some detail why this is so, and eloquently refutes the notion that fully integrated units are needed in all Triad regions and other views on the subject by various strategy gurus.

It is vital to understand that integral strategy in globalization does *not* call for an identical strategy in all corners of the world. True, Porter and others call for a differential strategy. But adaptation actually may increase the need for overall integral strategy that will minimize geographic and functional suboptimization and enhance the value contributions of the entire MNC. Yet it is also clear that integral strategy is not synonymous with centralization or total coordination.

Porter's general impact on strategic thought is superbly defined in Dan Schendel's concluding essay: By making managerial choice in an explicitly environmental context the focal point of analysis, Porter succeeded in turning Industrial Organization economics on its head, and made its findings useful in policymaking in the private sector (i.e., at the company level).

The global perspective is further applied in Sessions 3 and 4.

# GLOBAL COMPETITION AND THE LOCALIZATION OF COMPETITIVE ADVANTAGE[1]

Michael E. Porter and Rebecca E. Wayland

One of the seminal forces affecting companies in the postwar period has been the globalization of competition. As transport and communication costs have fallen, national infrastructures have become more similar, and trade barriers have eased, international trade and investment have grown markedly. The need for global, as opposed to domestic, strategies has become a given in a wide and widening range of industries.

As the globalization of competition has become more apparent, it is no surprise that research on international strategy has taken on greater prominence. This research, by and large, has concentrated on the power of the multinational company to create competitive advantage through its globalness. A global strategy, involving operations spread to many countries, has been seen as a powerful engine for reaping economies of scale, assimilating and responding to international market needs, and efficiently assembling resources such as capital, labor, raw materials, and technology from around the world. Authors as diverse as Ohmae, Reich, and Bartlett and Ghoshal see the global firm as transcending national boundaries. The national identity of a corporation must be replaced, in this view, by a strategic paradigm which knows no borders.

When considering the globalization of competition, however, one must confront an important paradox—although companies are competing globally and inputs such as raw materials, capital, and even scientific knowledge now move freely around the world, there is strong evidence that location continues to play a crucial role in competitive advantage. There are striking and persistent differences in the economic performance of nations, and of states and cities within nations.[2] The world's leading competitors in a wide variety of industries are all based in one or two countries, especially if industries are defined narrowly in ways that are meaningful for setting strategy and cases where government heavily distorts competition are eliminated. This geographic concentration is true not only in established industries such as automobiles and machine tools but also in new industries such as software, biotechnology, and advanced materials. Within companies, global firms have indeed dispersed activities to many countries, but they concentrate a critical mass of their most important activities for competing in each business in one location.

This paper aims to reconcile these seemingly contradictory developments. In order to understand the new international competition, we must recognize that the paradigm defining competitiveness has shifted from static efficiency to one based on continuous innovation and upgrading. In the new paradigm, the firm's home base for a particular business is where competitive advantage ultimately resides. Global strategies are ways of leveraging and extending home base advantages through sourcing inputs, accessing foreign markets, and selectively tapping specialized capabilities. We conclude by examining the implications of the new paradigm for global strategy and organizational structure.

## EVOLVING CONCEPTS OF GLOBAL STRATEGY

With the growing prominence of MNCs after World War II, there has been a stream of research on international business both in business schools and by economists.[3] The earliest work addressed the problems of doing business abroad and the sequence by which companies internationalized. In economics, a major contribution was the 1960 thesis by Hymer (and subsequent work by Kindleberger [1969]) which identify foreign direct investment as a manifestation of market imperfections. The focus was on the choice of foreign direct investment versus alternative organizational and market forms, such as licensing or exporting. Kindleberger's work saw a firm's decision to invest in a foreign country as driven by imperfections in product markets, imperfections in factor markets, economies of scale, and government policies.

A complementary stream of research examined in more detail the motivations leading firms to establish or expand operations outside their home country. Vernon (1966) examined the effect of product life cycles, particularly the need to enter new markets and lower production costs once products matured, demand became more elastic, and production processes more standardized. Caves (1971) highlighted the ability of MNCs to extend advantages due to differentiation and other intangible assets created in the home market to other country markets, thereby overcoming the inherent disadvantages faced by a foreign firm. Knickerbocker (1974) examined the growth of international investment within an industry as a "follow the leader" phenomena in which firms moved abroad in response to expansion by a competitor. Graham's (1974) complementary work saw international expansion as the result of an "exchange of threats," in which firms used their position in various markets to threaten competitors in the equivalent of a global chess match. Overall, this stream of research identified the advantages of firms with locations around the world in terms of their ability to gain economies of scale, to scan for new technologies or products, and to achieve flexibility in competitive gaming with rivals.

In the early 1970s, more attention was directed at theories of the multinational corporation itself. This work was broadly introduced by Johnson (1970) who broadened the definition of factors of production to include technological and managerial knowledge. McManus (1972), Buckley and Casson (1976), and Magee (1976) focused on the operation of the multinational corporation. Buckley and Casson, who are usually credited with the most pronounced influence, framed the MNC as consisting of a broad range of interdependent activities connected by transfers of knowledge and expertise. Rugman (1977) extended this work to examine MNCs as a means of internalizing markets for the transfer of intermediate products. The MNC form arises because these kinds of intangible assets—know how, brand names, and so forth—cannot be easily traded across borders via markets because of high transaction costs.

Dunning (1977) sought to integrate a variety of perspectives through his "eclectic paradigm" for explaining the existence of the MNC, encompassing ownership advantages, location advantages (immobile factors or trade barriers), and internalization advantages. Dunning also highlighted structural (e.g., trade barriers) and transactional market failures as determining the locations of activities across nations and the division of activities between multinational and uninational firms.

The management literature focused on the operations of the MNC, and how foreign subsidiaries could be better coordinated into a global enterprise. Perlmutter's (1969) work, for example, raised the distinction between ethnocentric, polycentric, and geocentric organizations, making the case that the geocentric form was superior. A critical challenge identified by more managerially oriented literature was the trade-off between global integration and local responsiveness. Prahalad (1975) and subsequent works by Doz, and Bartlett and Prahalad (1981) focused on how managers should address these trade-offs. Since country needs were different, the essence of global strategy was framed as how to reconcile the need to be responsive to national differences with the compelling benefits of global efficiency.

Some, notably Hout, Porter, and Rudden (1982) and Levitt (1983), saw the MNC not simply as a respondent to competitive forces but as having the capacity to transform industry structures through new modes of competing. Levitt's controversial but influential essay argued that international needs were homogenizing, but that multinationals could hasten the process through marketing activities. Levitt was making the case, then, that the efficiency/responsiveness tradeoff could be tilted in the global firm's favor. A similar and broader argument was contained in Hout, Porter and Rudden, who highlighted the proactive role of product design, the choice of production process, and other aspects of strategy in globalizing competition.

In general, this stream of research stressed the advantages of the multinational's *network* as a competitive advantage and how such a network could be managed. How and where the intangible assets that underpinned the MNC were created has not been addressed in the literature, and represents important questions stressed in our (1990) work.

## Toward a General Framework for Global Strategy

Our earlier research on global strategy (1986) sought to integrate these disparate streams of research into a unified framework for understanding the patterns of international competition across industries and the implications for the global strategy of firms, drawing on research in industrial organization as well as a newer stream of work on competitive strategy and the sources of competitive advantage.

This framework begins by recognizing that there is not one single pattern of international competition but many. The nature of international competition in industries can be arrayed along a spectrum. On one end are *multidomestic industries*, where the industry is present in many countries but competition takes place on a country-by-country basis with little or no linkage among them. Examples include most types of retailing, metal fabrication, construction, and many services. On the other end of the spectrum are *global industries*, in which competition in different countries is connected because a firm's position in one country is affected by its position elsewhere. Prominent examples are commercial aircraft, consumer electronics, and automobiles. In multidomestic industries, the "global" strategy should be a series of distinct domestic strategies. In global industries, however, firms must create integrated strategies involving all countries simultaneously.

Most issues in strategy are the same for domestic and global companies. In both cases, performance is a function of the attractiveness of the industry in which the firm competes and its relative position in that industry (Porter 1980). The firm's competitive position depends on its competitive advantage (or disadvantage) vis-à-vis its rivals. Competitive advantage is manifested either in lower cost than rivals, or the ability to differentiate and command a premium price that exceeds the extra cost of differentiating.

Competitive advantage cannot be examined independently of competitive scope, or the breadth of the firm's market target. Scope encompasses a number of dimensions including the product and buyer segments served, the degree of vertical integration, and the extent of related businesses in which the firm has a coordinated strategy. The array of geographic locations at which the firm competes is also a dimension of scope, which we concentrate on here. Competitive advantage is attained within some scope, so that the choice of scope is a central one in strategy. Both domestic and global companies must understand the structure of their industry, identify their sources of competitive advantage, and analyze competitors.

To understand the underpinnings of competitive advantage, we must decompose what firms do into the *value chain* (see Figure 1) (Porter 1985). A firm is a collection of discrete, but interrelated economic *activities*, such as products being assembled, salespeople making sales visits, and orders being processed. Activities involve human resources, physical assets, technologies, routines, and information. "Strengths," "competence," "capabilities," and "resources"—common phrases in discussions of strategy—are best understood in terms of particular activities in which the firm has an advantage, skills, physical assets, or technologies embodied in activities, or the ability to link activities or improve them over time.

A firm's strategy defines its configuration of activities and how they interrelate. The activity is the basic foundation of competitive advantage. Competitive advantage results from a firm's ability to perform the required activities at a collectively lower cost than rivals, or to perform some activities in unique ways that create buyer value, and hence support a premium price. Creating buyer value depends, in turn, on the influence of a firm on the activities of its channels and end users. Buyer value arises when a firm's activities (including the product itself) lower buyers' cost or raise buyers' performance relative to competitor activities. The required mix and configuration of activities, in turn, is altered by competitive scope. Broadly targeted competitors seek to gain advantages by sharing activities across an array of industry segments. Narrowly targeted competitors (which I term focusers) seek advantage through tailoring activities to the needs of a particular segment(s).

The value chain groups a firm's activities into categories, distinguishing between those directly involved in producing, marketing, delivering, and supporting the product and those that create or source inputs (factors) required

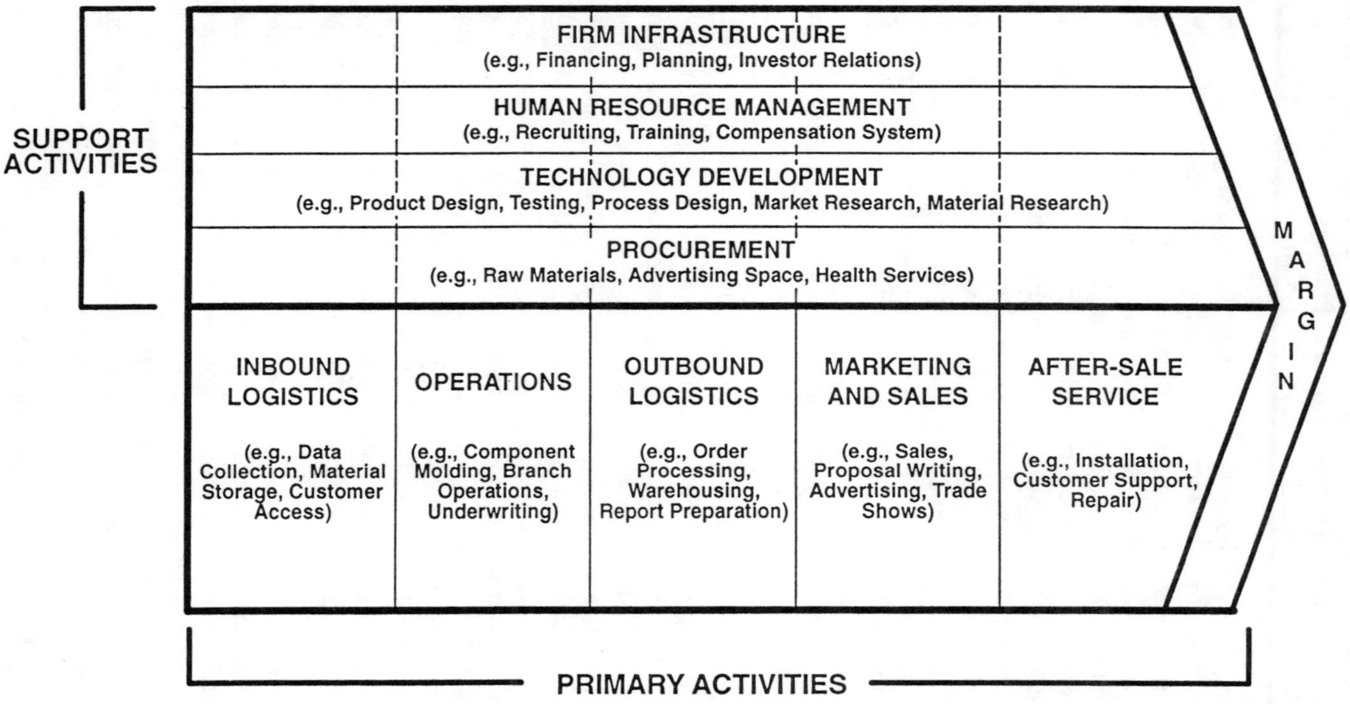

|  | | | | | MARGIN | |
|---|---|---|---|---|---|---|
| SUPPORT ACTIVITIES | FIRM INFRASTRUCTURE (e.g., Financing, Planning, Investor Relations) | | | | | |
| | HUMAN RESOURCE MANAGEMENT (e.g., Recruiting, Training, Compensation System) | | | | | |
| | TECHNOLOGY DEVELOPMENT (e.g., Product Design, Testing, Process Design, Market Research, Material Research) | | | | | |
| | PROCUREMENT (e.g., Raw Materials, Advertising Space, Health Services) | | | | | |
| | INBOUND LOGISTICS (e.g., Data Collection, Material Storage, Customer Access) | OPERATIONS (e.g., Component Molding, Branch Operations, Underwriting) | OUTBOUND LOGISTICS (e.g., Order Processing, Warehousing, Report Preparation) | MARKETING AND SALES (e.g., Sales, Proposal Writing, Advertising, Trade Shows) | AFTER-SALE SERVICE (e.g., Installation, Customer Support, Repair) | |
| | PRIMARY ACTIVITIES | | | | | |

*Figure 1.* The value chain.

to do so. Discrete activities are much narrower, and include such economic processes as field repair, in-bound materials, receiving and storage, and billing. The identity of individual discrete activities depends on the particular business. The ability to gain advantages in either cost or differentiation in an activity depends on underlying activity economics.

The concept of the value chain provides the way to highlight the strategy issues that are unique to global industries. While both domestic and global firms have value chains, the global firm has special latitude along two dimensions. The first is *configuration*, or where the activities in a firm's value chain are located. In a domestic company, all activities are located in a single country. In a global company, however, firms can choose where to locate each activity to enhance competitive advantage. Assembly can be in one country, and product R&D in another. The second unique dimension of strategy in a global company is *coordination*, or the nature and extent to which the conduct of dispersed activities is coordinated versus allowing activities the autonomy to tailor their approach to local circumstances. It is a firm's choice in these two areas which give rise to the unique competitive advantages from competing globally rather than domestically.

## Configuration

The international configuration of a firm's activities creates competitive advantage in two ways. The first is through choosing *where* to locate. Some activities, such as sales and distribution, are necessarily tied to the customer. A firm seeking to sell in a country must either establish its own activities or rely on others (e.g., distributors, joint-venture partners). Other activities, however, can be decoupled from the customer, giving the global firm greater discretion in the number and location of its activities. The global firm can, for example, locate activities in whatever country has a comparative advantage in that activity, such as low-cost labor, or a favorable supply of raw materials. Some multinational software firms, for example, have located debugging and software maintenance activities in India to access low-cost programmers. The location with comparative advantage varies by activity, giving the global firm the potential to gain competitive advantage by arbitraging comparative advantages across locations. There are other reasons for locating in a particular nation (or state) which I will examine later.

In addition to deciding where to locate, a global firm can also choose *how many* locations in which to perform an activity. The firm can concentrate an activity in one location to serve the world, or disperse the activity to several or many locations. By concentrating an activity, firms may gain economies of scale or progress rapidly down the learning curve. Concentrating a group of activities in one location may also allow a firm to better coordinate across them.

Dispersing activities, in contrast, may be justified by the need to minimize transportation and storage costs, hedge against the risks of a single activity site, tailor the activity to local market needs, facilitate learning about country market conditions that can be transmitted to headquarters, and respond to local government pressure or incentives to locate in a country in order to sell or produce there. Sometimes firms disperse one activity to a country in order to gain the ability (or permission by government) to concentrate others. Establishing local assembly plants in a variety of countries, for example, may allow a company to import scale-sensitive components to each country in which it has an assembly operation and hence concentrate its production of them. The global firm should disperse those particular activities which involve the *least* sacrifice in terms of economies of scale and learning, and the least need for close coordination with other activities.

## Coordination

The way that a firm coordinates its activities around the world determines its ability to benefit from a particular configuration. By coordinating methods, technology, and output decisions across dispersed activities, global corporations can achieve a number of potential competitive advantages. These include the ability to respond to shifting comparative advantage (e.g., raw material prices, exchange rates); to share learning among countries; to reinforce the corporate brand image for mobile buyers who encounter the firm in different places (e.g., McDonald's or Coca-Cola); to differentiate with multinational buyers who simultaneously deal with several of the firm's units; to gain bargaining advantages with governments through possessing the ability to expand or contract local operations; and/or to respond more effectively to competitors by choosing the location at which to do battle. Conversely, allowing each dispersed site to act autonomously and tailor its activities to local circumstances may be the source of competitive advantage in other cases. Where local needs and conditions vary and where there are few economies of scale and only local customers, a strategy involving high levels of autonomy for dispersed units is favored.

Coordination encompasses the setting of standards, the exchange of information, and the allocation of responsibility among sites. Coordination (which involves allocating responsibilities across countries such as worldwide responsibility for producing particular models) can unleash economies of scale. Coordination involving information exchange is needed to reap the benefits of worldwide learning. Coordination, then, can allow a firm to realize the advantages of dispersing its activities, just as a failure to coordinate activities can lessen those advantages.

Coordination across geographically dispersed locations involves daunting organizational challenges, among them language, cultural differences, and difficulties in aligning individual managers' and subsidiaries' incentives with those of the global enterprise as a whole. Some forms of coordination, such as allocating responsibilities for component production to different locations, require less ongoing interchange than others and are more readily implemented. A central issue in coordination is how and where information, technology, and other knowledge from disparate locations is *integrated* and reflected in products, processes, and other activities.

## Implications for Global Strategy

This framework allows us to understand and explain the patterns of global competition and think systematically about crafting a global strategy for competing in a particular industry. Some competitive advantages are location based, while others relate to the overall global network and the way it is managed. There is not one pattern of global competition, but many depending on the particular activities that are concentrated and dispersed, their locations, and how activities are coordinated. Competition in an industry globalizes when the competitive advantages of a global configuration and coordination across dispersed activities exceed the costs. The balance of these advantages and costs varies by activity and by industry.

In multidomestic industries, industry structure favors a highly dispersed configuration in which virtually the entire value chain is located in each country. There are strong benefits in multidomestic industries to allowing dispersed units nearly full autonomy. In global industries, concentrating some activities to serve world markets, and tightly coordinating among those activities that are dispersed, yields significant competitive advantages. As industry economics, buyer needs, and government policies change over time, the pattern of globalization will also change.

Even in global industries, there is no one type of global strategy. Strategies will differ in terms of which activities are concentrated and dispersed, where activities are located, and the nature and extent of coordination achieved. They also differ in the extent to which companies perform activities independently or rely on partners. Firms have an active role in shifting the benefits and costs of a global strategy. Firms can redefine competition through strategic innovations that increase the advantages of a global strategy or reduce its costs. Becton Dickinson, for example, created worldwide demand for disposable syringes in favor of reusable glass syringes. By being the first mover, Becton Dickinson was able to emerge as the world leader. In other cases, firms triggered globalization by pioneering new approaches to competing that increased economies, or invented product designs or production processes that reduced the cost of tailoring products to differing country needs. Many global industry leaders emerged because they were the first to perceive and act on these levers. Theodore Levitt's work on the globalization of markets is typically seen as arguing the merits of world products. Yet his essay is more important than commonly recognized in stressing the ability of the firm to *create* world products, by pioneering new approaches to segmentation and marketing rather than passively responding to preexisting needs.

### Recent Conceptions of Global Strategy

Recent writings on global competition and strategy have taken the argument about globalization to its ultimate limit. With global markets, global firms, and modern information and communications technology, recent work asserts that national borders have been transcended. Three leading works—by Ohmae (1985, 1990), Reich (1991), and Bartlett and Ghoshal (1989)—are each different but reflect this underlying perspective.

*Ohmae*

Ohmae's point of view is captured by the title of his 1990 book *The Borderless World*.[4] Ohmae sees globalization as having accelerated the tempo of technology commercialization, and equalized the flow of information to consumers in different markets. New process technology has caused a shift within corporations from labor to capital-intensive processes, and has decreased the advantage of tapping low-cost labor sources. The principal source of competitive advantage for corporations, then, has become the ability to gain economies of scale in order to amortize the fixed cost of developing and applying technology. This requires that a firm have access to global markets so that it can sell its products to consumers around the world.

Although demand has become more homogeneous and some global segments have emerged for high-priced products, Ohmae argues that distinctive differences among consumers remain, particularly in commodity products which are purchased frequently.[5] It is important, then, that firms become as close to their customers as possible by becoming "insiders" in major markets. This requires firms to establish *full business systems* (a complete value chain, in our parlance, including not only marketing and production but also administration and R&D) that is tailored to each particular market. As a market develops, an entire business system would thus be put in place for that area and, over time, tailored to meet specific local needs. Market-specific business systems should be managed through regional (rather than worldwide) headquarters to maintain flexibility and responsiveness. Regional headquarters should function relatively independently with only limited intervention from the corporate center. Ohmae sees the establishment of protectionist barriers as reinforcing the need for establishing a full business system in each part of the so-called Triad—North America, Europe, and Asia.

The agenda that Ohmae presents for firms encompasses five stages of globalization, ultimately achieving the goal of "global localization." In this final stage, all customers are equal, country of product origin and location of headquarters do not matter, and companies use regionally based headquarters to remain close to their local customers. Firms should shed the identity of their home nation in order to respond to customer needs and business system requirements of each market. Ohmae stresses the need to overcome a headquarters mentality that focuses excessively on the home country. Corporate managers should be "equidistant" from all markets, with equal emphasis on the importance of customers, suppliers, and consumer trends in each part of the Triad. Maintaining an insider status in each region is needed to access knowledge that may be present there. The corporate center should play a relatively limited role in business operations, focusing on establishing corporate values, providing consistent employee training throughout the world, and encouraging the creation of informal networks among regions. Global managers thus play an important role in focusing the operations, decisions, and attention of the organization on the particular needs of local markets.

## Reich

In Reich's conception of global competition, capital, information, and skilled individuals flow freely around the world through corporate "webs of enterprise" (Reich 1991). There are homogenized markets and free mobility across national boundaries. The only things not mobile are less-skilled workers and infrastructure. Competition has shifted from producing large volumes and gaining economies of scale to providing high value, in which competitive advantage is gained by transmitting information and ideas to serve small customer segments distributed around the world. Competition based on information and ideas has separated workers into "symbolic analysts"—or sophisticated problem solvers who are internationally mobile—and low-skilled or service workers bound to their home country. Because they cannot contribute to the new high value, expertise-intensive environment, low-skilled workers will face growing pressures on wages. In this environment, corporations become agglomerations of decentralized but interconnected activities that transcend national boundaries. Their products have no national origin but are "international composites," with R&D performed in one location, production in another, and assembly in a third. In our parlance, *each activity* is located in the country which offers the best combination of factor costs, lower-level skills, and government incentives.[6]

Reich's agenda is focused primarily on how policymakers should deal with the effects of globalization on different types of workers, yet his conclusions may also be examined from a corporate perspective. The most successful corporations will be decentralized federations of groups performing different activities, in which the groups are linked together. The home country of a firm is of minimal importance, and corporate headquarters may be located anywhere. In Reich's view, global managers play an important role in facilitating the rapid flow of information throughout the organization.

*Bartlett and Ghoshal*

Bartlett and Ghoshal's global competition is one where the "transnational" firm is destined to win (Bartlett & Ghoshal 1989). Their starting point echoes some of the earlier work on global strategy, which focused on the tension between responding to local differences and gaining global economies of scale. In their view, globalization has standardized many aspects of international markets yet has not eliminated differences among countries. Traditional corporate organizations, focusing primarily on either local responsiveness or global standardization, sacrifice important opportunities for competitive advantage. Corporations should forego traditional distinctions of national versus global organizations to become transnational. In this configuration, some activities are centralized at headquarters to gain economies of scale, develop core competence, and provide close management supervision. Others are centralized in other countries to reap scale economies, gain access to resources, or source low cost factors. Still others are decentralized to meet local needs and preserve flexibility.

In contrast to Ohmae, Bartlett and Ghoshal believe that corporations should not view each country as equal. Some countries have more sophisticated customers, more local rivalry, or more technological advances than others. Corporations can thus gain competitive advantage by locating core activities in the most sophisticated areas of the world and then coordinating among them. Strong national organizations that are located in strategically important markets should serve as "strategic leaders" for the entire corporation in developing and implementing organizational initiatives or competitive responses in their area of competence. Research and development could thus be led by the national organization of one country, product design by another, and sophisticated assembly by a third.

In this respect, Bartlett and Ghoshal agree with Reich that the *individual* activities in the value chain should be separated and dispersed around the world. The authors differ from Reich, however, in noting that different activities in the value chain require different levels of efficiency, responsiveness, and capabilities for learning. They note that within each activity, there is typically a distinctive "center of gravity" or force which determines the strategic demands for that activity. The most important activities should thus be located in an environment that is closest to this center of gravity, or in the most "sophisticated" location for that activity. Decisions about less important activities, such as product assembly, should be more strongly influenced by cost considerations.

# Global Competition and the Localization of Competitive Advantage

Because the home market may not offer the most specialized expertise nor the most cost effective location for many activities, firms should avoid excessive focus on the home market. In the Bartlett/Ghoshal model, as in that of Reich, coordination is crucial because core activities are dispersed around the world. Forging interdependent relationships among product, functional, and geographic groups is thus one of the most important tasks for global managers.

## The Three Perspectives Compared

If we relate these recent perspectives to our general framework for global competition, we see that each has a somewhat different view of the best configuration of activities globally and the nature of the required coordination.

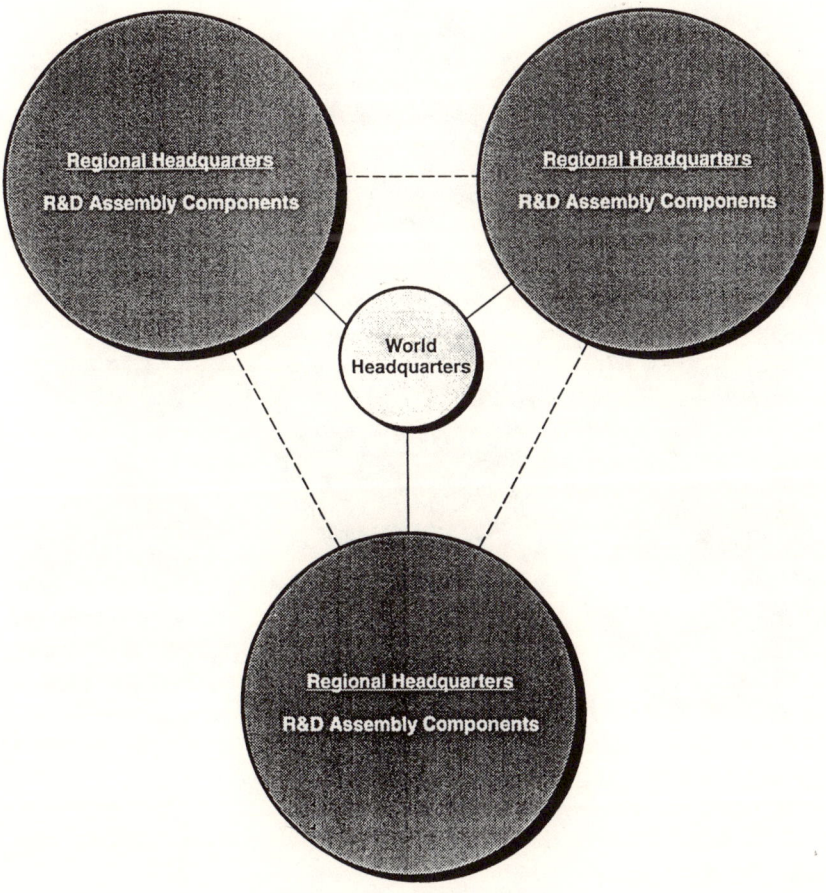

*Figure 2.* Ohmae model.

Implicit in each of the three approaches is a set of hypotheses about the costs and benefits of concentrating and dispersing various activities. Especially in the case of Ohmae and Reich, all industries are seen as following the same pattern of globalization and facing similar competitive challenges.

According to Ohmae, corporations should establish three integrated, regional firms each with a full value chain (see Figure 2). In this view, all activities should be dispersed to each of the three regions in order to gain market access and scale, and remain close to customers. Central and regional coordination in Ohmae's model is relatively loose. Corporate headquarters can be located anywhere as long as it treats each regional subsidiary as equally important. Informal interchange occurs across regional operations, but regional subsidiaries are largely autonomous and focus on the distinctive needs of their own market areas.

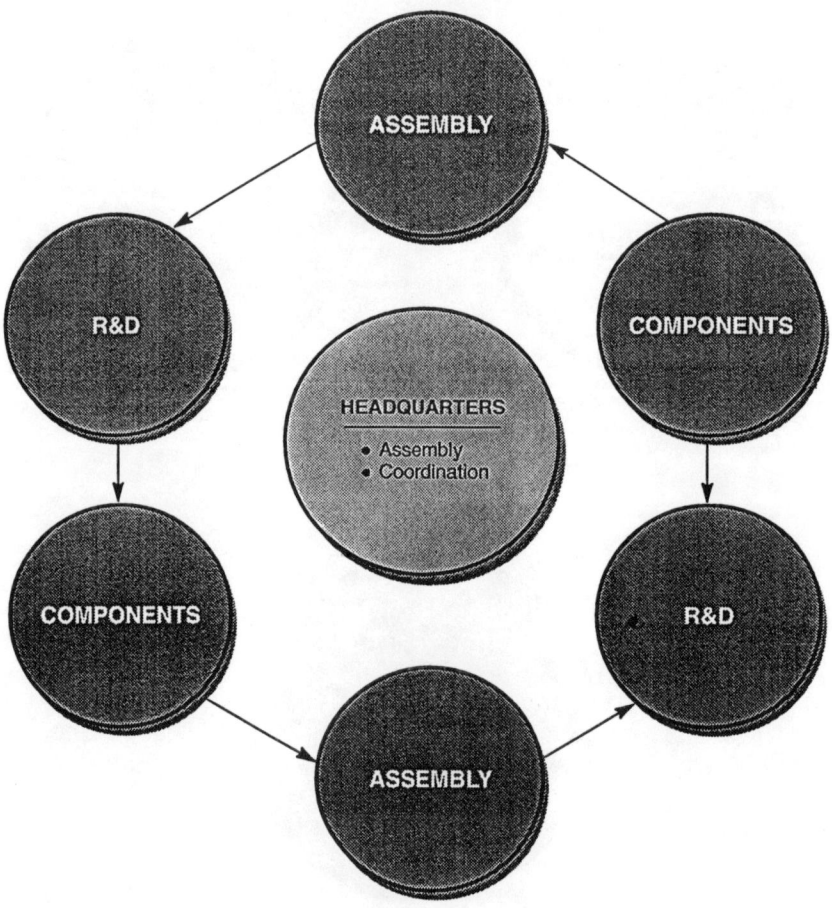

*Figure 3.* Bartlett/Reich model.

Reich, in contrast, envisions a configuration in which activities in the value chain are *individually* dispersed to the best location (see Figure 3). The location of each activity is determined by tax considerations, input costs, and skill availability in various geographic areas. The key to gaining competitive advantage is a superior ability to transfer specialized knowledge. Thus, it is coordination rather than configuration which drives competitive success. Most coordination is conducted by corporate managers who may be located anywhere in the world as long as they have access to worldwide communication and transportation systems.

The optimal configuration of Bartlett and Ghoshal combines aspects of both Ohmae and Reich, although it is closer in spirit to that of Reich. Activities in the value chain are separated and dispersed, but not quite as widely dispersed as in Reich. Activities are concentrated at home and in other more sophisticated locations, while other activities are dispersed more widely.

Overall, the transnational structure is specialized but dispersed, allowing firms to tap sophisticated capabilities around the world, foster worldwide learning, and serve customers in each local market. Coordination is thus also perhaps the most essential source of competitive advantage in Bartlett and Ghoshal's model, tying the various activities together. Overall, the focus of the literature on global competition has been on the ability of global companies to coordinate and transmit knowledge, capabilities, and other advantages through global networks, not where and how to create them.

## Case Studies of Global Corporations

To explore the fit between these views and actual corporate practice, we examined the international activities of three prototypical global corporations headquartered in Europe, Japan, and the United States, respectively. For each of these successful international leaders, we profiled their international operations and probed deeply into the international configuration and coordination of their activities.

An overall snapshot of the international operations of these three companies provides strong support for the globalness of strategy and the diminished role of the home country. Novo-Nordisk Group (Novo), headquartered in Denmark, is the world's leading exporter of insulin and industrial enzymes. Novo generates 96 percent of its revenues outside its home country and has strong positions in Europe, the United States, and Japan.[7] Twenty-seven percent of its employees are based outside Denmark and 19 percent of its total assets are located outside Europe. Novo has seven R&D locations and nine production sites outside Denmark. The company distributes its products in 100 countries, and has its own marketing subsidiaries in 43 countries. Novo sources animal pancreases, a key raw material for insulin, in more than 20 countries. It also sources its capital from around the world, funding 83 percent of its short-term debt and 54 percent of its long-term debt in currencies other than the Danish kroner. The company is listed on the London and New York stock exchanges.

Honda, headquartered in Japan, is the one of the world's leading producers of automobiles and is the world leader in motorcycles. Honda generates 61 percent of its revenues outside Japan and holds particularly strong market positions in Asia and North America.[8] Twenty-two percent of its employees and 39 percent of its total assets are based outside Japan. The company maintains production and assembly facilities in 39 countries and distributes its automobiles and motorcycles in 150 countries. Inputs and capital are sourced worldwide, with listings on the Tokyo and New York stock exchanges.

Hewlett Packard (HP), headquartered in the United States, is the world's largest and most diversified manufacturer of electronic measurement and testing equipment as well as a leader in other products such as printers, medical instruments, and computers. Hewlett Packard generates 54 percent of its revenues outside the United States.[9] Thirty-eight percent of HP's 93,000 employees and 50 percent of total assets are based outside the United States. HP operates 600 sales and support offices and distributorships in 110 countries. It is listed on stock exchanges in London, Paris, Tokyo, Frankfurt, Stuttgart, Switzerland, and the Pacific.

Globalization has led each of these firms to spread their activities around the world. Hewlett Packard's locational philosophy is instructive. Hewlett Packard locates low-skilled manufacturing activities with high direct labor content in low-cost areas, at an estimated savings of 40 to 75 percent compared to U.S. locations. For example, some component assembly and manufacturing for personal computers (PCs) is conducted in Singapore, and electronic component manufacturing is conducted in Malaysia. Hewlett Packard also locates some medium-skilled activities in lower cost countries. Some product and process engineering activities (such as manufacturing cost reduction programs) are conducted at the PC manufacturing facilities in Singapore, process engineering for some new electronic component products has been transferred to the manufacturing plant in Malaysia, and some software coding and maintenance has been sub-contracted to countries such as India, China, Eastern Europe, and the former Soviet Union where college-educated programmers are available at 40 to 60 percent lower cost than in the United States.

## THE LOCALIZATION OF COMPETITIVE ADVANTAGE

The view that global strategy has eliminated the importance of borders and the home nation is understandable, but incomplete. While the globalization of competition has indeed nullified some traditional sources of competitive advantage tied to location, such as access to raw materials, capital, or low cost labor, it has not eliminated the importance of location in competition. Location plays a profound role in the process by which the most important competitive advantages (including intangible assets) are created and sustained. Evidence from the performance of economies, the location of international industry leaders, and the location of industries within nations supports this view. So does a closer look at the global strategies of our three companies. If one merely counts up international activities, one is left with the impression of soon-to-be borderless companies. If one looks at the specific activities that are conducted at each location, a very different picture emerges.

The striking differences in economic performance of national, state, and local economies provides the first indication of the importance of location. The national origin of successful international competitors is the second. We examined patterns of international competitive success, initially in ten leading trading nations and subsequently in several others.[10] Across the hundreds of industries that were examined, including services and newly emerging fields such as software, advanced materials, and biotechnology, world leaders were typically headquartered in just a few and often only one country. Our three case studies fit this rule. Honda is not the only Japanese success story in the automotive and motorcycle industries—nine of the world's automobile companies and the four dominant global motorcycle companies are all based in Japan. Neither is Hewlett Packard the only successful U.S. firm in its industries—U.S. firms are preeminent in workstations, PCs, medical instruments, and test and instrumentation equipment. Novo-Nordisk is the world leader in insulin production—the result of the 1989 merger between two Danish-based companies (Novo and Nordisk Gentofte) that dominated insulin exports. Novo is also a leader in industrial enzymes, where other Danish firms also compete. If location were not important, one would expect the headquarters of leading companies in particular industries would be spread more widely.

Another manifestation of the importance of location is the geographic concentration of leading firms *within* nations. A particularly interesting example is the United States. Despite free trade among states, a common language and laws, and great similarities along many dimensions, the location of successful competitors in particular businesses is far from evenly distributed. Publishing is heavily concentrated in New York City; movies and television production in Hollywood; office furniture in western Michigan; pharmaceuticals in Philadelphia/New Jersey; hosiery and home furnishings in North Carolina; artificial hips and joints in Indiana—and there are countless other examples. Figure 4 illustrates just some of the many U.S. industry concentrations in a particular state or even city.

These "industrial Hollywoods" in particular fields can be found in every advanced nation, as has been further explored by Enright (1993a and 1993b).

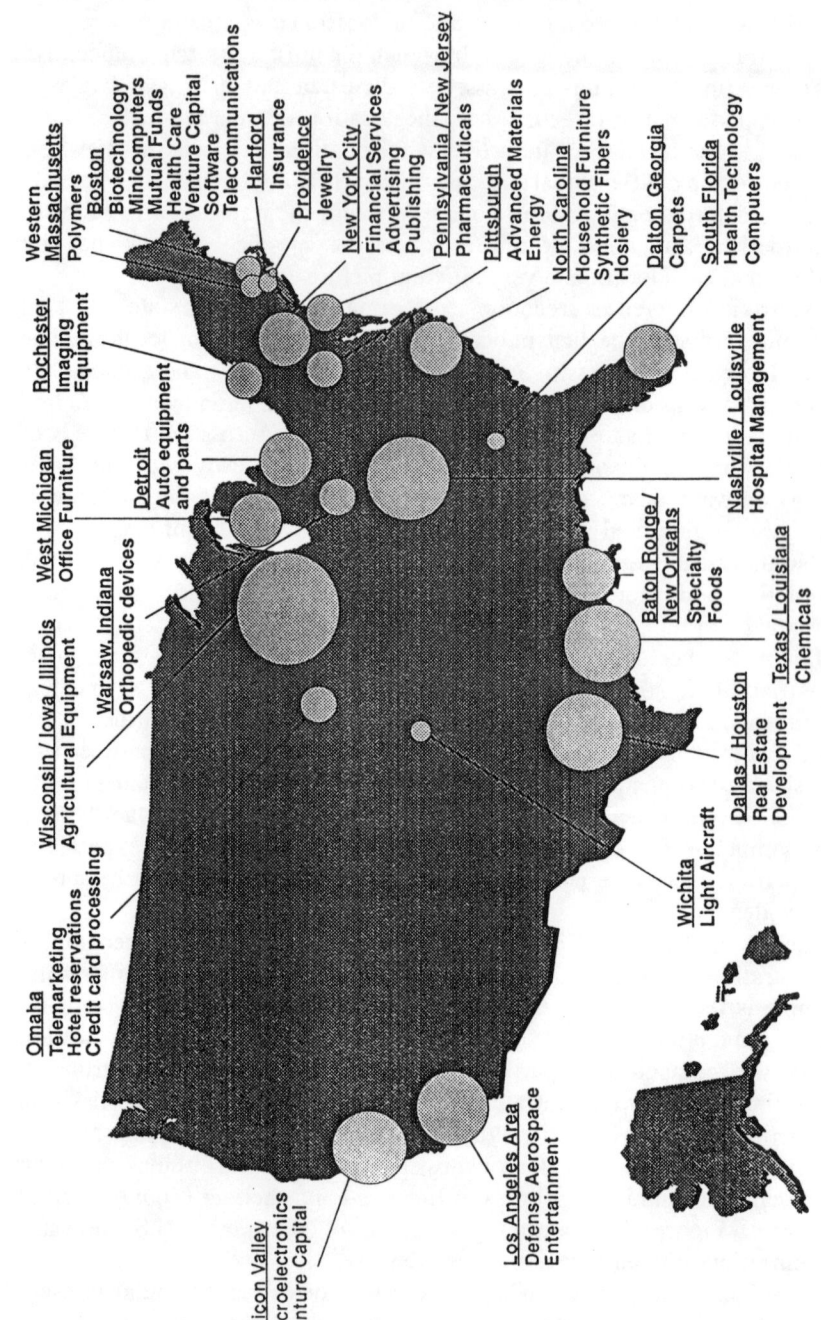

*Figure 4.* Selected regional clusters of competitive industries.

However, the U.S. case is a particularly important example because there would seem to be no economically relevant borders within the United States. Moreover, the U.S. economy—with its homogeneity among states—would seem to be a metaphor for what an integrated Europe or Asia could ultimately become. Yet even with similarities in wages and many other factors, location seems to play an important role in creating competitive industries.

Finally, the importance of location to competitive advantage is also manifested in the location decisions by multinational corporations. Statistical data provides the first indication. Although U.S. multinationals are extending their reach into international markets, the evidence shows that their home nation continues to play a strong role in manufacturing, core research, and high-skill jobs. In 1990, U.S. MNCs generated 69 percent of total sales in the United States, but the United States was the location of 76 percent of their total assets.[11] Despite widely acknowledged trends toward greater globalization, these percentages of U.S.-based sales and assets were higher in 1990 than in 1977. No less than 87 percent of corporate R&D spending of U.S. MNCs took place in the United States in 1990, a slight decline from 90 percent in 1980.[12] The United States was also the location of more highly skilled and paid jobs—employees of U.S. MNCs based in the United States commanded wages 17 percent higher than those based in other developed countries and 360 percent higher than those in developing countries.[13]

This broad pattern is confirmed by a close look at the international activities of global companies including our three case studies. Accounts citing widespread geographic dispersion of activities are misleading, first because of company diversification. Foreign activities span many entirely different product areas, while the activities in a given business are far less dispersed. More important, however, is to distinguish between the *types* of activities located in different countries. International firms tend to concentrate their most sophisticated activities in the home country, or if not there, in a single other country. While Novo-Nordisk markets its insulin products around the world and sources some inputs globally, it conducts its most strategically important activities in the value chain—all production and core product and process R&D—in Denmark. While Honda has extensive worldwide manufacturing and distribution, Japan remains the base for production of Honda's most sophisticated components, including all core engine research. Hewlett Packard's operations encompass over 16,000 product lines sold around the world, yet worldwide responsibility for each product line including core manufacturing, R&D, and decision-making, is concentrated in one particular location (HP refers to this as "worldwide re"). Moreover, multinationals relocate headquarters of particular businesses from one nation to another, apparently with increasing frequency. This evidence is hard to reconcile with the observations of writers such as Ohmae and Reich.[14]

## The Need for a New Paradigm

The apparent paradox between the globalization of competition and a strong national and even local role in competitive advantage can be resolved by taking a fresh look at the nature of international competition and the sources of competitive advantage in international markets. The paradigm that governs international competition has shifted. The old paradigm was one in which competition was based on static efficiency and the firm with the lowest factor costs (e.g., labor, raw materials, capital, infrastructure) or the greatest economies of scale won.

The changing nature of competition has overtaken this view. As Reich and many others have noted, globalization allows firms to source factors such as raw materials, capital, and even generic scientific knowledge in international markets, and to locate selective activities overseas to take advantage of low-cost labor or capital. Similarly, volume gained in the home market is far less important than the ability to penetrate world markets. Equally important to neutralizing the traditional role of location is technological change. Advancing technology has given firms the ability to eliminate, nullify, or circumvent weaknesses in local factors. Japanese firms, for example, have prospered in many industries despite the high cost of energy and space, through pioneering energy-saving technologies and space-saving innovations such as lean production. New technology is also diminishing economies of scale,[15] and/or allowing them to be rapidly neutralized by smaller but more innovative and dynamic rivals (witness the difficulties confronting General Motors, IBM, Phillips, and many other large firms).

In a world of rapidly diffusing information and generic technology where basic inputs are widely available, globalness alone is not sufficient to sustain competitive advantage. The only way a firm can retain its competitive advantages is to continuously innovate and upgrade its advantages to more sophisticated types. Innovation refers not only to physical technology but to ways of communicating, marketing, product positioning, providing service, and other forms of competing. The most dynamic and innovative companies outpace rivals, even those entrenched competitors enjoying low cost factors or economies of scale. Competitive advantage results from the rate of dynamic improvement, not static efficiencies. In the parlance of the earlier literature, the essential source of competitive advantage is the ability to rapidly create and recreate intangible assets that lead industry needs, not the inputs or scale the firm possesses today.

In this form of competition, the role of location changes profoundly. Firms operate globally to source inputs and access markets. Competitive advantage, though, comes from the process of innovation which is heavily localized at the firm's "home base," or the location of its strategic management team, the R&D to create the core product and process, and a critical mass of the firm's sophisticated production (or service provision), for a particular product line.[16] The home base is where the essential skills and technology reside, where inputs and information sourced from global activities are integrated, and where the most productive jobs are located. The location of ownership, or of the overall corporate headquarters, is far less significant than the location of the home base activities for each strategically distinct business.

## Location-based Foundations of Upgrading

The capacity to innovate draws heavily on the proximate environment in which the firm's home base in a particular business resides. Our research (1990) has highlighted four aspects of the national (or state or city) environment that take on particular significance: factor conditions, demand conditions, related and supporting industries, and the context for firm strategy, structure, and rivalry. These four attributes, which I collectively term the diamond, help explain why certain companies based in particular regions are capable of consistent innovation in particular fields, and why they relentlessly upgrade (see Figure 5).

### Factor Conditions

Factors of production are the basic inputs to competition, and include land, labor, capital, infrastructure, natural resources, and scientific knowledge. Globalization has made basic factors such as roads, bridges, or college-trained employees easily duplicated and available around the world. General purpose inputs, such as an educated work force and good basic infrastructure, are necessary to avoid a disadvantage but no longer sufficient for gaining competitive advantage.

Advantages arise from highly *specialized* pools of skills, applied technology, infrastructure, and even sources of capital that are tailored to the needs of particular industries. In the United States, for example, preeminence in software rests on unique pools of highly trained programmers and other computer science professionals, unparalleled research programs in computer-related disciplines, and well-developed and expert sources of risk capital for software firms (many American venture capital firms specialize in software). Hewlett Packard benefits from some of these in its computer-related businesses. Nations and regions do not inherit, but must create the most important factors of production for sophisticated competition. The presence of unique local educational, research, and other institutions that create specialized skills and technology is a potent source of competitive advantage.

More paradoxical is that selective *disadvantages* in basic factors, such as high wages or local raw material shortages, often lead to competitiveness through triggering innovation. In Holland, for example, a poor climate has

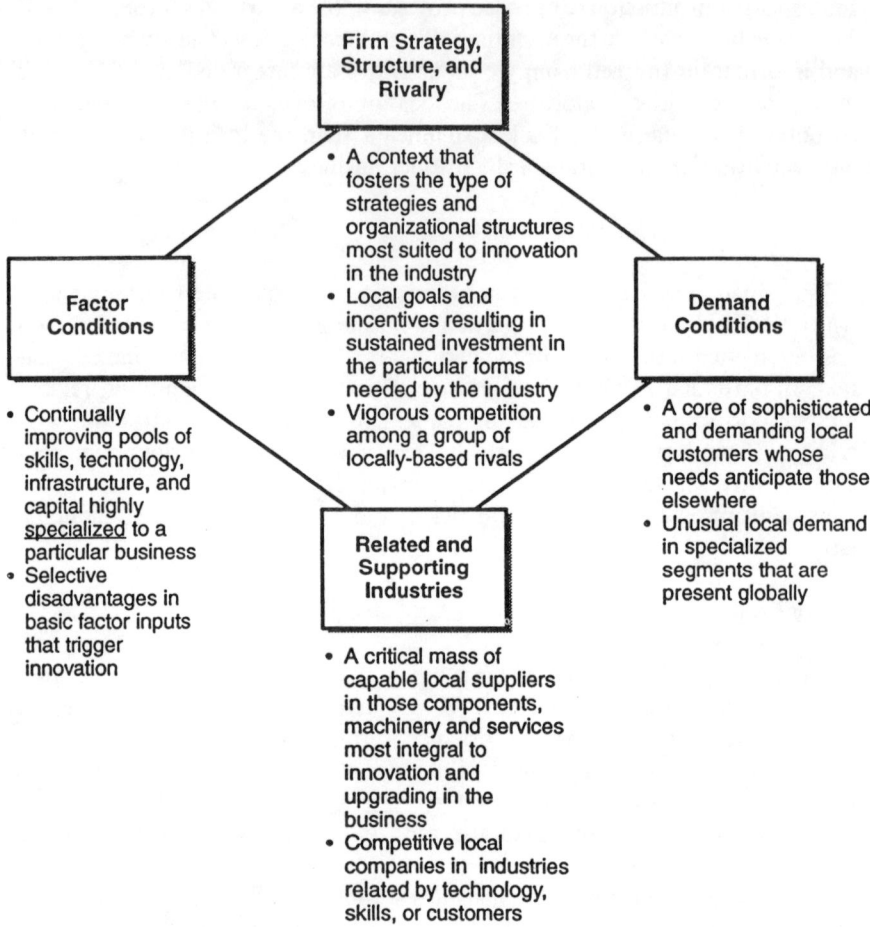

**Figure 5.** Selected location-based determinants of competitive advantage: The "Diamond."

led to innovations in such areas as greenhouse cultivation methods, breeding technology, and handling techniques for cut flowers, where the Dutch hold more than 60 percent of world exports. Conversely, the presence of abundant labor, cheap debt capital, and bountiful natural resources leads firms to use these resources less productively and be vulnerable to new global competitors.

*Demand Conditions*

National and international success grows out of having a core of local customers who are or are among the most sophisticated and demanding buyers in the world for their products or services, or who have unusually intense needs for specialized varieties in demand elsewhere. The size of the home market is far less important than its character. Sophisticated, demanding buyers provide a window into advanced customer needs; they pressure companies to meet high standards, and prod them to innovate and move into more advanced segments. Sophisticated home customers are particularly valuable if their needs anticipate or even shape those of other nations, and thereby provide "early-warning indicators" of global market trends. Local customers are far more likely to spur improvement and innovation than distant customers, because of high visibility, short communication lines, and the opportunity for joint working relationships. Unusual local needs for specialized varieties are important for similar reasons, because it causes firms to concentrate on improving in segments that are ignored elsewhere. All three of our global leaders benefitted from sophisticated demand at home. Novo, for example, sold to perhaps the most sophisticated group of doctors specialized in treating diabetes in the world, and operated in the context of a national health care system that provided generous reimbursement for new treatments.

## Related and Supporting Industries

Competitive advantage arises from the presence of a critical mass of competitive, home-based suppliers of those specialized components, machinery, and services that most drive progress in the business. Local suppliers are important less for access to inputs, which has been largely nullified by globalization, than for the advantages they provide in innovation. Suppliers and end-users located close to each other can take advantage of quick and constant flow of information, joint work on improvements, and mutual pressures to advance. Highly applied technology and specialized skills, which are hard to codify, accumulate. Companies have the opportunity to influence their suppliers' technical efforts and can serve as test sites for new developments, accelerating the pace of innovation. Honda benefitted from such a supplier network in both automobiles and motorcycles. General purpose machinery, standard components, and raw materials are less important to innovation. They can (and must) be sourced globally wherever they are the most cost-effective.

Home-based competitors in related industries, or industries with closely similar skills, technologies, or customers, provide similar benefits: information flow, technical interchange, and opportunities for sharing that increase the rate of innovation and upgrading. Japanese dominance in electronic musical keyboards, for example, grew out of success in acoustic instruments combined with a strong position in a wide array of consumer electronics industries.

*Firm Strategy, Structure, and Rivalry*

The circumstances and context of a nation or region influence how companies are created, how they are managed, and how they compete. Competitiveness grows out of a context that encourages the types of strategies and organizational structures that foster innovation in the industry (e.g., larger, disciplined, structured organizations in some businesses and smaller, fluid, family-owned companies in others). Also important are a context of social norms, tax incentives, patent laws, and prestige that encourage sustained investment by both individuals and companies in the skills, knowledge and physical assets needed in the particular business.

Among the most significant influences on innovation and dynamism is the presence of *local* rivalry. Honda, for example, faced competition from eight other Japanese auto companies, all of which competed internationally. Firms rarely succeed abroad unless they compete with some capable rivals at home. Rivalry among a group of locally based competitors heightens pressures to innovate and upgrade. Local rivals have comparable access to the home market, comparable local inputs, and similar basic circumstances. This nullifies these as sources of competitive advantage, and encourages upgrading. This is reinforced by a rapid flow of information, and fosters *relative* (versus absolute) performance comparisons which stimulate rapid improvement. The presence of local rivals works against comfortable dominance of the home market and pressures vigorous efforts to compete nationally and internationally.[17] Novo, for example, was pushed to export because it had to compete in the Danish and Scandinavian market with Nordisk, unlike most insulin producers who were effectively national monopolies. While individual companies have difficulty staying ahead for long, the entire local industry progresses more rapidly than competitors based elsewhere.[18]

*The Diamond as a System*

These four location-based sources of competitive advantage constitute a dynamic system which is as or more important than its parts. The effect of one part of the diamond on innovation depends on the state of the others. For example, having selective disadvantages in factors (e.g., higher energy or raw material costs) will not lead to innovation unless there is vigorous local competition to pressure investment to offset them and the technical and supplier foundation to overcome them. Conversely, vigorous local competition can degenerate into price cutting and harvesting if local customers have unsophisticated needs or the local context discourages investment. Serious weakness in any one attribute of the diamond will constrain an industry's potential for advancement.

The four determinants are also self-reinforcing. The role of local rivalry is illustrative. Vigorous domestic rivalry not only pushes companies to improve but also stimulates the development and renewal of unique pools of specialized skills and technology. Local institutions, such as universities and financial institutions, are encouraged by the presence of a number of rivals to adapt and support the industry's distinctive needs. Active local rivalry promotes the formation and upgrading of local supplier industries, as well as new related industries.

The sinews that hold the parts of the diamond together are the relationships among the entities that constitute it. Strong relationships and open information flow between firms, local suppliers, customers, educational and research institutions, and infrastructure providers, and between all those entities and government, weigh heavily in the rate of upgrading and innovation. Vertical collaboration, between customers and suppliers, is a sine qua non of competitiveness. Horizontally, between rivals, vigorous competition is a necessity for competitiveness. Some limited forms of horizontal collaboration in infrastructure areas (e.g., trade fairs, industry association training programs) can be beneficial.

Competitive advantage, then, grows not from a comfortable home environment but out of pressure and challenge. Nationally and internationally, competitive companies are those based in the most dynamic and most challenging home environment. Proximity to capable rivals, suppliers, sophisticated customers, and specialized factor providers leads to rapid information flow, faster accumulation of knowledge and skills, more fluid working relationships, and stronger pressures to innovate.

## Industry Clusters

Nations, regions, and even states are rarely competitive in isolated industries, but in entire *clusters* of interconnected industries, a prominent feature of every advanced economy.[19] A cluster is a grouping of industries linked together through customer, supplier, or other relationships. Both manufacturing and service industries are part of clusters, and are often closely interconnected. The seed of a cluster can come from unusual local needs, natural resource endowments, university areas of excellence, or acts of pure entrepreneurship. As a cluster forms, the industries which comprise it become mutually reinforcing. Aggressive rivalry in one industry spreads vertically and horizontally in the cluster through spin-offs or related diversification. Ready access to local suppliers, skill pools, and a base of sophisticated customers lowers the cost of entry.

Clusters widen as new industries develop upstream, downstream, or in related fields. New industries or segments involving advanced technology emerge, even from clusters involving mature industries. Less productive and innovative industries in the cluster, conversely, can shrink and decline. Through a cumulative process that often occurs over several decades, the nation, state, or region becomes a unique repository of specialized expertise, technology, and institutions for competing in a given field.

Clusters are often also geographically concentrated within a nation. Firms are all based in a particular region or city (recall Figure 4). This reflects the importance of proximity in motivation (through highlighting relative versus bold performance), the flow of information, the start-up of new companies, and the responsiveness of local institutions to a cluster's specialized needs.

## Location and Competitive Advantage

While competition is increasingly national and global, the crucial sources of competitive advantage are often local. Generalized factors such as capital, raw materials, and even scientific knowledge are highly mobile, and companies can readily tap low-cost labor anywhere through global networks. What is not mobile, however, are the critical masses of highly specialized and interconnected skills, applied technologies, firm home bases, supplier home bases, and institutions which reside in particular areas.[20] Firms based in these locations emerge as global leaders. Foreign firms are drawn to invest in these locations and to delegate world-wide responsibility for the products involved to their subsidiaries located there. Finally, individuals with good ideas and specialized skills are drawn to these locations because they offer the greatest excitement and rewards.

Because of the cumulative and self-reinforcing nature of the diamond and the time required to build specialized institutions, knowledge, and a critical mass of firms, there will normally be only a small number of favorable locations for competing in a particular business. The process of cluster formation and upgrading is not inevitable. Healthy diamonds are those where there is the most vigorous local rivalry, local institutions are the most responsive to industry needs, the climate for investment and new business formation is the most favorable (because this strengthens the feedback loops among the diamond's parts), and strong linkages form between firms, suppliers, universities and other actors. As an established diamond upgrades, it will attract specialized factors, customers, suppliers, and even firm home bases from around the world, often from weaker diamonds. In pharmaceuticals, for example, the Philadelphia/New Jersey diamond has attracted substantial investment by German, Swiss, British, and Japanese pharmaceutical firms because of its superior demand conditions and better access to specialized factors. Conversely, activities that become standardized will be dispersed to source cheap inputs or facilitate foreign market access. The most sophisticated parts of an industry, or of particular industry segments, will thus become concentrated in a particular location, making it difficult to develop or attract similar concentrations to other locations. Spillovers among parts of the diamond reinforce the advantages of established concentrations and make it more difficult to replicate them elsewhere. The cycle is interrupted only when major technological changes invalidate past skills, suppliers, and other local advantages, or when pressure to innovate diminishes because rivalry is eliminated or buyer sophistication lags.

A firm must locate its home base for business in a favorable diamond to truly access its advantages. Co-locating a critical mass of home base activities at one location fosters rapid progress by promoting communication, cross-functional coordination, and more rapid decision making. Firms benefit not only from spillovers within the local diamond but also spillovers within the firm. Co-locating the full range of core activities at a single favorable diamond is thus favored over dispersing these activities, even if dispersed activities are each located at a sophisticated location for that activity. Activity-specific advantages are outweighed by rapid cross-activity coordination from a single location and the ability of this configuration to better capture spillovers within a single diamond. Dispersing core activities widely to areas of functional excellence (as recommended by Reich and Bartlett and Ghoshal) rarely occurs in practice.

Proximity to a favorable diamond is needed to best access the diamond's innovation advantages. Proximity in physical, cultural, and institutional terms speeds the flow of information, facilitates vertical working relationships, and amplifies the pressure from rivalry and desire to improve relative performance. By having a critical mass of home base activities at such a location, the firm is better able to assimilate and benefit from local externalities that cut across many activities (functions).

Location within a strong diamond is difficult to offset by firms based elsewhere. Direct contact with knowledgeable customers, educational and research institutions, and suppliers, and proximity to the core activities of capable rivals, produces information and motivation benefits that cannot be easily duplicated or tapped unless a firm has a home base there. For example, it is difficult, if not impossible, to fully understand the Japanese customer as well as Japanese-based rivals when a firm's senior management and core R&D personnel are based in the United States. Mere access to components, machines, or customers yields no competitive advantage. What is needed, instead, is ready access to specialized knowledge as it develops and evolves over time, which results from proximity. Also, spillovers are strongest within a local diamond, and slow to be transmitted outside.[21]

While competitive advantage is heavily local, however, competition must be global. The firm's home base is the platform for global strategy, not the place where all of a firm's activities should take place. Companies must sell their products nationally and globally. Activities that are not central to the innovation process, such as final assembly, sourcing capital, and after-sale service must be dispersed to source low-cost inputs and gain access to foreign markets.

# A NEW CONCEPTION OF GLOBAL STRATEGY

This new paradigm for international competition carries strong implications for company strategy, especially for the design of approaches to competing globally. Some of the most important implications follow, illustrated with examples drawn from the three global companies profiled earlier.

## Setting Corporate Goals

Corporate goals must shift from solely static measures such as return on investment or market share to dynamic measures of the ability to improve. Continuous innovation and upgrading must be the central purpose of the enterprise. Companies that emerge as world leaders are those that can sustain innovation over decades, as have the three companies we profile.

Since their founding in the early 1920s, both Novo and Nordisk pioneered the most important innovations in the insulin industry. Nordisk pioneered mixing technologies and slow-acting insulin. Novo led in the development of highly purified insulin, and was the first truly global competitor.

An orientation toward innovation at Honda goes back to its founder, Soichiro Honda, who had a strong passion for creativity and originality. His philosophy of pioneering led to the development of the first mass market motorcycle, the CVCC engine, the Accord, and the Acura luxury car concept (the first among the Japanese companies), to name just a few achievements. An orientation to innovate also underlay Honda's actions after the 1970 Clean Air Act. It resolved to upgrade the fuel efficiency of its engines, rather than join U.S. competitors in battling against the regulations.

Hewlett Packard developed the first desktop scientific calculator in 1968, pioneered inkjet printing technology in 1984, and led with HP Precision Architecture in 1991, among a long list of innovations. The company was one of the first American corporations to adopt Total Quality techniques. More than half of HP's orders in 1992 were for products introduced in the previous two years.

Performance must be measured in terms of progress, not today's position. Corporate goals must be expressed in terms of long-term competitive position, not current profitability. Some of the most sustainable competitive advantages are those created through investing in intangible assets such as technology, supplier relationships, employee training or market access whose benefits are difficult to quantify and which diminish near-term profitability. Goals framed in terms of long-term competitive position are needed to overcome the pressures found in many U.S. corporations for short-term financial returns.[22]

## Creating an Innovative Organization

While the foundation of competitive advantage is the ability to innovate and upgrade, neither occurs naturally. There is a tendency in any organization to maintain past ways of doing things, and hone the ability to execute past approaches or just fine tune them. Innovation and change are disruptive, difficult, and unsettling. Internal and external feedback is more often negative than encouraging.

The principal role of senior management is to overcome those tendencies and motivate an organization to advance. Companies that are world leaders have a sense of urgency, and run a little scared. There is a constant focus on threats and challenges.

Part of the environment for innovation comes from internal management practices. Among the most important are those for performance measurement and capital budgeting. Performance measurement should stress *relative position vis-à-vis competitors* rather than current financial indicators. Capital budgeting should encompass not only physical assets but intangible assets such as R&D, training, relationships with suppliers, and information systems. Investments must be considered not as discrete projects but as a series of complementary investments across a variety of forms (Porter 1992).

However, it is rare that a leader can motivate innovation solely from within. Innovative companies are often those that systematically and culturally draw on pressures and insights from their local environment. To put it bluntly, most companies do not innovate unless they are forced to. Indeed, one can cast the role of a leader in terms of harnessing external pressures and information to motivate change in an organization.

One example is to set out to serve the most demanding local customers, even if they represent only a small part of sales. Another is to make a commitment to tackle the jurisdictions with the most stringent regulation. Avoiding them, conversely, sends a signal of complacency to the organization, and undermines the search for product and process improvements. Capable competitors are another potent motivator of organizational change. The most innovative companies often set capable rivals up for detailed study, and make bettering them a highly visible goal in the organization.

## Selecting Industries and Segments

The diamond provides a way of identifying the industries in which a firm can gain a unique competitive advantage vis-à-vis rivals based elsewhere, and those industry segments where home circumstances provide the most distinctive benefits. New business development should concentrate in these areas.

The principles of the new paradigm raise cautions about extensive vertical integration. Instead, a company should foster strong relationships with local suppliers of specialized machinery and inputs, while sourcing generalized and less technology-controlling inputs globally. Diversification should be more horizontal and along cluster lines. By diversifying into areas involving similar skills, technology, or customers, companies will not only better leverage their own internal assets but also the unique assets of their local environment, such as suppliers, research centers, and skill pools. HP's diversification from measurement and test equipment into information systems and medical instruments has followed those principles, in each case involving a field where the United States has unique strengths. Novo's move from insulin to industrial enzymes followed the same principles, as did Honda's diversification from motorcycles to automobiles. Innovations often originate at the interstices between industries and clusters, when related technologies and skills are combined. Honda, for example, got its start in automobiles based on small engine technology nurtured in automobiles, while drawing strengths from the fierce rivalry and supplier base of the Japanese automobile cluster.

## Setting Global Strategy

The diamond model casts choices about configuration and coordination in a new light. While recent research on global strategy has focused on the benefits of dispersing activities and global coordination, this is an incomplete view of the problem.

### 1. A Clear Home Base for Each Distinct Business

The ultimate source of competitive advantage is not the ability to compete globally, but the unique attributes of a firm's strategy and capabilities which draw heavily on its home base. Firms, then, must have a clear home base for competing in each strategically distinct business, where a critical mass of home base activities are located. A coordinating center is not enough. The home base should have clear worldwide responsibility in the business and serve as the integrating point for inputs, information, and technology obtained elsewhere.

The home base should be located in the most favorable diamond for the particular business. This may not necessarily be the country of ownership. The location of overall *corporate* headquarters is less significant. Failure to distinguish between the location of corporate headquarters and the location of business unit home bases is a principal cause of confusion in interpreting MNC global strategies.

Each of the three companies we profiled has a clear home base for each major business. Denmark serves as the home base of Novo-Nordisk's insulin business (and of both Novo and Nordisk's insulin businesses prior to the merger). Even though 95 percent of sales are generated outside Denmark, all insulin purification facilities, which comprise the most critical activities in the production process, are based in Denmark. Denmark has a large pig-farming industry, which has provided the crucial raw material. Insulin purification requires not only large investments but also highly specialized machinery, skilled technicians, and strong quality control systems. Denmark is home to critical suppliers of machinery and other specialized production inputs, in part due to its strong position in the dairy and beer industries which employ related technologies and skills. All Novo's core product and process research is also conducted in Denmark, which is home to an array of world-class diabetes research institutes and two leading diabetes hospitals. Danish demand conditions in insulin are also advanced. The advanced and generous health care system in Denmark provided early funding for new diabetes testing and treatments. Danish doctors not only examine patients but also conduct and monitor programs which train diabetes patients in their eating and cooking habits. Novo-Nordisk personnel interact directly with hospital doctors to gain quick feedback on the success of new products and on emerging issues facing diabetes patients.

Honda's most sophisticated activities in both motorcycles and automobiles are also conducted at its Japanese home base. Japan accounts for 76 percent of Honda's production capacity in motorcycles and 68 percent in automobiles. Foreign production plants are primarily assembly facilities, drawing on sophisticated parts sourced from Japan. Honda's Japanese motorcycle plants have an average capacity of 396,000 units compared to 75,000 for those located elsewhere. Automobile research and development is even more concentrated— 95 percent of R&D employees and *all* core engine research are located in Japan. R&D personnel based outside Japan must undergo two years training at the Tochigi Research Center in Tokyo before beginning work in their native country.

At Hewlett Packard, worldwide responsibility for each product line— including core research, the most sophisticated production activities, and decision-making—is concentrated in a particular location. Many product line home bases are located in the United States (the United States comprises 43 percent of physical space dedicated to marketing but 77 percent of that dedicated to manufacturing, R&D, and administration). Within the United States, product line home bases are concentrated in particular geographic areas such as medical instruments in Waltham, Massachusetts, printers in Boise, Idaho, personal computers in Palo Alto, California, and electronic components and instrumentation in San Jose, California.

## 2. The Role of Dispersed Activities

The dispersal of activities from the home base should serve one of three purposes. The first is *sourcing basic factors* such as cheap labor, raw materials, or capital (adjusted for taxes). Here, the firm seeks to exploit the comparative advantage of various locations. Firms must take advantage of global markets to efficiently source inputs that do not affect the innovation process. Second, activities should be dispersed to *securing or improve foreign market access*. Locating selected activities near markets signals commitment to foreign customers, and allows responding and tailoring offerings to local needs. Dispersing to secure market access often includes some production activities, to produce tailored product varieties, and some R&D activities, to support compliance with local regulations and product adaptation to local needs. However, modern flexible manufacturing systems and the increased power of information and communications technologies are working to lessen the need for dispersed activities, as customization to serve local needs can be more easily accomplished from a single facility. Greater harmonization of technical standards and diminishing trade barriers have the same effect.

Activities may also be dispersed in order to respond to actual or threatened government mandates, as has been the case with Japanese auto and consumer electronics assembly in the United States. In responding to government pressures, dispersing some less scale- or innovation-sensitive activities can allow the firm to continue to concentrate others. The goal should be to deal with government mandates at the least possible sacrifice to efficiency and especially to the rate of innovation.

Third, firms should disperse activities to *selectively tap particular skills or technologies* that are not available at the home base. In tapping the capabilities of other diamonds, it is important not to replicate or seek to replace the home base, but to supplement it. Ultimately, the aim is to develop capabilities in important skills or technologies at home to facilitate more rapid progress. Relying too heavily on advantages sourced elsewhere, conversely, threatens the capacity to innovate. Overall, the principle is to disperse *only* those activities needed to achieve these three classes of benefits.

Alliances with firms based elsewhere can be tools to more effectively or more rapidly gain these benefits. Market access is often enhanced by a local partner and the ability to tap advanced skills and technologies in another location may require a partner's well-established local presence. Alliances, however, complicate coordination and can slow innovation. The best alliances are highly selective, focused on particular activities and on obtaining a particular benefit, and often temporary. A firm cannot rely on a partner for assets crucial to competitive advantage.

Our case studies illustrate all these motivations. Novo sources its main raw material, pig pancreases, from 20 countries. Worldwide sourcing not only gives Novo-Nordisk access to larger supplies but also smooths price fluctuations. Novo also funds 83 percent of its long-term debt in currencies other than the Danish kroner, and taps foreign equity markets. To facilitate market access and lower transport costs, Novo dispersed four insulin processing plants to France, South Africa, Japan, and the United States. These plants—the only ones which operate outside Denmark—are not full-scale production facilities but add water to concentrated insulin crystals imported from Denmark and then package products for final sale. Dispersing these less scale-sensitive processing plants allowed Novo to continue to concentrate its more scale-dependent primary production in Denmark. To improve access to local medical communities and government health care systems, Novo established marketing joint ventures with local companies in a number of countries. Finally, Novo established a limited number of highly specialized research and development activities outside Denmark to tap particular skills or technologies not available at home. Zymotech, based in Seattle, Washington, was acquired to access expertise in genetically engineered insulin (a U.S. strength), and a Japanese research facility was established as well. After repeated delays in gaining regulatory approval in Denmark, Novo-Nordisk established a genetically engineered insulin production facility in Japan, where approval was more rapid. Yet Novo had not ceded this core technology to foreign operations, but has built up its own genetic engineering capabilities in Denmark. The company is transferring the knowledge acquired in the United States and Japan back to its Danish home base, and established genetic insulin production there as well.

Honda has also dispersed non-home base activities for all three reasons. Automobiles are assembled in 11 countries and motorcycles in 30 countries to reduce transportation and tariff costs and to source lower-cost labor. To ensure continued market access in the face of rising concern over Japanese automobile imports, Honda has invested $2 billion in the United States in two assembly plants, a manufacturing facility for engines, transmissions, and suspension parts, an engineering center, and a research and development facility. Honda's U.S. activities are focused on cost reduction and adapting products and processes to the U.S. market, with innovation centered in Japan. Honda also has a joint venture with Rover in the United Kingdom oriented toward securing access to the European market. Finally, Honda taps styling expertise available in California, and high performance design capabilities in Germany, via small local design centers which transfer knowledge back to the Japanese home base where they are incorporated into model development.

## 3. Coordinating and Integrating Dispersed Activities

Unlocking the full competitive advantage from dispersed activities requires that they be coordinated, and that learning and technology gained from dispersed activities be integrated at the home base. While all three of our case studies are illustrative, Novo's case is particularly interesting. Novo's global procurement, production, and marketing activities are tightly coordinated from Denmark. All marketing subsidiaries, agents, and distributors use consistent promotional materials and are trained in consistent selling approaches. Novo works hard to ensure a common image worldwide, which is reinforced by periodic international physician conferences on diabetes sponsored in Denmark.

Coordinating subsidiaries, and integrating ideas at the home base, requires an organizational structure, systems, and norms that support frequent and open information exchange and decision-making that address the goals of the global business unit rather than individual subsidiaries. These attributes are difficult to achieve. While a full discussion of solutions is beyond the scope of this paper, some of the key ingredients include information and accounting systems which are consistent worldwide to facilitate exchange of information and comparisons, active efforts to facilitate mutual learning and personal relationships among subsidiary managers, and an incentive system that weights overall contribution in addition to subsidiary performance.[23]

## 4. Upgrading the Home Base

An important part of a firm's competitive advantage resides in its local environment, not within the firm itself. Without a fundamentally healthy home base, the capacity to rapidly innovate will diminish. The firm will be unable to assemble the resources and capabilities most essential to competitive advantage. Dispersing sophisticated production or outsourcing critical components and machinery will improve performance in the short run, but threaten the firm's ability to innovate in the long run.

Firms should support specialized training programs, and promote university research in areas that are relevant to their particular business. Local suppliers should be nurtured and upgraded (depending heavily on foreign suppliers nullifies a potential competitive advantage). Unfortunately, few companies see their local environment as a vital competitive resource. In the United States, for example, many companies take their suppliers for granted, and see education and training as the responsibility of government. Industry associations can play an important role in sponsoring training programs, funding research on enabling technologies and standards, and collecting market information.

Our case studies illustrate how global leaders take an active role in upgrading their home environment. For example, Nordisk established the Nordic Insulin Fund in 1926 to support insulin research projects in Scandinavia, and established the Steno Memorial Hospital in 1932, specializing in research and treatment of diabetes. Novo founded the Hvidore diabetes hospital, and the Hagedoorn Research Institute in 1957 to conduct basic research on diabetes. The Novo Research Institute was created in 1964 to investigate the causes and origins of diabetes.

Today, the Steno Diabetes Center and Hvidore Diabetes Hospital treat 6,000 diabetes patients and conduct 25,000 diabetes consultations each year. Novo-

Nordisk also sponsors international conferences on diabetes in Denmark, bringing together local experts and specialists from around the world (Enright 1989).

The history of the Danish insulin industry illustrates the power of active local rivalry between two companies which motivated continual innovation. The risk is that their merger, while achieving static efficiencies, will undermine dynamism. The parent is aiming to address these risks by keeping the two operations separate. The broader principle, however, is that the presence of local rivals creates advantages. Seeking to eliminate local competition is normally misguided.

## 5. Product Line Home Bases at Different Locations

As a firm's product range broadens, the home bases for some product lines may be located outside its home country. A firm should locate the home base for new product lines in the country with the most favorable home diamond in that particular segment of the business. (Figure 6 illustrates the resulting configuration schematically.) This approach is far superior to replicating production and R&D activities for the same products in several countries, which is inefficient and dulls innovation. Ohmae's triad model, in which each regional subsidiary concentrates on serving its home market, gives up important advantages in terms of specialization. Instead, each regional subsidiary should *specialize* in models for which it has the most favorable diamond, and serve those segments worldwide. Instead of dispersing activities individually, as the Bartlett/Reich model suggests, groups of activities comprising product line home bases should be located in countries with favorable diamonds.

Hewlett Packard provides an interesting example of these notions. Its worldwide operations encompass a number of product lines, each with a distinct home base that has worldwide responsibility. Research and development, sophisticated manufacturing, and key decision-making is concentrated at this home base, with regional subsidiaries responsible for some process-oriented R&D, product localization, and local marketing. Engineers at the home base with specialized expertise are designated worldwide experts, and transfer their knowledge either electronically or through periodic trips to subsidiaries. Responsibility for personal computers and workstations is based in California—home to almost all of the world's leading workstations and personal computer firms. The medical instruments group is based in Massachusetts, the location of some of the world's leading research hospitals and numerous leading medical instrument companies. Inkjet printer operations are concentrated in Vancouver, with localization for regional markets and assembly in Barcelona and Vancouver. Worldwide responsibility for a new line of compact inkjet printers is based in Singapore. This line combines printer

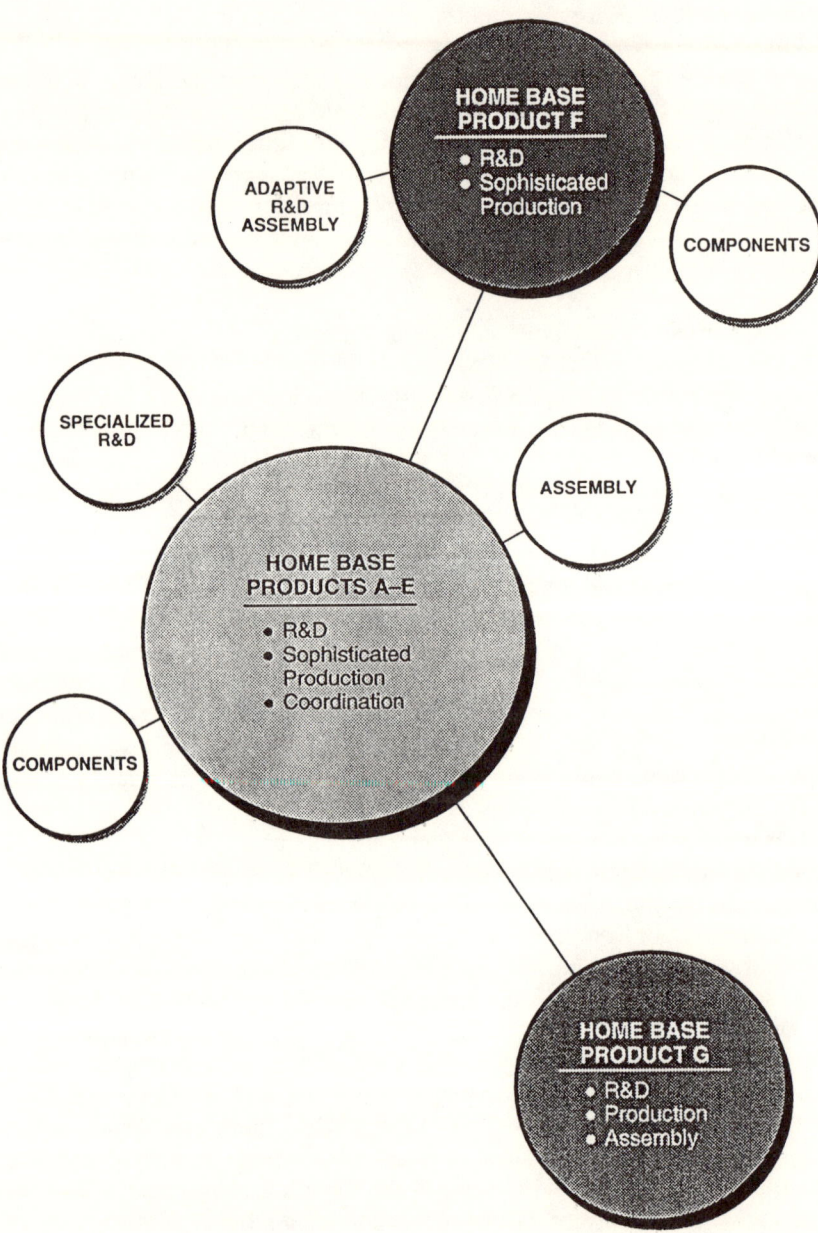

*Figure 6.* The home base model of global strategy.

technology transferred from Vancouver with Asian expertise in designing space-saving office products.

Honda's home base for automobiles has been entirely in Japan. However, it is beginning the process of creating a product line home base in the United States. "Project DW," an initiative to develop an Accord station wagon, is based in the United States. Adapted from a sedan designed and engineered in Japan, the station wagon was conceived, designed, and developed in the United States. This was because the United States is considered to be the leading market for station wagons, and has a network of established suppliers of specialized components. Honda's California R&D design facility created the models and life-sized mock-ups of the wagon, the Ohio R&D facility fabricated the metal prototype, and major production tooling, including stamping dies, was made by Honda Engineering in America. Honda has stated that the United States will become its world headquarters for station wagons, and that U.S. designers and engineers will continue to develop and upgrade the product. American Honda also has worldwide responsibility for development of a two-door Civic coupe.[24] By the end of the 1990s, American Honda plans to export 70,000 automobiles from the United States to more than 20 countries.

## 6. Preserving National Identity in Business Units

A firm's national identity in a business is not something to shed, as some observers have suggested, but something to preserve. Competitive advantage arises from distinctive attributes of the firm's home environment in a business, which place an imprint on the firm and shape how it competes. This identity and culture, and the company characteristics it connotes, are also crucial to foreign customers. Most Americans, for example, do not want to buy a German car from a car company that is acting American.

When accessing foreign markets, a firm must adapt by tailoring its product to local needs and being sensitive to local business practices. Yet it should not lose its distinctive identity which should be preserved and inculcated in foreign subsidiaries. At Honda, for example, managers hired to run international subsidiaries must first undergo two years' training at the Japanese home base.

## 7. Relocating the Home Base

If the attractiveness of a firm's home base for a particular business deteriorates because of changes in customer sophistication, new supplier needs, ineffective local institutions, or other reasons, the first response should be to upgrade at home. If such efforts are exhausted, a firm may need to relocate its home base to a location with a more favorable diamond. The shift of home bases from country to country is occurring with increasing frequency in multinational companies. As global competition exposes firms to the world's best rivals and nullifies advantages in capital, raw materials, and labor, the penalty of an unfavorable home diamond is increasing. Yet relocating a home base must take place reluctantly, because it involves becoming accepted as a true insider in a new environment and culture.

Firms rarely shift the home base of the entire company at once. Instead, they relocate the home base of a particular product line or business segment where the home diamond is least favorable. One common catalyst, and enabler, of such a shift is the acquisition of a foreign firm already established in a more vibrant diamond. This provides the critical mass for a new home base, which over time gains increasing worldwide responsibility and decision-making for a business. For example, Nestlé has relocated the world headquarters for its confectionery business to England, centered around the acquired Rowntree MacIntosh company. England, with its sweet-toothed consumers, sophisticated retailers, advanced advertising agencies, and highly competitive media companies is a more vibrant environment for competing in mass market candy. Similarly, Nestlé has moved its world headquarters for bottled water to France, the most competitive country in this industry.

Although each of our case study companies continues to enjoy a strong home diamond in its principal businesses, not all firms are so fortunate. The Canadian manufacturer Northern Telecom, for example, has shifted its home base for digital central office switching equipment from Canada to the United States.[25] Northern Telecom manufactured and installed the first local digital switch, the DMS-10, in the United States in 1977. The subsequent AT&T divestiture and mandate for equal access reconfigured the U.S. diamond for telecommunications service and equipment, and led NTI to expand its U.S. operations dramatically. By 1991, Northern Telecom had relocated its world headquarters for central office switching to the United States. NTI now conducts all research and development activities in the United States for this product line, with over 1,000 employees. Virtually all central office switching manufacturing is also conducted in the United States, involving 7,000 employees and 2.2 million square feet located at NTI's major plant in North Carolina.

The rationale behind Northern Telecom's move to the United States can be seen in the strength of the U.S. telecommunications equipment diamond. Highly specialized factors are uniquely available in the United States compared to Canada, including sophisticated software engineers and world class university and research programs in computer science and telecommunications. American buyers and end-users are among the most sophisticated in the world, and the existence of 20 to 25 major independent switch buyers leads to intense competition which encourages customers to continuously upgrade their central office switching capabilities. American firms in integrated circuit manufacturing and systems level software design provide strong capabilities in related industries. The local rivalry within the U.S. market is intensified by the high commitment of focused U.S. competitors and the openness of the

U.S. market to foreign rivals (in telecommunications equipment, governments have tended to protect local markets and support monopoly suppliers).

Another interesting example is described in Wesson (1993). He describes the shift of Hyundai's home base in personal computers from Korea to Silicon Valley, as Hyundai discovered that it simply could not keep up from a Korean base. With all competitors sourcing low-cost parts internationally, the only competitive advantages were in the rapid introduction of new models that met evolving custom needs and the ability to successfully access evolving distribution channels. Here, the United States was far ahead of other locations.

Wesson's thesis also documents another corollary of the new global paradigm. Foreign investment (FDI) has traditionally been seen exclusively in terms of exploiting home base advantages or sourcing inputs. Wesson employs statistical evidence to confirm the prevalence of home base *seeking* FDI, or FDI directed at accessing sophisticated advantages of other locations or relocating the home base. Yet where and how the intangible assets that underpin competitive advantages are created and renewed proves more important than the ability to transfer them.

## CONCLUSION

Since the 1950s, globalization has exerted an ever increasing influence on corporate strategy. The traditional paradigm of comparative advantage has been superseded, and it is tempting to conclude that corporations have come to transcend national boundaries. Aggregate statistics confirm the popular view that firms are increasingly global in their sales and operations.

Yet deeper research reveals the striking localization of competitive advantage. This apparent paradox can be explained by adapting a new paradigm of international competition, based not on static advantage such as input costs or economies of scale, but on the ability to innovate and upgrade. This paradigm must guide a new generation of thinking about global strategy in which localization and globalization are integrated in wholly new ways.

Localization was once seen as a necessary evil to be balanced against the compelling benefits of a global strategy. Instead, there are two different roles of localization: innovation and adaptation to local circumstances. The home base location is often the root of competitive advantage. Global strategies can extend this advantage through input sourcing, accessing new markets, or tapping particular information or technologies. To play this role, however, dispersed activities must adapt to local needs and customs. This new synthesis, which recognizes the complex roles of location in competitive advantage, will drive competition in the coming decades.

# NOTES

1. This paper draws on research by Hernan Cristerna, MBA 1993, and has also benefitted from joint work with Michael Enright and with Örjan Sölvell and Ivo Zander (Stockholm School of Economics). We are also grateful for helpful comments by David Collis, Hans Thorelli, participants in the Integral Strategy Collegium at Indiana University, and participants in the International Business Group seminar at Harvard Business School.

2. Among nations, for example, Japan, Italy, and Korea have been prospering during recent decades in terms of world trade and per capita income, while other nations have been stagnating. Within countries, some states are consistently more prosperous than others. In Germany, for example, Baden Württemberg is the performance leader. In the United States, Massachusetts and New Jersey have ranked in the top 10 states in terms of GDP per capita for the last 10 years, consistently outperforming states such as Arkansas, West Virginia, Utah, and others. Some states such as Georgia, Virginia, and New Hampshire have gained markedly in the per capita income ranking while others such as Michigan, Indiana, and Oregon have fallen.

3. For summaries of the literature in these areas see Calvet (1981), Caves (1982), Ghoshal (1987) and Kogut (1991).

4. See also Ohmae (1985 and 1987).

5. Note that Ohmae's argument vacillates in terms of its stress on global customers (with similar needs around the world) and national differences. This draws into question his imperative of establishing full business systems in each major market to respond to customer differences (see below).

6. The exception to this free mobility is what Reich terms *symbolic analyst zones* which are locations of sophisticated problem solvers concentrated in a particular area to create a rapid flow of informal communication. Such symbolic analyst zones may be located anywhere in the world, but once established, they are difficult to duplicate. A firm's global web may extend across a variety of symbolic analyst zones (for example, one for a particular type of R&D and one for sophisticated production); however, no one zone will be predominant.

The relationship between these symbolic analyst zones and my (1990) concepts of clusters and home bases will be explored later.

7. Information on Novo is based on Enright (1989) and field research.

8. Figures taken from recent annual reports and other corporate filings.

9. Figures taken from recent annual reports and other corporate filings.

10. See, for example, Porter (1990); Crocombe, Enright, and Porter (1991); Porter and Monitor Company (1991), and Sölvell, Zander and Porter (1991).

11. Estimates taken from updated data presented in Tyson (1991) based on Mataloni (1992).

12. Data reflect the level of R&D spending rather than the composition of R&D activities. Our field research, and that reported in Sölvell, Zander, and Porter (1991) indicates that a large amount of the R&D conducted by foreign affiliates is related to product adaptation or production process modification rather than research on core products and processes.

13. Authors' updating of Tyson (1991) using 1990 data.

14. Additional evidence comes, ironically, from Asea Brown Boveri (ABB), a case Reich (1991) discussed, and we have studied in some detail (see Cristerna 1993). ABB has multiple operations located throughout the world, but global responsibility for establishing business strategy, selecting product development priorities and allocating production among countries for each product line is based in a particular geographic location. Leadership for power transformers is based in Germany, for example, electric drives in Finland, and process automation in the United States.

15. See, for example, Jaikumar and Upton (1993).

16. This group of activities, which vary in composition from industry to industry, will be termed "home base" or "core" activities.

17. Thomas (1993) confirms this result in pharmaceuticals, where the firms facing local rivals (and strict product approval regulation) were the most innovative.

18. Some observers have cited collaboration rather than competition as an important basis of competitiveness, referring most often to Japan and to the industrial districts of Italy. This view confuses *vertical* collaboration with buyers, suppliers, and local institutions, which diamond theory stresses, with horizontal collaboration between competitors. Such collaboration is rare in successful Japanese and Italian industries (*keiretsu*, for example, do not contain direct competitors), and limited to general infrastructure not products and process. Japanese and Italian industries contain numerous rivals who compete fiercely.

19. Clusters are also present in developing economies, although they normally lack depth in terms of machinery, producers, advanced components, and sophisticated services. See Porter (1990), Chapter 10.

20. See also Kogut (1991). Such location-based advantages are inconsistent with Reich's views of mobile resources, information, and technology. His notion of symbolic analyst zones, which is focused only on skilled employees, is an effort to bridge this inconsistency.

21. Given the dynamic nature of competition and the benefits available to early movers, speed of knowledge transmitted bodes large as a competitive advantage or disadvantage.

22. For a description of these pressures, their causes and effects, see Porter (1992).

23. For a useful discussion of organizational issues in global companies, see Bartlett and Ghoshal (1989).

24. Honda's movement toward greater local content is related to establishing new product line home bases.

25. Wesson (1993) further develops the Northern Telecom case.

## REFERENCES

Bartlett, C.A., & Ghoshal, S. (1989). *Managing Across Borders: The Transnational Solution.* Boston: Harvard Business School Press.

Buckley, P.J., & Casson, M.C. (1976). *The Future of the Multinational Enterprise.* London: Holmes and Meier.

Calvet, A.L. (1981). "A Synthesis of Foreign Direct Investment Theories and Theories of the Multinational Firm." *Journal of International Business Studies, 12,* (Spring-Summer): 43-60.

Caves, R.E. (1971). "International Corporations: The Industrial Economics of Foreign Direct Investment." *Economica, 38*: 1-27.

Cristerna, H. (1993). "The Role of Home-Based Advantages in Global Expansion: Five Case Studies," Unpublished MBA research report, Harvard Business School, May.

Crocombe, G.T., Enright, M. & Porter, M.E. (1991). *Upgrading New Zealand's Competitive Advantage.* Auckland: Oxford University Press.

Doz, Y., Bartlett, C.A., & Prahalad, C.K. (1981). "Global Competitive Pressures and Host Country Demands: Managing Tensions in MNCs." *California Management Review* 23 (Spring): 63-74.

Dunning, J. (1988). "The Eclectic Paradigm of International Production: A Restatement and Some Possible Extensions." *Journal of International Business Studies, 19,* (Spring): 1-32.

Dunning, J., & Rugman, A.M. (1985). "The influence of Hymer's Dissertation on the Theory of Foreign Direct Investment." *American Economic Review, 75,*: 228-232.

Enright, M.J. (1989). "Novo industri," Harvard Business School case 9-389-148.

Enright, M.J. (1993a). "Organization and Coordination in Geographically Concentrated Industries." In D. Raff and N. Lamoreaux (Eds.) *Coordination and Information: Historical Perspectives on the Organization of Enterprise.* Chicago: Chicago University Press for the NBER.

Enright, M.J. (1993b). "The Determinants of Geographic Concentration in Industry," Harvard Business School Working Paper 93-052.

Ghoshal, S. (1987). "Global Strategy: An Organizing Framework." *Strategic Management Journal, 8,* (September-October): 425-440.

Graham, E.M. (1974). "Oligopolistic Imitation and European Direct Investment in the United States." Doctoral dissertation, Harvard Business School.

Hamel G., & Prahalad, C.K. (1985). "Do You Really have a Global Strategy?" *Harvard Business Review, 63,* (July-August): 139-148.

Hout, T., Porter, M.E., & Rudden, E. (1982). "How Global Companies Win Out." *Harvard Business Review, 60*: (September-October): 98-108.

Hymer, S.H. (1976). *International Operations of National Firms: A Study of Direct Investment.* Cambridge, MA: MIT Press (from 1960 doctoral dissertation).

Jaikumar, R., & Upton, D.M. (1993). "The Coordination of Global Manufacturing." In Bradley, Housman, and Nolan.(Eds.). *Globalization, Technology and Competition: The Fusion of Computers and Telecommunications in the 1990s.* Boston: Harvard Business School Press.

Johnson, H.G. (1970). "The efficiency and Welfare Implications of the International Corporation." In C.P. Kindleberger (Ed.). *The International Corporation.* Cambridge, MA: MIT Press.

Kindleberger, C.P. (1969). *American Business Abroad.* New Haven: Yale University Press.

Knickerbocker, F.T. (1974). "Oligopolistic Reaction and Multinational Enterprise." Harvard Business School Division of Research.

Kogut, B. (1984). "Normative Observations on the International Value-Added Chain and Strategic Groups." *Journal of International Business Studies, 15,* (Fall): 151-167.

Kogut, B. (1985). "Designing Global Strategies: Comparative and Competitive Value Added Chains." *Sloan Management Review, 27,* (Summer): 15-28; and "Designing Global Strategies: Profiting from Operational Flexibility." *Sloan Management Review, 27,* (Fall): 27-38.

Kogut, B. (1991). "Country Capabilities and the Permeability of Borders." *Strategic Management Journal, 12,* (Special Issue, Summer): 33-47.

Krugman, P. (1983). "The New Theories of International Trade and the Multinational Enterprise." In C.P. Kindleberger, & D. Audretsch, (Eds.), *The Multinational Corporation in the 1980s* pp. 57-73. Cambridge, MA: MIT Press.

Levitt, T. (1983). "The Globalization of Markets." *Harvard Business Review, 61,* (May-June): 92-102.

Magee, S.P. (1976). "Technology and the Appropriability Theory of the Multinational Corporation" In J. Bhajwati (Ed.), *The New International Economic Order.* Cambridge, MA: MIT Press.

Mataloni, R.J., Jr.(1992). "U.S. Multinational Companies: Operations in 1990." *Survey of Current Business, 72,* (August): 60-78.

McManus, J.C. (1972). "The Theory of the International Firm." In C. Pacquet (Ed.), *The Multinational Firm and the Nation State.* Toronto: Collier-Macmillan.

Ohmae, K. (1985). *Triad Power: The Coming Shape of Global Competition.* New York: The Free Press.

Ohmae, K. (1990). *The Borderless World: Power and Strategy in the Interlinked Economy.* New York: Harper Business.

Perlmutter, H.V. (1969). "The Tortuous Evolution of the Multinational Corporation." *Columbia Journal of World Business, 5,* (January-February): 9-18.

Porter, M.E. (1980). *Competitive Strategy: Techniques for Analyzing Industries and Competitors* New York: The Free Press.

Porter, M.E. (1985). *Competitive Advantage: Creating and Sustaining Superior Performance.* New York: The Free Press.

Porter, M.E. (1986). "Competition in Global Industries: A Conceptual Framework." In M.E. Porter (Ed.), *Competition in Global Industries.* Boston: Harvard Business School Press.

Porter, M.E. (1990). *The Competitive Advantage of Nations*. New York: The Free Press.
Porter, M.E. (1992). *Capital Choices: Changing the Way America Invests in Industry*. Washington, DC: Council on Competitiveness.
Porter, M.E., & Monitor Company. (1991). *Canada at the Crossroads: The Reality of a New Competitive Environment*. Ottawa: Business Council on National Issues and Government of Canada.
Prahalad, C.K. (1975). "The Strategic Process in a Multinational Corporation." Unpublished doctoral dissertation, Harvard Business School.
Reich, R.B. (1990). "Who is Us?" *Harvard Business Review, 68,* (January-February): 53-64.
Reich, R.B. (1991). *The Work of Nations: Preparing Ourselves for 21st-Century Capitalism*. New York: Alfred A. Knopf.
Rugman, A.M. (1980). "Internalization as a General Theory of Foreign Direct Investment: A Reappraisal of the Literature." *Weltwirtschaftliches Archiv, 116,* 365-379.
Rugman, A.M. (1977). "Do Multinationals have a Future? *Futures 10,* 243-246.
Rugman, A.M. (1981). *Inside the Multinationals*. London: Croom Helm.
Thomas, L.G. (1993). "Spare the Road and Spoil the Industry: Vigorous Regulation and Vigorous Competition Promote International Competitive Advantage." Emory University Working Paper.
Tyson, L.D. (1991). "They are Not Us: Why American Ownership Still Matters." *The American Prospect, No. 4,* (Winter): 37+.
Vernon, R. (1966). "International Investment and International Trade in the Product cycle." *Quarterly Journal of Economics, 72,* (May): 190-207.
Vernon, R. (1979). "The Product Hypothesis in a New International Environment." *Oxford Bulletin of Economics and Statistics, 41,* 255-267.
Wesson, T. (1993). "The Determinants of Foreign Direct Investment in U.S. Manufacturing Industries." Unpublished doctoral thesis, Harvard Business School.

# DISCUSSION

## James K. Baker, Chair

*James Rush:*
 Is there maybe a paradox in the home base in that, although it is set up to promote and enhance innovation, *over time there may not be enough diversity of thought within a home base* to allow for renewal?
*Porter:*
 That is a very interesting question. It is true that there are well documented examples of home bases essentially becoming insular and then declining. I hesitate to say it, and I will say it quietly, maybe Detroit is an example. In Britain there used to be some centers, Lancaster and places like that, that just fell apart. What this conception I have suggests that in one of these locations, like Hollywood or Boston in biotechnology, there are a lot of companies, a lot of suppliers and at least a certain core of sophisticated users. They are all in the same place and all of them are global. The suppliers do not just supply Hollywood, they supply many places. The users do not just operate there; they compete world-wide. One source of diversity of views is the sheer number of different players that are located there, and the fact that all of them are international. Hopefully they are getting stimulation from that.

 What we find is that these clusters, or home bases, implode when one of two things happens. For one thing, for whatever reason, rivalry stops. That is, instead of having AT&T and Northern Telecom banging away at each other, we end up having the U.S. steel industry, where everybody (at least before the recent mini-mills) was in a kind of cozy arrangement, and they really were not banging against each other any more. Therefore, the pressure for dynamism erodes. The second reason that one of those bases might fall apart is that *some non-incremental change happens in either technology or demand.* That means that the specialized skills or technology that have been created there are no longer relevant. For example, an industry goes from a mechanical industry to an electronic industry. You need totally new suppliers, new customer needs, and most sophisticated customers may no longer be in the former base country. The answer is that these things do change. That is why nations gain and lose position in particular businesses. It also may mean that firms over time may have to think about migrating certain businesses. We are seeing more and more that multinationals are shifting home bases for *particular* businesses; I could list you dozens of cases studies here. I think we will see more of that as multinationals start to understand that this spread-everything-around-the-world, coordinate-like-hell model does not work. This more subtle in-between model says you don't do everything at home, and you don't spread everything out and coordinate like crazy. It is kind of an interesting combination.

I think one of the things we need to do is more research on failure. I have done a lot of research on success, and I think we need to understand a little better the dynamics of failure. I am right now studying a sample of Japanese failures. I thought it would be great for all of our egos and motivations if we understood Japanese failures. It turns out that Japanese have tried and failed in software, aerospace, financial services and so on. We can learn a lot from those failures.

*Rajan Varadarajan:*

Can there not be *multiple favorable diamonds* (to use your term) worldwide for certain products and services?

*Porter:*

There can be, but my hypothesis is that there is only room for a couple, like two, or three, but not many. The reason lies in these *agglomeration economies.* You do need to have a number of companies there, a number of suppliers there, and given scale economies, and so forth. One cannot support more than a small number. Typically, in an industry you see two or three places. In the case of Japan often there would be a couple of locations where there would be really successful companies, but not 10, 20, or 50. What one sees in the case of multiple locations is a tendency towards specialization. So, for example, the German car cluster has a very different character and model range and competitive philosophy than the Japanese car cluster. By the way, there is a car cluster in the UK, most of the Indy cars are made there, and most of the formula one cars. So you see multiple locations, but if you look very carefully you often see sub-specialization within the model range and within the strategies.

*Harvey Hegarty:*

When I looked at your map of the distribution of industries, and listened to what you were saying about competitive advantage, it struck me that part of *competitive advantage in many cases is being close to and being able to see your competitor*. I guess this brings an awareness that if you are not up on the next technology, somebody else is going to be?

*Porter:*

Absolutely, very well put. I would say two things. First, I would say that the behavior required for advantage, which I argue is innovativeness, dynamism, and change, is that this behavior is unnatural. It is the normal human condition to enjoy where you are and do what you have been doing. So you need pressure, you need stimulation and information all the time. Being close to that competitor and being able to see them, we find in this research, is very important. It goes even further than that. You go to the world centers in particular businesses, and it is more than just being able to see your competitors and their building. It is ego. It is pride; it is being part of the same community. It is getting razzed at the club. Out of sight, out of mind. That is absolutely right. I think we have gotten ourselves so worked up about globalness and the advantages of modern communications, and how we can all work at home and be networked together, that we have forgotten some very powerful points about the reality of the human innovation process. Think of sports, science, and the arts, great things happen in clumps. There happen to be a bunch of German tennis stars right now. That is no accident, because they all play with each other. The young ones see the Boris Becker and the others are all great. So they say, Gee, I am German, they are German, I can do it. They try a little harder. Great scientific breakthroughs, Nobel Prize winners, they are not randomly spread around the globe. Anyway, I could go on and on about this. A natural human condition is to want to be modern, but also to want to be different and to be unique, and I think that somehow maybe we lost sight of that. I think we will see more local identity and less EC identity. Bo Arpi is going to talk about some of these issues later in this meeting.

*Michael Schundler:*

I can see if I want to build a product I look for the diamond in which that product is dominating, and I pick that area site for my headquarters. I see the other example you say where the technology has changed and the diamond is no longer appropriate because the skill requirements have gone from mechanical to electronic. That is great when I am after the fact, but what happens when I am going into the picture and want to create a whole new product using a whole new set of technologies that don't exist. Do I build the diamond? *How do I get the diamond if it does not exist as yet?*

*Porter:*

I guess what you have to look for is where is the best emerging *critical mass?* Where is the best foundation? For discussion purposes, let us just use a wild example. Let's assume that you want to start a computer company. You have this conception of massively parallel processing. The Minneapolis Cray Data model is not massive parallelism, but rather having all these hyper-sophisticated chips that run very fast; you don't process in parallel, you process very fast through the same super-cooled chips. That philosophy and set of skills and support has been circled around Cray and the surrounding area. But if you believe in massive parallel processing, then Cray-Minneapolis might not be as good a place. So you look around the United States and ask where are some of the foundations. You look for heavy duty software expertise, because running these things in parallel is the really hard part. And you look for communications capability, and so forth. What you may conclude is that the computer industry, once almost wiped out in Massachusetts and moved to Silicon Valley, is going to move back to Massachusetts. Because as we get to the parallel computer concept, we have the local area network dominance, the software, computer science skills in Massachusetts. I think that the answer is that if you are building a new product and you don't see a recognized center, you have to either find one that is a foundation, or create one. Note that we find many examples in history of how companies that, maybe randomly, got located in a certain place, started to recognize that there were constraints to their capacity to improve—and they actually literally created ways of easing those constraints. For example, they prevailed upon local university research departments to sponsor training institutes, or they put suppliers in business to make particular components. The firm has latitude in not only changing its own strategy but in influencing the quality of its proximate environment as well.

# III THE GLOBALIZATION OF AMERICAN TELEPHONE AND TELEGRAPH

# EDITOR'S NOTE

Due to actual or perceived antitrust restrictions in 1925 and 1975, AT&T for a period of almost 60 years confined its overseas engagement largely to international long distance calls and standardization efforts. Randall Tobias headed the almost incredibly fast transformation of the new AT&T into a global operation. In addition to the fact that telecommunications infrastructures were expanding everywhere, he provided three motivating forces in guiding the process: (1) AT&T's prime customers (i.e., leading U.S. multinationals) were themselves globalizing, (2) even though the U.S. home market; it was not large enough to support the enormous R&D costs necessary to be a leader of the industry, and (3) the U.S. market was being invaded by foreign competitors.

In the restructuring of all of AT&T, delegation of authority to business units became a key principle and one particularly well suited to the globalization thrust, where flexibility, speed and adjustment to local customer concerns were the key to success. In addition, the acquisition of NCR doubled the number of AT&T employees outside the United States to 50,000, literally overnight. A king-size challenge was the cultural change, and reeducation, required of senior AT&T executives used to the idea that the domestic market was the only one that really counted. For purposes of coordination and integration, an International Policy Council was created, and AT&T España was used as an experiment in multinational matrix management.

Of special interest is the search for what Tobias calls "the Holy Grail of synergy" in the far-flung and diversified global AT&T, an effort to which Tobias devoted special attention.

# THE GLOBALIZATION OF AMERICAN TELEPHONE AND TELEGRAPH

Randall L. Tobias

Thank you, Dick [Richard D. Wood, Chair of the Session], very much. It is a real delight to be with you today. I told Mike I changed much of my speech and much of my strategy after listening to the first hour or so. Indiana University is an ideal host for a conference such as this one, and Indiana itself is the perfect setting, thanks to the international activities of a number of farsighted executives like Dick Wood of Eli Lilly and Company and Jim Baker, of Arvin. This state has long had a global outlook, and because Indiana University has for so long been focused on globalization, the state has become a magnet for students from all parts of the world. Many of you may not be aware of this, but much of the credit for Indiana University's focus on globalization goes back a very long time to IU's chancellor, former president and former dean of the School of Business, Herman B. Wells, who has been around a little while and celebrated his ninetieth birthday this year. Dr. Wells was largely responsible for pouring the foundation that has enabled the building of this first class institution. He was deeply involved in the formation of the United Nations and deeply involved in the globalization of the curriculum. He has traveled extensively. I spend some amount of time in Thailand, where we have significant activities, and there is a story of Bangkok, whether it is apocryphal I don't know. But it is a story of a couple of Hoosier business people who got off of the airplane in Bangkok, got into the back of a Thai cab, and began talking about Indiana. At this the Thai taxi driver turned around and said, "Excuse me, are you from Indiana? Do you know Chancellor Wells?" I would not doubt that that is a true story.

Certainly no less visionary in the world of global business is Hans Thorelli, so it is a real pleasure to be a part of this conference that he has put together. Hans asked me to describe AT&T's globalization and suggested a number of questions that I might want to address. For example, how did the philosophy of globalization emerge in the first place at AT&T? What is the suitable balance between centralized coordination and local initiative? How do we achieve desirable levels of integration while still pushing decision-making downward in the organization. Those are all very good questions—questions my colleagues and I find ourselves grappling with every day as a matter of practical necessity. I have spent a lot of time listening to and reading and trying to learn as much as I can from people who have worked, studied, and written in this area. I have spent time with Ken Ohmae and with David Nadler and C.K. Prahalad, who were featured recently in *Business Week*. I have read much of what Michael Porter has written. The problem I have with all of that is that there is also in the world in which I live a human dimension of egos, of willingness to work together, of changing environments, imperfect knowledge, and so indeed our approach to globalization is a dynamic one. It is dynamic enough that it will probably be different tomorrow based on some notes I took this morning. It is a little bit of all of the above and all of the things that you saw on that chart. But it is certainly not a world that I would describe with any degree of orderliness as one might conclude by viewing charts such as those we looked at. What I would like to do is spend a little time giving you some background thought and information about AT&T. And then I think perhaps the real substance of what we might share together may come out of the dialogue we might have later on.

Let me begin with a little history. You might think that AT&T is brand new to the world of globalization and international markets. We are in fact returning to markets that we entered successfully more than a century ago. Alexander Graham Bell invented the telephone in 1876, and late in 1876 he made the first telephone call that was made in Europe from Browns Hotel in London where he had taken his invention to try to raise venture capital. By 1925, AT&T had developed far-flung overseas manufacturing operations that stretched from London to St. Petersburg to Shanghai. But in that year, with rumors in the air of possible U.S. antitrust action in the air, we sold off then almost all of our international businesses to a company called ITT and limited our focus to developing the telecommunications network in the United States. We continued to provide international long-distance service through partnership agreements with telephone agencies throughout the world, and to some degree this kept us in touch with world markets, as did our active involvements with international organizations that were promoting cooperation and common standards. But we did not otherwise do business in the international marketplace until the 1970s, and then only on a very limited basis. Ten years ago, as I am sure you are well aware, to settle another antitrust suit and to gain freedom from government restrictions, AT&T agreed to divest itself of its local telephone company operations, including companies such as Illinois Bell, New York Telephone, and Indiana Bell. With the breakup of the Bell system, we began then in earnest to reenter the global marketplace, and for this purpose in 1980 we created a subsidiary company called AT&T International. There were some compelling reasons at that time for AT&T to begin to think about markets outside our traditional home markets in the United States—reasons far more compelling than those that motivated our predecessors in the 1880s.

First, our biggest and best U.S. customers, the U.S.-based *Fortune* "100" companies were increasingly globalizing their operations, and they were looking to us for the support to tie their operations together. Second, the U.S.-domestic market, large as it is, was clearly not going to be big enough to support the huge R&D costs that would be necessary for companies that want to be major players, particularly in the supply of infrastructure to the telecommunications industry. Third, with the breakup of the Bell system, foreign competitors began to concentrate on the U.S. market, requiring us to respond in-kind if we were not to be kept continually on the defensive. Fourth, the development of a telecommunications infrastructure was becoming a priority in every corner of the world. Government leaders discussing their infrastructure priorities used to talk about roads, sewers, electricity, and water. Now they talk about telecommunications and information infrastructure. Computers and communications have gradually become an integral part of virtually every business and industry from agriculture to retailing, from travel to financial services. To compete effectively, businesses need access to advanced voice and data networks. And nations that want to attract and retain businesses must have an advanced telecommunications infrastructure, and they are recognizing that.

Little wonder that the nations of the world will spend as much on telecommunications equipment during the decade of the nineties as they did cumulatively in all of the 115 years since Alexander Graham Bell invented the telephone. It is estimated that spending on telecommunications infrastructure may well reach $200 billion a year by the turn of the century.

In a related trend, nations are increasingly coming to see that privately owned telecommunications (indeed privately owned companies in general) can do better than government agencies in providing services that have historically been viewed in many countries as a responsibility of the central government.

Japan, the United Kingdom, Mexico, Venezuela, and other countries have privatized their telecommunications systems in recent years to enhance their performance and to enable them to attract private capital and in general to improve their national economic competitiveness. Indeed, some privatizations are likely to take place around the world in the next two to three years.

In addition to privatization, many nations are liberalizing the rules that govern telecommunications and are permitting some degree of competition in services, equipment, or both. And where they are not moving down that path, customers are increasingly placing pressures on them that will inevitably cause more and more competition to be permitted in the industry. Governments are discovering that, to improve the quality and to lower the cost of telecommunications, nothing works better than a competitive marketplace. And as markets around the world open up, there are increasing opportunities for a variety of service and equipment providers.

During our reentry into the international marketplace, we certainly made our share of mistakes and false starts, and we are still doing that. But on balance, I think our performance has earned at least acceptable marks, particularly when you measure what we have done in globalization in the last decade against the backdrop of the other challenges that we have faced in the years leading up to and following the breakup of the Bell system, which was arguably the largest industrial reorganization in history. In the mid-1980s, we had to manage our way through a very difficult period of cultural and organizational adjustment after spinning off the local telephone companies, which had represented about three-quarters of AT&T's assets and had been the primary focus of our planning and our operations. We also had to deal with operational problems. We had to resolve regulatory issues. We had to cope with technology, which was changing at a blinding pace, and we had to create within the firm a very new mindset, a new competitive outlook among people who had never really understood what it was like to be in a real business with all the dynamics of a competitive marketplace.

Following divestiture, it soon became evident to us that our work force was much too large—at least 25 percent too large. So from 1984 to 1987, we eliminated almost 70,000 jobs. That number is now over 100,000 that we have eliminated through downsizing activities through the last decade, a very painful experience.

As we emerged from this transition period, we established three broad goals for the firm. One was to do what was necessary to focus on and strengthen our traditional core businesses. These include, first, long-distance communication services, both within the United States and connecting customers in the United States with other parts of the world; and, second, the telecommunications equipment businesses for consumers, for providers of telecommunications services such as telephone companies and others. That was our first focus. Our second was to solidify a position in the network computing business to recognize the coming convergence of computing and telecommunications and our need to have a position in the computing side of computing and telecommunications. The third goal was to focus on the need to expand beyond our traditional U.S.-based markets.

In looking at the strengths and weaknesses of our core businesses, we came to see that our management structure was far too monolithic. We had come a long way since the days of the Bell system in slimming down, but the cold truth was that organizationally we still resembled the Queen Mary more than something like the squadron of speedboats that we were hoping to become. Hans Thorelli very properly sites the dangers of suboptimization to local and functional units when companies decentralize, and I certainly agree. But I have to tell you that, as the year 1988 unfolded, it was apparent that we were at the extreme opposite end of the centralization-decentralization spectrum.

We were running AT&T at that time almost as a single huge organization, clearly well beyond human scale. Our business units were business units in name only. They were really sales and marketing groups with little or no control over how their products were manufactured, sold, developed, priced, serviced, or advertised. We tended to deal with those things in functional areas all concentrated in New Jersey. These units had little control over corporate overhead in general, and our centralized staff groups were much too large, much too bureaucratic and had much too much power and control. Indeed, one of the things we at AT&T introduced at this point was a whole new concept that the corporate headquarters and the headquarters organizations in the business units existed to add value and to support the business units. Because, believe it or not, the cultural mindset was more that business units existed to serve the needs of the central core. We had a situation in which many people were empowered to say no and could kill a project, but very few people were empowered to say yes.

In 1989 and 1990, we began restructuring all of AT&T, creating 20 or so global business units and making them our basic organizational building blocks for the future. Soon they had pretty much full authority over the resources they needed to address their markets. They controlled their own R&D, product management, sales channels, pricing, advertising, and their manufacturing. In what was for us an equally radical move, we shifted literally thousands of staff jobs from corporate headquarters into the business units that they were meant to actually serve. We urged the business units themselves to begin to explore ways to divide themselves into smaller sub business units in order to get more focus on their market, customers, and competitors. Initially when we unveiled this new approach, there was a great deal of concern within AT&T about a loss of synergy, about a fear of fragmentation of the kind that Hans Thorelli has cited. During that period, in replying to such concerns among our own people, I kept trying to find ways to describe this. I often found myself using the analogy of symphony orchestras or football teams. While cooperation and synergy are crucial to their success, the key prerequisite for success must begin with strong individual performance. You are unlikely to have a winning football team or great orchestra if you make it up of mediocre players. Or, to put it more plainly as I finally began to do, eight rocks cannot be made to float by simply tying them together.

We told our managers therefore: let us focus first on the individual performance of our business units, and then let's concentrate on how to build and find the synergy between and among those elements of our business. Today, nearly four years after we implemented this approach, I think there is virtually unanimous agreement within our company. The business unit approach that we have been working to implement has been a success far beyond our expectations. The structure that we put in place and all that flows from that have given us great improvements in flexibility and speed, qualities of critical importance in the intensively competitive markets in which we operate. The structure gives us better control over our costs and puts power and authority and responsiveness in the hands of people closest to our markets and our customers.

Of course, a simplified clear-cut structure also makes it obvious just how well or how poorly individual business units are performing in terms of financial measures or market share or whatever. By the late summer of 1990, it had become painfully obvious that our computer systems business was still some years away from having the kind of scope and profitability and the scale that we sought. It was clear to us that we needed to stop the drain on our resources but indeed accomplish the goal we had set out to achieve. So within a matter of weeks, we concluded that the only way to reach our objective was to acquire a computer company. We focused our attention on NCR, a company we had been in fact looking at for several years. By May of last year, NCR's management and board had overcome what I would call their initial reluctance. Their stockholders accepted AT&T's offer, and a year ago this week the merger was consummated. In addition, in a single stroke the acquisition of NCR doubled the number of AT&T employees who worked outside the United States to about 50,000. It increased the number of countries in which we do business to about 130. By mid-1991, we had moved aggressively to address the first two of the three priorities that we had laid out at the beginning of the decade. That is, we had taken a number of steps to strengthen our core business, culminating in the restructuring that set them up as focused business units with global responsibility. And we had taken a significant step—$7.5 billion dollars worth—to develop a base in what we hope will be our network computing business.

So, finally, we were ready to give substantially greater emphasis to our remaining priority—international business—and we have done so with increased vigor during the last 14 or 15 months. Perhaps our most notable accomplishment has been our progress in changing the mindset, the priorities, and the share-of-mind attention among AT&T's leadership with respect to globalization. In some matters a bottom-up approach works fine. I think there are other endeavors—particularly those involving huge resource allocations, priorities, and emphasis—where the CEO has to be the strategist and leader. He must make it very clear where we are going and what we are going to do and within those parameters create an environment for the collaboration and participation that makes it possible for everyone to help with that vision. I think that corporate strategy organizations can be very helpful in facilitating that process, but the task is not theirs. Rather, I believe it is the key job of the senior leadership of the business. That is what we have been trying to do during this period of time.

We have also come to realize that we had adopted the youth soccer approach to the disposition of our resources. I don't know how many of you have ever had the experience of coaching a soccer team of six- or seven- or eight-year-olds, but they all have one characteristic in common. You have two sides, you have this huge field, and they are all crowded around the ball. That is kind of what our leadership was doing with their time and resources. We were all spending too much time crowding around the same ball, as opposed to looking how better to deploy our time and attention. So accordingly, in addition to my other responsibilities as vice chairman of the board, Bob Allen asked me to assume explicit responsibility about 15 months ago for all our operations, our planning, development, and all our activities outside of the United States. That action among other things sent a signal to our leadership that we were indeed serious about understanding what it means to globalize, what it means to be a global company, what we are trying to do, where we are trying to go, where we begin, how we measure success, what targets we are shooting for, and so forth. It sparked us to re-examine the way that we were managing much of what we were doing, and particularly outside the United States.

During our reentry into the global marketplace in the early 1980s we had, as I mentioned earlier, created an international division as the vehicle for the focus of much of what we were doing outside the United States. For the short term, in the early part of the decade, that division got the job under way, establishing an AT&T presence world wide, setting up sales channels, and maintaining or building ties with governments. But the division did not gain real power or control of resources. In a corporation as large as AT&T, it is very difficult to advocate something if there are no levers to pull. Indeed, the existence of an organization called AT&T International had an unintended negative consequence. Inadvertently, it prompted the leaders of our so-called global business units to believe that activities outside the United States were primarily the domain of AT&T International and that the mainstream of AT&T's people and resources could really stay focused on our home market. Indeed, I think we in senior management saw that we had been as guilty as everyone else in giving practically all our attention to the U.S. market and treating our globalization as a stepchild or an afterthought. We have taken several actions in the last year that have been, I think, effective in beginning to change the mindset of not only our senior management but management throughout our company in getting the appropriate people to think about globalization.

First, we have given a great deal more emphasis to the global roles of all the five operating groups that compose all our business units. The global components of their current and long-range business plans are getting a great deal more attention. Second, we have created an operations committee, made up of the heads of these five groups, and made the members accountable for the day-to-day operations of their businesses globally and not just in the United States. The chairmanship of this group rotates among the members. The committee is accountable to the CEO, Robert Allen, for our domestic U.S. focus and to me for our focus outside the United States. Likewise, we have given greater emphasis to the global accountability of our 13-person, management executive committee, which is our top level policymaking group. For example, the head of our global government affairs organization, which in a business like ours is sometimes critically important, is now spending a great deal more time focused on the non-U.S. aspects of his responsibilities.

Next, on the AT&T agenda is the creation of geographically based operating units that will complement our global business units.

Our business units operate very autonomously in each country outside the United States. We have very little integration, interface, and leverage across the totality of the businesses we may have in a given country, but there is an enormous amount of control and direction from the United States. We do not think that will work going forward. To echo something that Michael Porter was talking about, we also believe that we must change the mindset that requires that the headquarters of our business units and the headquarters of the corporation be identical, and we must also change the mindset that the headquarters of the business units have to be in the United States.

For example, we are in the process of moving the headquarters of the global business units for telephone sets that are corded to France. The reason is that the market for corded telephones is going to be largely focused in Europe. Wireless technology, cordless technology, is moving along with such speed in this country that we are already selling more cordless and wireless products than corded products.

In Spain, we have taken a first step toward the creation of geographically based units by setting up a national organization called AT&T España. It has P&L responsibility and shares responsibility with the global business units that do business in Spain in ways that we are still trying to define.

We are using the experience that we are gaining in matrix management in Spain to set up other country and regional units elsewhere around the world. I don't believe we are going to find that a cookie cutter approach is going to work, but there are certain principles that are certainly going to be very helpful to us. Perhaps the Holy Grail of integrated strategic planning is the illusive notion of synergy. I will tell you that, in recent years, the term synergy has gotten a black eye at least within AT&T because of some of the issues I talked about earlier. The role of potential synergy prompted a lot of unwise, unprofitable, and unfocused activities. Perhaps we had too much of a view that weaknesses in the fundamentals can simply be overcome through synergy. So, we are mindful that the hunt for synergy can sometimes be a trap, and we are trying to be very careful not to force it. Nonetheless, our business units are all engaged in activities that have common technologies or related technologies, and we think there is significant opportunity for core competencies, for synergies, for collaboration across the firm. Finding that right mix, however, is somewhat difficult. We have found some examples in the newly independent republics of the former Soviet Union where there is no money and an acute need for modern telecommunications equipment. We have begun both in Armenia and in Ukraine to put together approaches where we are making our equity investment in the form of network equipment from our equipment unit. As the telecommunications infrastructure in the country is created, it can be paid for by the international long-distance revenues that are now generated by the infrastructure that we build, thus creating a flywheel. You could achieve the same end through joint ventures, but I think our approach is somewhat easier. We hope that, in developing countries, this is going to be a helpful way to go.

We also expect synergy and integrative strategic planning to come into play on a longer term basis as our business units cooperate and collaborate in finding applications for the major new technologies of the nineties.

The three most significant of these technologies that we see are wireless communications, video, and the related technologies of speech recognition and speech processing. In the next decade these technologies will profoundly affect the way all of us communicate with one another. And the way we exchange information, the way we run our businesses, or run our universities. AT&T Bell Laboratories has been a leader in all three of these technologies and in the basic technologies upon which they rely, such as microelectronics and photonics. These technologies are already being applied throughout our various businesses. NCR, for example, has introduced an automatic teller machine with a two-way video, and, when necessary, ATM customers will be able from those machines to deal face-to-face with real human beings. Recently we began delivering our videophone 2500, which is a picture phone that operates over ordinary telephone lines, and we hope it will begin to fulfill the prediction made by John Mayo, the president of our Bell Laboratories, who has been saying that he believes that video technology will be in the 1990s what the fax machine was in the 1980s.

For global businesses, certainly international videoconferencing has become almost commonplace, and applications are under development or entering the marketplace in a number of related areas. We are also starting to see major new applications of wireless technology and speech recognition and speech processing, and a flood of advanced applications will be hitting the marketplace in the next few years from AT&T and a broad range of companies, large and small.

All of which bespeaks the need for the holistic approach that Hans Thorelli calls on us to consider. In AT&T's case, we are certain that synergy can be created as our business units and country units learn to collaborate in bringing new applications to their customers. But we are equally certain that synergy will not just happen by itself. It will require a great deal of work in figuring out how to integrate these strategies. Strategies that will call for the creative insights, combined insights, and capabilities of both global business units and market geographic customer-focused units working together. It is our belief that, with this sort of integrated approach, we will be able to find the Holy Grail of synergy and make AT&T an organization that indeed will be greater than the sum of its individual parts. Thank you very much.

# DISCUSSION

## Richard D. Wood, Chair

*The Chairman Wood* asked Randall Tobias, "How do you get an organization to think of the United States as one piece of a world mosaic" within AT&T's global strategy?

*Tobias:*

This is an issue that I am beginning to believe is more critical to the acceleration of our activities outside of the United States than we initially recognized it to be. And I suspect that at some appropriate point along the way, we're going to need to set up some disaggregated focus on the U.S. market through some form of U.S. operations. The problem is that many of our people in senior levels can really influence where we deploy resources, where we're going to take the risks, where the best people are going to be deployed, and so forth. They are the same people who are accountable for things on a global basis. But because the success or failure of their business in the United States is such an overwhelming part of what they do, they can quickly get unfocused.

Thus, we have tried to change the role, definition, and use of time of our management executive committee, and we have begun to think of our corporate headquarters as a global corporate headquarters and disaggregate out of what we used to think of as the corporate headquarters those people—and it's most of them—who are not focused on global activities but on the U.S. market. I certainly wouldn't want to suggest that organization changes per se are the critical factor, but I am a believer that you can put organizations in place that can inhibit your ability to get done what needs to be done and that's the thing that we're wrestling with.

*Samuel Felton* asked, "To what extent have you modified your performance, measurement, and reward systems to facilitate your objectives?"

*Tobias* emphasized the importance of the "human dimension" of strategy. He indicated that it "may be the primary limiting factor in the relative success" of strategy, and he is paying a lot of attention to measurement and reward systems. He also suggested that organization structure is of critical importance but is not an easy challenge to solve.

*Tobias:*

It's easy for me to say glibly from 30,000 feet that the success of our cordless telephone business in Spain is the shared accountability of the president of AT&T España and the global president of AT&T's cordless telephone business unit. I mean that's the sort of statement that vice chairmen make. Now, when you come down from 30,000 feet, we have this decision to make in the next 15 minutes, and I want to do this and you want to do that. How are we going to measure success and how do we break the ties and how do we keep all that moving? I've more questions than answers, but I believe accountability and decision-making power are also critical elements in what we're trying to do.

*Michael Schundler* proposed a challenge to Tobias regarding structures with *joint accountability*: "Doesn't a tiebreaker encourage executives to focus their attention on him rather than on their customers, because whoever the tiebreaker is, he is the one that's going to influence the decisions made?"

*Tobias:*

Yes, and that's why we're putting a lot of emphasis and effort into teams and leaderless groups. We don't want to reward the kind of performance that causes people to constantly escalate the issues instead of getting them resolved.

*Edward Bowman* suggested that IBM had problems similar to AT&T in terms of decentralization and globalization, yet until now they do not pay the penalty that you pay internally for laying people off. They have a somewhat different method of moving people out. How important is this to AT&T and how can you reconcile these two issues of the human factor?

*Tobias:*

You pay an enormous penalty for layoffs, but with all due respect to IBM, I'm not certain that putting off the inevitable questions of cost structure, which is what they're doing, is the better solution to the problem. We have done a number of very creative things with respect to our people, yet it is not enough. We are putting an enormous amount of emphasis on something we call "the common bond," which is a set of values of how we live in the corporation, how we work with each other, how we treat each other, how we respect the individual. We have not begun to scratch the surface, however, on the challenges of retraining and transitional mechanisms that help people get their lives focused in some different direction. We've been through difficult times in the last decade, and I'm not happy about all the steps we had to take. But I do believe it was a necessary thing for us to do.

Discussion

The other side of this equation is that the way we keep from having to do that in the future is to find ways to grow our business rather than simply focusing on the downsizing and cost-cutting that we were, I think by necessity, focused on in the early part of the decade. You are absolutely right in the sense that it's going to take a long time to rebuild the trust and the teamwork and the feeling of dedication that existed before we found ourselves in this mode. I hope that companies which will face some of the challenges that we have been through are beginning to work on those things today as opposed to waiting until the ox is in the ditch.

When prompted by a participant to provide examples of the key success factors that have allowed AT&T's business units to be successful so quickly, Tobias highlighted a few more human resources issues.

*Tobias:*

One of the things we did initially was symbolic, but it had enormous ramifications. We turned all of our organization charts upside-down. We put the chairman on the bottom, we put the customers on the top, we put the presidents of the business units on the corporate organization charts on the top layer and put everybody there to support them.

"Second, to cover corporate headquarters expenses, we put *a contracting mechanism* in place in which we established *categories of corporate headquarters expense, some of which required the headquarters units to obtain funding from the business units.* These headquarters groups heretofore had thought that the units of the business serving customers were there at the pleasure of the corporate headquarters. Now they found themselves asking, "Wait a minute, where are my customers? I didn't know I had any customers." For example, people who were doing compensation studies or market research had to find somebody in the company who was willing to say, "Yeah, that's adding value to what I'm doing, and we're willing to pay you the following amount next year."

"We put some protective mechanisms in this process early to give us a transition period. Even so, the approach certainly helped address the cost issue. More importantly, it dramatically changed behaviors, because it began to get everybody in the company to think about customers when they came in the door every morning."

A participant asked if anyone would comment on any change in Washington regarding the attitude of helping business internationally. It was suggested that the countries where business and the government work together very closely may be the leaders.

In agreement with earlier remarks by Michael Porter, *Tobias* suggested that "there are few, if any, examples of companies that do lack competition in their home market and at the same time have found a way to be world class in what they do." He indicated that in the infrastructure industry a number of companies that are doing very well today are going to have trouble a decade from now, as in many cases they are doing well mainly because they sell to the government-owned (monopoly) telecommunications company in their home country.

Using the example of switching equipment, *Tobias* suggested that the high charges per line to state-owned firms are covered by monopoly rates charged to customers in the country of service. In contrast, the same equipment may be sold to telephone companies in the United States for a fraction of the cost.
*Tobias:*

But in AT&T's case, we don't have the protective home market to enable us to do that, and that's one of the things that has driven the massive amount of cost cutting we have gone through. Regarding governments that are helping equipment manufacturers currently through some of what they are doing, I'm not sure they're really addressing the problems that are going to occur in the long term.

On the other hand, historically we have had a somewhat adversarial relationship generally between the U.S. government and business. I can cite a number of examples where that is changing, however. The current administration [Bush] has been extraordinarily helpful to us in things we have been trying to do around the world.
*Marjorie Lyles:*

What are you doing to manage your relationships with other firms, in particular, joint ventures and cooperative relationships? Have you learned anything special from the AT&T-Philips joint venture?

*Tobias* indicated that his view on joint ventures was "not necessarily shared by all [his] colleagues."
*Tobias:*

Too often people try to put together joint ventures where the two parties to the joint venture have exactly the same [competitive] objectives in mind, and they spend all of their time looking over their shoulder because (1) they really don't want this partner, (2) they'd really prefer to go it alone, and (3) as soon as they can figure out a way to get rid of them, they're going to go ahead alone. And I think that is a characteristic of many joint ventures that we entered early on. Philips was a good case in point.

AT&T is engaged in a number of various-sized joint ventures around the world. According to *Tobias*, successful alliances will become increasingly important.
*Tobias:*

"Some have worked well, but many have not. I think there are a number of characteristics shared by the alliances that work. For example, they have a clear focus and a clear shared understanding up front of what people want to do and how they're going to work together. Going forward, particularly in our industry, collaborations are going to be of critical importance to our success. We need to serve the needs of multinational customers all over the

## Discussion

world. We cannot do that and do not wish to do that alone. We've got to find ways to collaborate, and that's a new part of the teaming paradigm that we're spending a lot of time working on."

*Thomas Hustad* posed a question about integration of corporate objectives across strategic business units (SBUs):

You spoke earlier of the need for senior-most executives to set the tone, an overarching umbrella for strategy. I'm interested how the company achieves some complicated patterns of integration and such. It seems to me as you talked about migrating from the importance of fax technology to video technology there might be a way to examine the question. Fax technology is old, yet it only bloomed when the infrastructure of the installed bases of machines grew rapidly to make it possible to send faxes to the people you wished to reach, often in decentralized work environments. So video becomes a major program element for you. It may well be that there's a parallel infrastructure lesson to be learned there. Left to its own devices *one of those retardant SBUs* (as you characterize them, 'I don't make money, I'll never make money') *might want to recover costs, price the thing very high and retard infrastructure development while the corporation has as an objective to drive the development of that technology to build the infrastructure and support the growth in sales.* So, at AT&T how does that get worked out?

*Tobias:*

It doesn't get worked out very well, and we're working on it. It's a very key issue. One of the risks is the other side of the answer to an earlier question: if you have a business unit, it has all this power and is very much under earnings pressure or market share pressure or whatever. Their inclination (if you don't provide the support and the coaching) may well be to not pay for things that they can't afford this quarter or this month but which are important to our success two or three years from now.

There are also issues particularly in technology where something like video may require a commitment of resources today that our communications services people, who focus on long distance for residence customers, don't think these customers can afford. And the infrastructure people who make switching equipment to sell to cable companies and telephone companies and so forth don't think they can afford it; and NCR can't afford it, and so forth. But somehow collectively we could all afford it. And in many cases we can't afford *not* to do it. So how do you deal with that?

We've settled now on about six core initiatives. Video is one of them. We have a group of representatives from various parts of the business who are charged with figuring out how we can get a nucleus together of activities around video that may fit in the businesses that exist today, or in new businesses that need to be created to address these opportunities.

*Denis Mentha* asked about integrating AT&T's strategies within the international group and how the core initiatives are funded across the international units.

*Tobias:*

Our budgeting process is still evolving. But in simple terms, core initiatives are the kind of projects that are getting funded at the corporate level, and they are linked back to the profit & loss units as a tax. We tend to describe it in our business, as "what you pay for the privilege of being able to put the AT&T brand name on the product or service that you put in the marketplace." Tobias suggested that AT&T's practice facilitates growth of brand equity:

*Tobias:*

It is our belief that people want to add value to the brand, and the brand ought to be more valuable next year than it was this year as a result of those people who have been permitted within the firm to use it. And this is one of the ways we get that done.

*Hans Thorelli* asked Tobias to suggest synergies from AT&T's acquisition of NCR. "The acquisition of NCR doubled your overseas employees. How will the integration of NCR and AT&T be accomplished, and what are the potential synergies from the acquisition?"

*Tobias:*

Briefly, we acquired NCR with several objectives in mind. One of which was to fix the problem I described earlier. Clearly, another objective was to harvest the synergies of the convergence of computing and communications going forward. The first priority was to do the reverse acquisition. In fact, I think the NCR people were quite startled to come out of this acquisition to sort of discover that rather than them having been acquired, they were acquirees. Because the first thing we did was turn the AT&T computer business over to them, and they spent about six months to a year rationalizing the products and sorting through the people issues and so forth. And that has gone very, very well. To this point, we have operated NCR very much with AT&T in a holding company role and NCR over here on the side. But the other thing we have done is to let AT&T and NCR people around the world begin to find each other, work together, find things that made sense. They are now building a customer-driven head of steam that we're going to begin to rationalize. It is going to help deal with the human resistance of bringing these things together because the approach is customer driven. It's driven by people who are finding synergies in resolving customer problems, and pretty soon it's going to have so much momentum that we couldn't stand in the way of it even if we wanted to.

# IV INTEGRATION OF A GLOBAL ENTERPRISE: THE SIME DARBY EXPERIENCE

# EDITOR'S NOTE

A sign as good as any of the economic emancipation of the developing countries is the recent rapid emergence of MNCs headquartered in these nations. As this new genre of MNC is not yet widely known (and far less researched), we were especially pleased to have Tunku Ahmad Yahaya, CEO of the largest MNC based in Malaysia, conduct an intensive session.

The documentation from the session is presented in four parts: Ahmad Yahaya's presentation, the following open discussion, an interview by the Editor, and, finally, a description of Sime Darby Berhad. The reader unfamiliar with this MNC might wish to read this description first.

The crucial theme in Ahmad Yahaya's remarks is his rationale for the developing-country MNC: It relies on networking with MNCs from the heavily industrialized countries for technology transfer, and in return provides its own intimate knowledge about culture and markets in the developing country, or in the present case, the Southeast Asia region, and, in the Sime instance, local funding as well. The linking of these two factors would seem to constitute the key challenge in developing integral strategy for Sime Darby.

# ORGANIZING FOR INTEGRAL STRATEGY FORMULATION AND IMPLEMENTATION:
## SIME DARBY OF MALAYSIA

Tunku Ahmad Yahaya

Perhaps the first point I would like to make is that very few companies are truly global and Sime Darby is certainly not a global organization in the fullest sense of the word. Business today, however, is truly international and extends through and beyond national frontiers and boundaries as readily and as easily as picking up a telephone, reading a fax, or jumping on an airplane. I think it was Groucho Marx who said that one man in a thousand is a leader of men and the other 999 are followers of women. And the essence of his remark, which applies equally to the business world, is that once a business trend or path has been opened up, 999 out of every 1,000 businessmen tend to follow it. The herd instinct is endemic in the business community and the business trend today is undoubtedly in the direction of globalism. This does not mean necessarily that the companies themselves have yet fully come to adjust to this global concept. Sime Darby, for example, has businesses, factories, and offices throughout the ASEAN and the Pacific region and is what I would call a notably strong regional organization. Sime Darby also does business all around the world, and even has offices and people located in countries outside the Asia-Pacific region and readily qualifies as an international or multinational company, but not yet as a truly global organization, not in my book anyway.

There have always been, in the 20th century that is, a number of companies that operate globally, such as Goodyear, Coca Cola, ICI, Shell, Esso, Lever Brothers, Ford, and there are many more, especially Japanese companies, coming into the game today. The companies which are entirely global are relatively few when compared to the numbers of companies that do business internationally.

Sime Darby is a regional group and I myself am a regionalist. At a business conference a few months ago, where I first heard Professor Michael Porter speak, I expressed the view that the quickest way to establish an international free trade world, if that is ever going to be possible, would be by following the regional grouping route. The U.S. Administration is opposed to regional trade groupings because they believe they represent a barrier to free trade. And yet, the U.S. has only recently created a new economic grouping with the North American Free Trade Association, and Europe is already in place with the European Economic Community, which is clearly an economic grouping or trade block. I am in favor of an East Asia-Pacific group which would include Japan. This would, or could be, the first step towards some sort of link-up between the North American Free Trade area and the East Asia- Pacific group, and eventually a second link up could, or would be, between this enlarged grouping and an expanded European Economic Community grouping. I would suggest that this is a more practicable and likely route to a free trade world which most of us want to see come to pass than continuing with a never-ending round of inconclusive GATT talks.

But to get back to the subject I have been asked to speak on, namely Sime Darby and its experience in the integration of a global enterprise. Maybe as an introduction I should tell you a little bit about the Sime Darby Group. Although Sime Darby has been around for almost 100 years now, the problem of organizing an integrated strategy has only in recent years become important. Sime Darby, like all the best vaudeville acts, started out as a duet with Mr. Sime, a Scot, playing the entrepreneurial role, and Mr. Darby, an English banker, providing the financial backup. Mr. Darby left the act very early and Mr. Sime continued on his own in the direction of rubber plantations and trading in which they had started. Sime Darby was never one of the established blue chip plantation companies and in fact developed a reputation in the industry as a corporate hustler, a reputation which over the years I think we have managed to live down, though I still encourage our corporate executives to be entrepreneurial in their thinking. By the way, an American friend of mine never fails to remind me that entrepreneur is the French word for hustler!

The Sime Darby appearance on the Malaysian equity scene occurred when a few corporate executives in the private sector, of which I was one, got together to look at the possibility of developing a Malaysian multinational. In other words, rather than sit on the steps of the multinational corporation club, bemoaning how we were being exploited by the members inside, we thought we ought to find a way to join the club and get involved in the action ourselves. It just so happened that Sime Darby, a company listed on the Kuala Lumpur and London stock exchanges, turned out to be the corporate vehicle for which we were looking.

At that point in time, more than 60 percent of Sime Darby pre-tax operating profit was coming from plantations. In the last financial year, 1991 to 1992, out of a pre-tax profit of 775 million ringgit, $300 million U.S. dollars, less than 10 percent came from plantations. And in the previous year when commodity prices were not so good, the figure was less than 5 percent. In effect, therefore, over the past ten years, we have changed Sime Darby from a Malaysian-based plantation company into a regional conglomerate, no longer dependent on the vagaries of commodity prices. And we have done this whilst maintaining a base of close to 200,000 acres of prime tropical agriculture. This is something that we value for the group. We have built up, in other words, the other businesses throughout the region without moving away from, or sacrificing, our plantations-based inheritance.

Over the past five years our attention has been concentrated, firstly, on developing a system of management for a regional conglomerate. Learning how to manage a conglomerate in itself is difficult enough in the sense of monitoring and keeping tabs on its various business activities. But in our case, it is further complicated by the fact that these businesses are spread geographically throughout the Asia-Pacific region. Then having created this regional conglomerate, our attention was next directed to the problem of how to integrate such an organization, how to create a Sime Darby corporate philosophy and culture that would translate across national boundaries and have a meaning for our managers and staff throughout the region. And finally, and perhaps most importantly of all, how do we do all this and keep the action going to produce the sort of growth and profitability we are seeking for the group, and which our shareholders have come to expect.

Here I am going to make a few specific points on integration and related issues, and briefly develop them from Sime Darby's experience over the years. The first point I would like to make is one of the areas where I find difficulty in following Professor Porter's arguments that the global executive is not an essential part of the system. *I believe that to become a regional company doing business internationally, and even more so for a truly global company, you have to have international executives.* That is, executives who understand and are comfortable doing business internationally. And here, I would say that developing-world companies are at a disadvantage in the sense that companies from the major industrialized and developed world have a much bigger pool of experienced international executives to choose from. But as I understand it, even these companies themselves have difficulties in finding such executives in sufficient numbers. I think Professor Porter made the point that it would be unseemly for a German executive to shred his sort of German identity. I don't think that really is the point. I think the point is more a case of finding the people that can relate to overseas operations, whether it is overseas from the United States, or overseas from Malaysia. I think we have all had experience of executives who are outstandingly good in a particular district, or a particular region, but when they are transferred out of that to a different environment, they don't perform well at all. In the international field, the international executive I believe is a very key part of the requirements for going global.

I would like to give a couple of examples to illustrate this point, particularly since I respect so much the arguments and way in which Professor Porter puts over his talks. A few years ago we were approached by one of the universities in the United States and asked whether we would support a scheme to employ MBA scholars when they finished their course. The idea was that these scholars would come and actually find working employment in companies throughout the region. In this sense we were a very good target because we have operating companies throughout the whole of the Asia-Pacific region, and we agreed to join in the scheme and take some of these executives.

These days it is not so easy to get employment permits and to go through all of the procedures that go with immigration, particularly at the lower levels of management. But, in the end, we managed to place five MBA executives in Singapore, Hong Kong, the Philippines, and Malaysia. They were all matched in their specific areas of abilities and everything was fine. But when we came closer to the day when they were "officially" qualified by their universities, one by one all five of them disappeared; they either got better jobs or their mother-in-law didn't want them to go to the Philippines, and so forth. All five dropped out, and I understand that the experience was very similar in companies that had agreed to take on some of the other MBA executives. Thus, in spite of the fact that everyone agreed from the U.S. side and from the developing world side that this was a very good scheme, it failed simply because you could not get these people to go international. So I think it is important to bear that in mind. The other point I would like to make is that personally I believe that the Peace Corps scheme conceptually was brilliant, and that it was ahead of its time and foreshadowed the trend towards a globalized political and business world, which we are now facing in the immediate future, if not the present time.

It provided the United States with a corps of intelligent young people with *working experience*, I make that point very strongly, and an understanding—intimate knowledge—of the people and the operations of a number of countries around the world. The MBA Scholar scheme, in a sense, was an attempt to revive the Peace Corps concept in a small way. But unfortunately it lacked the public spirited appeal of the earlier model. No one approves of the creation of an elitist group within an organization, but in this case I would suggest that there was very little choice.

There used to be an old saying, I am told, that went something like this, "If you want to get ahead you have to wear a hat," and I think it is true today that if you want to get ahead in the global business race you have to have a cadre of international executives: international executives, that is, with something of the pioneering spirit, people who are not looking for the soft option in the traditional domestic market. I believe that in the affluent society where people are more comfortable at home and reluctant to move, these people are not easy to find. They are not easy to find even in Malaysia; one of the biggest problems we have is in finding people who are prepared to move overseas, where all the problems of education of their children and so on, have come into play. But for the global company I think you have to have those people one way or another. And the only way that I can see that it can be achieved is by recruiting and treating them somewhat like an elite group.

I think it is also worth noting that Japan has no difficulty in identifying and recruiting such executives. This I think is very interesting, because when Japanese companies first started to move on a global basis, the people that they sent overseas to represent their companies knew a lot about the product and their company, but as international executives they had very little feel for how to do business in a global arena and they were not very good. You might even say that the first groups were disastrous, but in terms of the Japanese tradition, they persisted and persisted and persisted. Today, the Japanese executives that you see scurrying around all over the place in Europe and in Southeast Asia, and I assume also in America, are very international in their dealings and understanding of the situation. I think that this is interesting and worth noting.

My second comment would be that there is no such thing in my experience as a formula for success as a regional or global company. There are certain fundamental management principles which would apply just as readily to a one-product company operating out of Indiana as it would to a major international group. But I don't think that there is any special laid-down formula. In this sense *the global corporation will have to develop its own corporate philosophy and culture, its own organizational structure and system of incentives, and its own checks and balances to suit its own business, and its own businesses in the various countries in which it is going to operate.* There is no cut and dried formula for success in the global race, anymore than there is a documented system for managing people or running a business. Shell and Esso in my experience do things very, very differently, but they both enjoy very substantial success as global operating companies in the oil business.

In the Sime Darby system we give a lot of authority and responsibility to the man running the business, the division, or the region. But he does this against the background of a very tight business plan which the managing director and his team develop in their own way and which in turn comes under scrutiny by the executive directors of the board before being finally cleared with the group chief executive officer. In other words, the Sime Darby business plan is a team effort starting at the grass roots level and moving right through the organization, a true business plan—not, I would add—a finance director's forecast. We also have a strong financial reporting system and a head office group management audit department. We are not so much interested in the standard internal audit procedure but rather, we emphasize a true *performance* audit by a management audit team which comes from head office and carries with it a lot of authority. Our audit and accounts committee, which consists of the chairman, the chief executive, the finance director, and one executive director, goes through the group head office management audit very carefully. And, as far as I understand, it really is taken very seriously on the ground.

These policies give the Board of Directors the confidence to allow the person who is running the business to really run the business. We give the man in charge the authority to run the business, but we make sure that the managing director has done his homework in advance, and that we have the checks and balances in place to keep him moving in the right direction.

Clearly, synergy and conglomerate are in a sense incompatible. This is true in the case of the Sime Darby conglomerate: the businesses are different, the geographical locations of these various businesses are widely spread out, and are based in several different sovereign countries. *In order to create synergy and integration within the group we go out of our way to inculcate and foster a Sime Darby culture and develop a cooperative team spirit amongst the various divisions and regions.*

At the same time, in my opinion, head office control must be absolute. Genghis Khan or Napoleon in style it may be, but it should never be seen in that light down the line. The divisional director has to have the confidence in the head office so that he or she will not hide his problems, or feel he has to stand on his head to get attention. I once worked for a managing director who firmly believed that in order to get the capital expenditure approval to run the business he had to shave the truth by deliberately overstating the sales and the profit forecasts. As a young manager I was shocked at the time, but later on when I became managing director for the same company, I discovered that in that organization the only way you could get the capital investment you needed approved in order to run the business, was to present the "top side" picture, and then run like hell to make it happen!

The Sime Darby system is to control the financials against the background of the business plan, but never to allow head office to intervene unless there is really a need. If there is a problem, let it surface and be acknowledged, but leave it to the divisional or regional directors to sort out. If he cannot sort it out, he will call for backup from head office, in the best tradition of U.S.

management practice. If he really cannot handle the situation himself, and does not call for head office backup in sorting out the problems which will inevitably follow, you have to wonder whether he was the right man for the job.

*The Sime Darby Group corporate culture is focused on the region,* and in this respect I believe we have succeeded. We have not yet attempted to really bring in the operational units outside the region. They are part of the Sime Darby family group, but they have an "adopted" status at present, rather than a direct blood relationship. It is for this reason that I say that although we operate internationally as a group, we are not yet a truly globalized company. Our resort company operation in Florida and our health care company based in Seattle both operate independently, reporting to a divisional managing director who acts as a sort of guardian. Similarly our company in Queensland, holding the Caterpillar franchise for two Australian states and Papua New Guinea, acts independently but at present lacks the full authority to run the business, and reports to the director of operations in Kuala Lumpur who takes responsibility for the operation at the management committee level.

Total global integration in the Sime Darby Group will come, and it will follow the system which we have developed in our regional operations. But when we move, we shall move carefully towards the truly global company status, confident that it is easier to expand an established and proven regional culture to meet a global requirement than it would be to go cold turkey globally. Thank you very much.

# DISCUSSION

## James A. Henderson, Chair

In response to a question about synergies within Sime's tire business, *Tunku Ahmad* replied the following:

We have three tire factories, two in Malaysia and one in the Philippines. We bought the B.F. Goodrich factory in the Philippines when they decided that they wanted to sell out, and we bought the Dunlop factory in Malaysia when the breakup of the Dunlop group started. We also acquired a smaller factory in the north in Kedah which manufactures Sime tires. So we have three factories, one in the Philippines, which now manufactures Sime tires also, because B.F. Goodrich has been taken over by Michelin, and we had a problem with the rights to the name, so we switched in the Philippines to Sime tires. We still maintain the Dunlop brand name in Malaysia for tires, and we operate a second tire factory making Sime tires.

The ultimate objective of the tire company in Malaysia is to become one of the international players in the large earthmover tire field. This should be possible for several reasons, primarily because scale in the manufacturing of earthmoving tires is not a big factor. When you have to build a five-ton tire, you have to move it around a lot, put it in the pot and cook it, and you have to take it out with overhead cranes and those sort of things. So it is not possible at this stage to automate the process to turn them out in the way that you can run car tires through. And we do not have to have that large market which is essential for car tires or truck tries. But we do have natural rubber, and earthmover tires are 100 percent natural rubber, generally speaking, for reasons of heat build up. We are a rubber producer, so there is some synergy there.

and Sumitomo is the poor relative, so to speak. So they have an ambition as most of the Japanese companies do to catch up with the big guy. They have ready-made equipment in our factory, which produces the ultra-large, earthmover tires. They have given us fantastic technological support in meeting Bridgestone's standards, and that has been great for us.

*Tunku Ahmad* briefly described Sime's distinguished board of directors and ownership structure, and how they affect regional and local operations:

Firstly we have a board, 12 members, of which we have only three executive directors: the chief executive, the finance director, and the director of operations for the Malaysia core businesses. So there are three executive directors, and there are nine non-executive directors. These non-executive directors come from outside, including the chairman. Our chairman is a former governor of the Malaysian Central Bank. We have as non-executive directors the former head of the Singapore Monetary Authority, Mr. Michael Wong Pakshong; Dick Romulo, son of the famous General Romulo from the Philippines; Haroen Al Rasjid from Indonesia, who is the chairman and CEO of P.T. Caltex, Indonesia; Mr. Anand Panyarachun from Thailand, the last Prime Minister; David Lee from Hong Kong, the chairman of the Bank of East Asia and with very good connections with China; the rest are Malaysians—former Chief Secretary of the Ministry of Trade and Industry, a lawyer, and a local businessman. So we are a regional company both in terms of our aspirations and locations and also in terms of our board.

When I said I was one of a group of executives who was part of the idea to create a Malaysian multinational company, unfortunately we did not have the money at that time to back up the idea. If we had had that, we would be very rich today. But, we went to one of the institutional investors in Malaysia, the PNB, and they backed us in this enterprise at that time. They now own about 30 percent of our equity. The Kuwait Investment Authority owns 5 percent, they used to own 15 percent, but they have been reducing their share recently. Of the other 65 percent, about 30 percent is held in Singapore by private investors and 35 percent in Malaysia with private investors.

Answering a follow-up question about how Sime Darby's stocks were traded, *Tunku Ahmad* explained that the holding company's firms were listed on various exchanges and that Sime's listings serve as a check and balance for local/regional management:

Sime Darby Berhad is publicly listed in Malaysia and London. (We withdrew the listings in Singapore and Hong Kong because there was not sufficient business in those areas to justify listing.) Most of our other companies are listed. For example, Consolidated Plantations is a public-listed company in London and in Malaysia. Tractors Malaysia, which holds the Caterpillar franchise, is a Malaysian public-listed company, as is Sime UEP, our property development company. Sime Darby Hong Kong Limited is a public-listed company in Hong Kong. Sime Singapore Limited is a public-listed company in Singapore; Sime

Darby Philippines, Inc. I think, is a public-listed company in the Philippines. This we believe, is part and parcel of the checks and balances. Because we give so much authority to the person running a business in our system, the public listing and the requirements of the listing is a deterrent to sort of running off with the till.

*Hans Thorelli* asked about the advantages and handicaps of developing country-based and industrial country-based entities for alliances in multinational firms. *Tunku Ahmad* replied that many opportunities exist, and each party in the venture must contribute some unique asset:

I think the benefit for a company coming from an industrialized country is the *technology*. I think there are tremendous joint venture opportunities and deals available for people that really have the technology in the developing world. I suppose in the past the U.S. domestic market has been so big and so strong that very few of the middle-size U.S. companies have ever bothered to look outside America. Why should they, if they are doing so well in the States alone? There are opportunities for companies that have technology to go abroad, and everyone in the developing world now understands that no one gives the technology away for nothing. There is no such thing as a free lunch, as they say. So they are aware that there has got to be a deal, there must be some quid pro quo from the developing world. One of the things that we appreciated fairly early on was that we have to bring something to the party in order to get reasonable joint venture arrangements, and we have concentrated on saving up our money so we are very cash rich. We bring two things to the party. We bring (a) the ability to fund from our own resources anything that we move into, and (b) to those companies that are coming into the region for the first time, we bring a specialized knowledge of many of the countries in the Asia-Pacific region.

# AN INTERVIEW WITH TUNKU TAN SRI DATO' SERI AHMAD YAHAYA, GROUP CHIEF EXECUTIVE, SIME DARBY BERHAD

Hans B. Thorelli

*What are the key sources of synergy in the Sime Darby conglomerate?*

Clearly, "synergy" and "conglomerates" are in a sense incompatible—in fact this is true of the Sime Darby Group. The businesses are different, the geographical locations of our businesses are widely spread out and cover several different sovereign countries. We do work hard, however, to create a synergy in the Group, and the way we do this is through the people. We go out of our way to develop a Sime Darby spirit and a degree of cooperation between the various divisions and regions, although the businesses themselves differ widely. At the same time, we attempt to develop a sense of "friendly" competition between the various divisions. How do we do that? It begins with the Group Management Plan and is continued at the monthly Group Management Committee meeting where Divisional/Regional Directors report on their own operation and listen to the reports of others.

*What is the risk you may be spreading yourself too thin in terms of businesses and/or regions?*

We rely very much on the judgement of the Divisional or Regional Director in running the businesses of the Group profitably and in determining what resources he needs to run his business. This is done through the Annual Management Plan and updated monthly.

*Do you think that developing countries (LDCs) have so much in common that an LDC-based multinational corporation has a major advantage over a Europe- or U.S.-based multinational active in the LDC?*

Of course, an MNC from an LDC has an inherent advantage over an MNC from a developed country operating in the same LDC. That is an advantage which flows from having what in golf would be called "local knowledge." This is also illustrated in the competitive world of sports where the home team is always recognized as having a comparative advantage. It is the local knowledge and contacts which give the LDC-MNC a natural competitive advantage when playing at home. Now, the countries in the SE Asia region have sufficiently much in common that an MNC based in one of these countries may have a competitive advantage in several markets in several SE Asian countries over an MNC based in an industrialized nation.

*Do you feel there is a Southeast Asia-wide consumer loyalty to Southeast Asian enterprises (even though they may be based in another Southeast Asian country)?*

No, I do not think there is a regional consumer loyalty—if anything there is a Western brand name bias. Japan may be something of an exception in this respect, but Malaysia, like most other regional markets, reflects an established brand preference and loyalty.

*Does the Sime Darby Group have a special Strategic Planning and/or New Ventures unit?*

The Sime Darby Group has a Corporate Planning Department to organize and coordinate the Group Management Plan exercise. The Management Plan is a three-year operational business plan. It goes further than being a mere financial budget, and the intention is that it evolve naturally from the grassroots right through the organization involving management at all levels.

Long-term strategic planning in a sense follows from the three-year consolidated Management Plan. This, however, is the responsibility of the Group Chief Executive, the Director of Operations and the Group Finance Director, all of whom are members of the Sime Darby Berhad Board. The long-term strategy is initiated by these three executive directors, formulated by the Executive Committee of the Board and approved finally by the Sime Darby Berhad Board.

*Regarding Sime Darby's insurance business, what is the relative merit of in-depth specialization on Malaysia as compared to offering insurance throughout the Southeast Asian region?*

The Sime Darby Group is always on the lookout for regional business opportunities, that is, a business activity which can be established and developed on a regional basis, taking advantage of the Sime Darby Group's connections and favorable reputation throughout the region. Insurance is an example of such a business opportunity. The Malaysian insurance business would not be large enough to become a core business activity for the Sime Darby Group. Insurance as a regional business for the Sime Darby Group means taking advantage of the Group's regional presence and its many business contacts and supporters.

*Are you regretting your entry in the UK insurance market?*

We are confident that over time the Sime Darby Group is capable of establishing and developing a regional insurance business. In spite of the many setbacks which we have received during the initial learning process we have no regrets about moving into this business on a regional basis. If we have any regrets at all it is in regard to extending the insurance business into the UK. Every conceivable natural and unnatural disaster seems to have taken place in the UK from the time when we first established an insurance company in London. In this sense, we very much regret having become involved in insurance in the London market, and we now appreciate even more that our strengths lie in the Asia-Pacific Region.

*What are your future plans for entering markets in Europe, Japan or the United States? And why would you enter?*

In essence, any further plans which we have for entering markets in Japan or the USA would be directed towards supporting our regional core business activities. It may well be necessary for us to become more directly involved in marketing and distribution activities for our export products in Europe, North America and Japan in the future. But again, this would be in support of our regional business activities.

*Are headquarters of all businesses in Malaysia? Or do you have Group-wide headquarters for any line of business in other regions?*

The Sime Darby Group has a mixture of divisional and regional business operations. Each independent business unit or profit center is headed by a Manager responsible for the total operation. These business units or profit centers are then grouped either into a divisional business operation or a regional operating unit with Divisional and Regional Directors responsible for the total operation, reporting to either the Director of Operations or the Group Chief Executive. The business units therefore are run independently by an individual responsible for the total operation and located where the business operates.

Sime Darby Berhad in Malaysia coordinates and consolidates these operating business units.

*Do you have a matrix-type organization, where, say insurance in Hong Kong reports both to a general Sime office there and also reports to the Group-wide insurance general office in Malaysia?*

Insurance is the only Group divisional operation where its accountability is spread over the whole region. In the case of insurance there are separate individual insurance operations in Malaysia, Singapore, Hong Kong and Thailand, and these operations all report to and come under the control of the Divisional Director—Insurance.

*What language is "lingua franca" in your overseas operations?*

The "lingua franca" in all our overseas operations is English.

*To what extent (and how) do you try to give a "local" flavor to your regional operations?*

As a matter of policy we try to introduce into the various regional operations the maximum amount of local involvement compatible with the requirements of security and control in the operations of a subsidiary company. All other things being equal, if we can find the right local national to head the operation we would do so. The tendency, however, is to train and build-up a local national with service at Sime Darby Head Office in preparation for taking over the running of the company. If the company is run by a local national, the likelihood is that the Finance Director would be a Sime Darby career-man, though this would not exclude the person being a local national.

In addition, Sime Darby policy would be to seek a listing of the company on the local stock market, not because we are looking for financing, but because we want to have a local financial involvement in the business. At all times, the intention would be to establish the operation as a local company and follow the aspirations and best interest of the local community, while, of course, maintaining optimum long-term profitability objectives.

*In joint ventures, do you insist on majority ownership?*

As a general rule, the Sime Darby Group operates on the basis of a minimum 51 percent equity control in any of its business operations. This policy, however, is not cast in stone and minority interest equity stakes have been taken in certain business ventures. As a general rule, however, whenever Sime Darby takes a minority equity interest, it usually insists upon having a management agreement which gives it management control. Again, this is not always the case, but in those instances where Sime Darby has taken a minority interest without management control, it is with partners who are extremely well known to the Group and where the management responsibility is clearly defined. Such cases, however, are very few and far between.

*Is technology transfer to Sime Darby what interests you most in considering joint ventures and strategic alliances with multinational corporations from the industrialized nations?*

In my opinion there is no such thing as free technology transfer, or, if there is, then it needs to be looked at very carefully. No one gives away his technology without getting something back in return. I don't think that is being too cynical, it is merely a fact of life, and anyone who believes otherwise is being naive. It is apparent that in the world today technology is the thing which gives a company and a product the competitive edge. In certain instances for a small operation, it is not worth spending money on research and development, and generally it is more a case of the company not having the money to even start to become involved in R&D. Such companies have no choice if they wish to stay in the business but to buy into the technology. In some cases it may be possible to learn from the experience of others by hiring the necessary people. In other cases while it may be too expensive for a company to cover the whole field, it might be possible to concentrate on one particular product or special area in the business. Sime Darby Group experiences illustrate these points:

1. Sime Darby could never afford to spend the amount of money needed to build up and maintain a technical presence in the tire business, so we have to buy it.
2. But while we buy the basic, fundamental, up-to-date technology, we are building our own research center, firstly, to do all the applied technical testing work which goes into tire manufacture, and, secondly, designating off-the-road or earthmover tires as our special area for fundamental research. Having three tire factories in the Sime Darby Group, this becomes financially possible because this is not an area where production volume is so important. It is also difficult to automate a process which involves building large tires weighing around five tons, moving them around and finally cooking them. Also, these tires are generally made of natural rubber, though contrary to most people's thinking, this is only a minor item in the cost of manufacture, though it is an advantage having natural rubber on tap, so to speak.
3. In the case of the management of major leisure resorts, we would like to learn this technology and transfer it to developments in our region. And where are the best designed, organized and managed, large scale, leisure resorts in the world? In the USA. This is the reason why we have acquired Sandestin, in order to learn from the people that run this operation how to manage such an operation. We do not have a project on the drawing board at the moment, but we know we are going to be in this business in the region in the future.

*What is Sime Darby's philosophy about "maximization of shareholder value" and the stock markets? What are your long- versus short-term perspectives?*

Clearly, it is in everyone's interest to improve the company's stock market price over time for the simple reason that this keeps the shareholders happy and reduces the pressure on the management from the financial media. It is as well to remember, however, that it is not possible to please everyone all the time, and it is not practicable to do so. Fortunately, we are not burdened with quarterly reporting and, frankly, we do not worry very much about the share price so long as the operations and the management of the company are progressing well.

*What "hurdles" must a proposed new investment overcome in order to be approved by Sime Darby's management?*

Ideally we are looking for business opportunities that can be exploited on a regional basis, which, in essence, represents the Sime Darby Group's strength. New business opportunities arise basically from Sime Darby operating companies, though occasionally Head Office comes up with a proposal which is looked at in principle and then passed on to the appropriate operating company to investigate further on a more practical down-to-earth basis.

Other investment prospects come from people or companies wishing to establish a joint venture with Sime Darby or initiate an approach for which they themselves do not have sufficient financing. In much the same way, these are looked at by the Group Planning Department, and if the project passes this preliminary general scrutiny, it then goes to one of the operating companies for a more businesslike appraisal. There are many considerations taken into account for assessing the project, but the one criteria which is fundamental is the financial test. The project must have the long-term potential of providing a minimum of 20 percent return on funds employed. This is the basic guideline, though I must confess that a good deal of human judgement goes into this assessment, and other considerations tend to influence this assessment.

*What are the challenges or advantages to assembling half a dozen automobile makes in the same Sime Darby plant?*

There is an advantage in having a Motor Group with franchises which cover a range of different types and models. There is the advantage of scale in terms of meeting overhead expenses and also the advantage of bringing a degree of variety within the range. This situation has worked extremely well for us in Malaysia, Hong Kong and Singapore, all of which are relatively small markets.

*It has been suggested that there is a relative absence of marketing skills and consumer orientation in Southeastern Asia; "selling" as such, is meant to be "selling to the dealers." To what extent may this be changing–and why?*

We are short of managers with international standard marketing skills, and this is a handicap to us in promoting our products in overseas markets. It is also a problem for us in our own market, although this is changing with consumer orientation becoming increasingly important. Previously under the old system, the main emphasis in the marketing plan was directed at the dealers. The consumer played very little part in the marketing plan thinking, and even the advertising and promotional campaigns were seen as support for the dealers, rather than as a pitch to the consumer. This is changing now, because of the incredible progress made in mass communications, and, in a sense, because people are better informed and hence smarter. They no longer accept everything the dealer tells them. Consumer marketing is now an important consideration, with television the most powerful media in the region.

*Who are your key competitors? Are they primarily MNCs based in developing or industrialized nations?*

Sime Darby operating companies have competition in all the areas in which they operate, normal, healthy, business competition. But Sime Darby as a whole does not have direct competition other than the usual media-related competition in terms of earnings per share and price earnings ratios relative to other listed companies. I see competition as being head-to-head stuff like Pepsi against Coca Cola, or Caterpillar against Komatsu, or BMW against Mercedes, or Michelin against Goodyear. Sime Darby experiences competition at the operating level, but at the Holding Company level in Sime Darby Berhad, we have no direct head-to-head competition other than in meeting the challenge of performance. We do not see ourselves competing against other multinationals or conglomerates, because none of them could duplicate our organization precisely. They are only competitors in the media or financial press sense. I am not saying that does not matter to us, but we would not waste a lot of management time or money on that sort of competition.

*Some of your philosophy about human resource development was recently published in the Wall Street Transcript. How would you summarize the importance of management training for Sime Darby?*

Human resources development and management training are becoming increasingly important for Sime Darby, particularly for its operations in Malaysia and in the Asia-Pacific region. Taking a regional macro view for the moment, it is apparent that the demand for technical personnel at all levels is going to increase significantly, and from this point of view, the governments themselves must do something about education and training to meet this basic need.

In the case of Malaysia, it is being suggested that this has to start with the curriculum at the primary school level. Given the scale of this demand for trained technical personnel, the government on its own cannot meet this demand. The government can only lay the groundwork and point the way. In pointing the way which the private sector needs to follow, the government must then offer the sort of incentives which will induce the private sector to play its part in the training and development of people in the human resources field.

In the case of Sime Darby, we have established an Education Trust Fund which offers scholarships at the secondary school and university level. We have also recognized the fact that being involved in business internationally we need to produce executive staff and managers who can operate comfortably in an international environment. To meet this need, we have a special program for undergraduate education at Cambridge University, and in addition, we have an extensive overseas business school training program. In this respect, we have sent executives to a wide range of business schools in both Europe and North America, and our conclusion is that it is virtually impossible to say that anyone is better than another. Our experience leads us to conclude that it is a matter of matching the person to the course and style of the business school. Not everyone benefits from the training program at the Harvard Business School, and in much the same way a person who would get maximum benefit from the Harvard Business School might not respond to a more leisurely academic approach in one of the continental business schools, or a more hands-on, mixed approach from an Australian-style business training program. It is a matter of "horses for courses" as they say in the horse racing world.

# SIME DARBY BERHAD:
## A DESCRIPTION

The Sime Darby Group is one of Southeast Asia's largest conglomerates with a market capitalization of US$2.6 billion. The Malaysian-based regional MNC operates more than 200 companies, employing about 30,000 people in 12 countries. The company is listed on the Kuala Lumpur Stock Exchange and the International Stock Exchange in London. Turnover in the year ending 30 June 1991 was US$2.1 billion with a pre-tax profit of US$251 million.

The Group consists of five core business activities, namely, plantations and commodity trading, manufacture and marketing of a wide range of tires and related products, heavy equipment and motor vehicle assembly and distribution, property development, and insurance services. Four of the five core business activities are public-listed companies in Malaysia. In addition, the Group has sizeable investments managed by public-listed companies in Singapore, Hong Kong, the Philippines, and Australia, as well as other subsidiary companies in Japan, United Kingdom, USA, Indonesia, Thailand and Brunei.

Principal activities by territory and as a percentage of turnover and profit contribution in the financial year 1991 are shown in Table 1.

Table 1. Principal Activities by Territory

| | Malaysia | Singapore | Hong Kong | Philippines | Australia | Other | Percent of Sales | Percent of Profits |
|---|---|---|---|---|---|---|---|---|
| General Trading | * | * | * | | * | * | 45 | 32 |
| Manufacturing | * | * | * | * | * | | 14 | 10 |
| Property Development | * | * | | | | * | 8 | 15 |
| Heavy Equipment, Distribution | * | * | * | * | | * | 14 | 15 |
| Oil & Gas Equipment | * | | | | | | 6 | 4 |
| Insurance | * | * | * | | | * | 4 | 1 |
| Plantations | * | | | * | | * | 9 | 6 |
| Net Investment Income | | | | | | | - | 17 |
| | | | | | | | 100% | 100% |
| Percent of employees | 82 | 5 | 8 | 3 | 0.5 | 1.5 | | |
| Percent of turnover | 61 | 14 | 20 | 2 | 1 | 2 | | |
| Percent of profit | 69 | 10 | 17 | 3 | 1 | | | |

## Says CEO Tunku Ahmad:

Whilst many of Sime Darby's business activities are based in Malaysia, the real strength of Sime Darby is that it is a regional group. To realize the full potential of this strength, Sime Darby's extensive operations are organized and structured to benefit from sound and professional management of the holding company, while allowing its parts to retain their respective autonomy. I see...the Asia Pacific region as...one of the main areas of growth in the world over the next five years. From that point of view, Sime Darby is pretty well placed as a group.

Given Sime Darby's connections and favorable reputation throughout the region, the Group is an attractive business partner in Southeast Asia. A broad range of globally recognized names have joined forces with the Group. Sime continues to seek additional joint venture partners who can build on its existing regional network and knowledge of the market.

"There was a time when plantations really represented the Sime Darby Group. That's no longer the case...the Plantations Division...represents less than 10 percent, closer to 5 percent of the group profitability." This contribution is unusually low, due to the "pretty miserable" commodity prices. However, "the 200,000 acres of prime tropical agriculture on which the Plantations Division is based is still a pretty good platform for a multinational conglomerate." Oil palm, rubber, cocoa, and fruit crops are managed in

Peninsular Malaysia, Sarawak, Sabah and Indonesia. This division has moved into commodity trading and downstream processing activities such as marketing of such crops and the refining and packaging of vegetable oils and specialty fats. The years 1990 to 1991 witnessed further vertical integration in the latex area, into manufacture and marketing of gloves and condoms.

The Tractors Division has two key activities: (1) the Caterpillar franchise, whose sales tend to move in tandem with commodity prices, and (2) the assembly plant, which involves Ford, BMW and Land Rover vehicles and Scania trucks, as well as sales, distribution and credit facilities. Mazda and Suzuki passenger cars are also assembled under contract. Vehicle sales move in parallel with the economy as a whole, lately quite strong.

Property Development is chiefly attending to the "tremendous demand for middle-class housing in Malaysia." The Property Division has developed Southeast Asia's largest township built by a single developer and is in the process of building industrial estates for modern warehousing and light industry.

DMIB Berhad (Sime's manufacturing division) is based on the former Dunlop Tire Factory, which was the first such plant in Malaysia. This division manufactures and markets a broad range of automotive, earthmover and aviation tires. It is Malaysia's largest tire producer and the largest exporter of tires in Southeast Asia. DMIB was the first company in the world to retread the B747-400 aircraft tire for commercial airline operations. Its other activities include the manufacture and marketing of mattresses, sealants, adhesive and golf balls. Sime also has a tire plant in the Philippines (the former B. F. Goodrich plant).

"Insurance... is one of those businesses which gives us the opportunity to operate on a regional basis, and here we are pretty confident that in the long run insurance as a regional business will be a good business for Sime Darby Group." On the other hand, the UK insurance in the past has been more of a challenge than an opportunity. The Group is looking for potential partners in insurance.

The diversified activities of the Malaysia Region which are considered as having significant potential for future development include manufacturing, trading, services and oil and gas. The manufacturing activities cover tires and building and industrial products, such as furniture, tile, sanitary ware, sports goods, batteries, security equipment, packaging, and paint. The trading operations consist of agency lines in consumer products, electronic equipment, building materials and engineering products. Services include travel, security and computer software and systems applications. The oil and gas division provides engineering and fabrication services to the petroleum industry.

The regional operation in Hong Kong is very important, also because of its relations with China Resources, a major PRC trading company. The Australian operation is fairly new and modest, focused thus far on Western

Australia. The Philippine and Singapore regional operations have suffered due to current world recession. However, Tunku Ahmad is very bullish about the future prospects of the Southeast Asian region.

# V DYNAMICS OF INTEGRAL STRATEGY

# EDITOR'S NOTE

Like Michael Porter, George Day is fascinated by competitive advantage (or "superior capabilities"). But while Porter emphasizes the substance of advantage, Day is even more concerned with the organizational processes building superior capability, as well as the internal dynamics required to renew it in rapidly changing environments. And while Porter's essay is primarily looking at advantage from a corporate perspective, Day is more immediately concerned with applying a customer-oriented perspective. Day manfully struggles with the apparent paradox that while organizations have a need for stability and continuity in strategy, their viability may require continuous improvement, or, frequently, even transformation of strategy. Ultimately, he seems to see integral strategy as a key means of resolving this dilemma.

George Day makes a valuable contribution by making a distinction between assets (roughly equal to resource endowments) and capabilities of an organization. Being the integrative glue that enables the assets to be deployed advantageously, capabilities are embedded bundles of skills and knowledge which, in a seamless organization, ensure integration of activities and assets, and also enable the organization to learn and improve continuously. At the micro level we see 3M's new product teams as a means of building and capitalizing on this kind of capability (Hershock). Distinctive capabilities are seen as adding to superior customer value and/or finding multiple, synergistic applications, thus speeding the firm's response to environmental change or new market opportunities. Day's essay is replete with practical illustrations. Market sensing and learning capability, notably in understanding and satisfying customers, is of utmost importance. This places a premium on networking and standing relationships externally, and, often, on integrative process management within the organization.

In supplementing Day, Everett Shorey went even further in stressing the dynamics of strategy. He, too, focused on strategy as process, rather than content. He inveighed against the common view of strategy as a fixed road map. Shorey instead used the analogy with the sailor, who constantly makes minor (occasionally even major) adjustments on the wheel to reach his destination. In other words, we should look upon strategy as a continuous process, once the mission ("destination") has been defined.

# BUILDING SUPERIOR CAPABILITIES FOR SERVING CHANGING MARKETS

George S. Day

## INTRODUCTION

An integral strategy is the outcome of an on-going struggle to balance the need for stability and continuity of the strategic thrust, while continuously improving and innovating in response to changing customer requirements, unforeseen competitive moves, and emerging technological possibilities.

The virtues of stability of a competitive strategy, and the attendant continuity in programs, investment commitments, and organizational structures and systems, are compelling. With long experience in executing a strategy comes proficiency and a greater possibility of shared understanding across functions. The more durable the strategy—provided it has a history of success—the stronger the underlying values, beliefs and behaviors of the organization. Stability is reinforced by enduring, and irreversible investment commitments that help to secure a strong competitive position. These large commitments, to technologies, distribution systems, or manufacturing processes for example, effectively "lock-in" the firm to a strategic path. The resulting assets and know-how are long-lasting, and because of their specialization cannot readily be used for other purposes (Ghemawat 1990). In stable market environments, where these commitments matter the most, they add to the momentum. However, this also produces inertia in the face of the need to change. When changes are made that eventually overcome this inertia, they are often half-hearted defensive adjustments to shifts in market requirements, or to counter competitive moves.

Few firms can now afford to wait for competitors to make a move, for new customer segments to fully emerge, or for new business systems to prove their worth. Instead of the cost of change being the determining factor, firms are having to consider even higher costs of waiting. The most identifiable cost is the loss of competitive position during the time it takes to be persuaded that a real change is needed, combined with the inevitable lag between making the decision and seeing the results. A more subtle cost of waiting is incurred when the eventual strategic move, which is taken for defensive or catch-up purposes, is transparent to competitors. These competitors are well-equipped to counter this strategy, or move to a new basis of competition in anticipation of changing market requirements. This is the plight of the U.S. auto makers who continue to chase the moving target of their Japanese competitors but never seem to catch up or surpass. Finally, there is the cost of opportunities that were missed by waiting. These are most evident in short life cycle electronic markets where a six-month delay in entry may reduce the profitability of a new product by 50 percent.

Companies seeking to avoid being disadvantaged through slow and inadequate responses are shifting from an emphasis on continuity of strategy toward enhancing their capability to anticipate and adapt to volatile markets and technologies. This is proving a difficult adjustment to make, for an overemphasis on continuous change leads to instability, organizational confusion, bewildered customers who no longer understand the competitive position, and a loss of strategic integrity as functions work at cross-purposes.

The purpose here is to describe possible approaches and frameworks for maintaining a healthy balance of continuity and change. Our interest is in the capabilities of organizations that have become superior at anticipating market changes and taking adaptive steps to retain or capture customers while thwarting their competitors. This approach will complement the burgeoning literature on capabilities management by studying capabilities from the "outside in," rather than following the predominant "inside out" approach which has emphasized the ability to coordinate manufacturing and processing skills or integrate multiple streams of technology. Success then comes from marrying these two classes of capabilities.

## Why Emphasize Capabilities from the "Outside In?"

The argument for highlighting the ability of a business to anticipate and respond to market changes is that these are the issues that preoccupy senior

**Table 1.** Importance of Business Issues
Percent of 270 senior managers who rated issue as extremely important on a 5-point scale

| Issue | Percent |
|---|---|
| Improving customer satisfaction | 68% |
| Implementing Total Quality Management | 50% |
| Developing more competitive strategies | 44% |
| Improving the flow of successful products | 38% |
| Responding to environmental regulations | 32% |
| Responding to changing economic conditions | 28% |
| Improving R&D effectiveness | 27% |
| Improving sales force effectiveness | 24% |
| Developing foreign markets | 24% |
| Using information to better advantage | 22% |

Based on interviews by Arthur D. Little, 1991.

management. This is what Arthur D. Little found in the middle of 1991 when they interviewed a sample of 270 senior managers of U.S. companies (see Table 1 for a summary of the results).

Three of the top four issues dealt explicitly with the ability to cope with market changes: improving customer satisfaction, developing more competitive strategies, and improving the flow of successful products. By contrast the bottom three of the overall list of 16 issues were evaluating diversification opportunities, restructuring the organization and financial restructuring. Fewer than 10 percent of respondents rated these as extremely important—a revealing indication that cost-cutting and financial engineering will not be the earnings drivers in the coming decade.

What underlies the emergence of these issues of competitiveness and adaptability? Many reasons have been advanced; an illustrative sampling would include:

- intensifying competition as the structural barriers—geographic, regulatory, scale and technology—that used to protect industries like steel, banking, automobiles and retailing are breaking down or have already gone;
- competition looming from new directions—especially from firms with capabilities that could be effectively transferred, as AT&T did to enter the credit card market;
- strategies that have become similar and predictable in many industries. Most regional banks focus on affluent customers and small businesses, and most airlines emphasize business travelers. With so many rivals pursuing the same customers the difference lies in the ability to anticipate their emerging needs and respond quickly;
- technology that permits firms to produce more and more varieties, and offer the customer the possibility of a customized offering—leading customers to expect precise tailoring of products to fit their requirements;

- the advantages of pioneering or early entry are eroding as markets fragment and offer new places for competitors to enter—whether through private labels, alliances, or internal markets.

The result is that few competitive positions are secure, and the only sure defense is to anticipate shifts in market requirements, and develop layers of advantage ahead of competition.

## THE CAPABILITIES APPROACH TO STRATEGY

A compressed history of scholarship and practice in the field of strategic management would show three phases of development. During the first phase, roughly corresponding to the seventies, the emphasis was on the *outcomes* of strategies. Much was made of market share strategies, the relationship of market share and profitability was debated (and continues to be debated), and the share-growth portfolio matrix became a popular tool for managing resource allocation in multi-business firms. The experience curve relationship of prices, costs, and cumulative output was an important building block during this period. For the first time there was a clear, straightforward explanation of differences in competitive performance. This was a prelude to a broader-based interest in the *positional advantages* firms had achieved through lower costs or superior customer value. During this second phase, which peaked in the mid-to-late eighties, the dominant paradigm was industry structure analysis, as epitomized by Porter's (1980) influential "five forces" model. Not only were these competitive forces shown to shape the present and prospective profit potential of an industry, but a firm could use the model to help find the position in the industry from which it could best defend itself or take actions to influence the forces in its favor.

By the late eighties, a third phase was emerging as attention shifted to the *sources of advantage*. This represented a renewed recognition that positional and performance superiority are derived from superiority in the skills and resources a business is able to deploy. These were not new ideas, for an emphasis on building distinctive capabilities or competencies can be found in Schumpeter, Penrose, and Selznick (1957) and was featured in the business policy frameworks of the sixties. Although useful insights came from these early frameworks, in practice the lack of a thorough theoretical understanding meant that the outcome was usually a lengthy and indiscriminate list of strengths and weaknesses.

Why the resurgence of interest in the sources of advantage as currently manifested in the capabilities approach? An early effort to capture their importance was the "skills" component of the McKinsey 7-S framework, which was seen as the most distinctive encapsulation of the organization's way of

Building Superior Capabilities for Serving Changing Markets    167

doing business. It was included because the other six components were not capable of defining important differences between firms, and seemed to contribute to superior performance. However, because this component often "fell between the cracks" in more reductionist analyses of systems, structures, and strategies, its importance was not appreciated (Peters 1984). A more obvious trigger of the change in emphasis was the recognition that the ability of Japanese firms to rapidly and continuously innovate and consistently manage quick response systems was rooted in their capabilities. The stark contrast of the success of the long-run capabilities approach of NEC with the relative stagnation of the portfolio approach of GTE in the eighties (Prahalad & Hamel 1990) could not be ignored. Meanwhile, the Baldridge Award was having a steering effect by focusing attention on processes rather than outcomes; and practitioners and scholars (deGeus 1988 & Senge 1990) were revealing the contribution of learning capabilities to the adaptiveness of firms in turbulent markets. Indeed, some have argued (Grant 1991) that a business should be defined more by what it is capable of doing rather than by the markets it serves or the needs it seeks to satisfy. If these markets are volatile and new competitors, technologies, and customer requirements are continually changing market boundaries, then enduring success depends on building an organization which can continuously infuse products and services with new sources of value as well as seek new market opportunities.

Confirming evidence of the need for greater attention to capabilities comes from empirical research on corporate performance. For example, there is a striking difference between the relatively poor performance of conglomerates pursuing unrelated diversification and the firms that use their capabilities to identify attractive acquisition opportunities in related areas, value them properly, and manage their integration effectively. This conclusion is reinforced by the experience of companies like 3M, Honda, Raychem, and Casio that grow steadily and profitably by developing and exploiting their internal capabilities. With this impetus, it is not surprising that scholars and practitioners are together working to better understand why and how capabilities contribute to these firm-specific differences.

## Characteristics of Strategic Capabilities

The potential usefulness of the capabilities approach has been impeded by semantic and conceptual imprecision, and serious difficulties in identifying the distinctive capabilities that contribute to a superior competitive position. Identifications are often *ex post* using a circular logic that leads to the conclusion that successful firms have some unique capabilities which make them successful. Such speculations are interesting, but hardly satisfying. Notwithstanding, there is a slowly evolving consensus as to the functions and defining features of capabilities.

## Sources of Potential Advantages

How does a business achieve and maintain a superior competitive position? The question is at the heart of the strategy development process and largely defines the field of strategic management. The emerging answer distinguishes two interwoven sources of advantages: assets and capabilities. *Assets* are the resource endowments the business has accumulated. An indicative list would include past investments in the scale, scope, and efficiency of facilities and systems, past strategic choices about the degree of integration, financial condition, brand equity representing the favorable carry-forward of past experiences of customers, as well as the consequences of the location of activities for factor costs and government support. As illustrated in Figure 1, *capabilities* are the glue that holds these assets together and enables them to be deployed advantageously.

Without capabilities, assets will be passive or under-utilized. The turnaround in the performance of the Walt Disney Company between 1985 and 1987 illustrates the possibilities. Much of the improvement in financial performance came from accelerated development of land holdings carried at very low book values, plus exploitation of the vast film library, and greater utilization of Disney's film production capability through the formation of Touchstone Films.

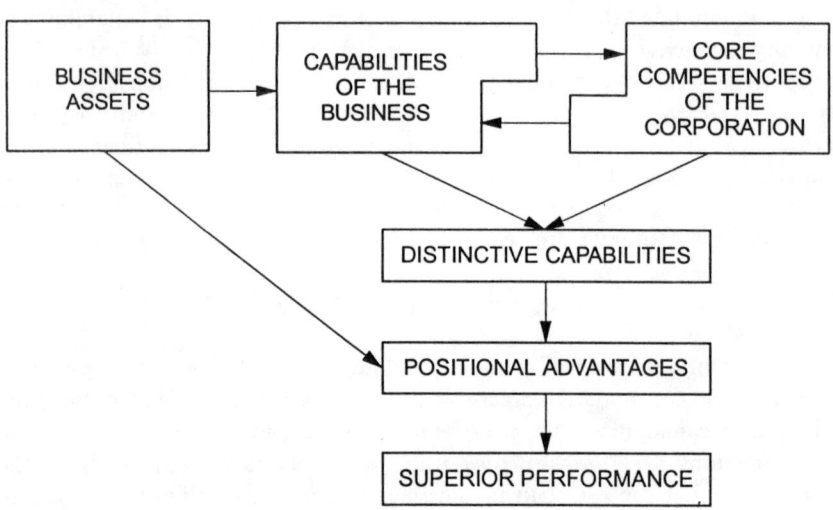

*Figure 1.* Sources of competitive advantage.

## Identifying Capabilities

A capability is a complex bundle of skills and knowledge, coupled with a commitment to working across organizational boundaries, that ensures superior coordination of activities and superior utilization of assets, while enabling the organization to continuously learn and improve. Thus, capabilities are what the organization does; the embedded skills and knowledge enable the organization to do these things.

Because capabilities are deeply embedded in the organization and contain a large component of tacit knowledge, they may be difficult to identify. Current practice suggests that the best way to overcome this problem is through a detailed mapping of the organizational processes in which the capabilities are employed. These maps usually show that capabilities and their defining processes span several functions and several organizational levels, and involve extensive communications. Because important processes link a number of organizational activities, there may not be a well-defined owner who is responsible for managing and improving them.

New product development processes demonstrate most of the attributes of complex processes, and also illustrate the gains that come from properly identifying how they work. Recently, a large manufacturer of complex telecommunications equipment undertook a post mortem to learn why it had taken four years to bring their latest offering to market. The stakes were considerable since the new system was a year late, and did not respond to an important shift in customer requirements for wide-area networking. What the process map revealed was a series of loosely linked activities that were disconnected from the market. Only one market study was undertaken at a very early stage in the process. Thereafter, the team became enmeshed in the details of technical development, prototype testing, costing, regulatory, and budget approval activities. As time passed and the product concept evolved, there was no effort to revalidate key assumptions about customer needs and expectations. Overall the organization demonstrated a weak development capability in this process, as manifested by a lack of critical skills and coordinating activities, poor communications, and an inadequate capacity for learning and adapting.

One consequence of the complexity of capabilities, and the array of skills and knowledge to be harmonized, is that a strong capability should be difficult for competitors to imitate—and certainly cannot be as readily acquired as a new numerical machine tool or software program. Thus the competitive advantages from a capability that has taken a number of years to hone to the point where the firm can outperform competitors is not likely to be quickly eroded. This point was recognized some years ago by Marvin Bower, the legendary leader of McKinsey & Co., during a rumination on the risks of having agencies and consultants serve competing clients and possible disclosing privileged information:

As a matter of realism, the interests of competing clients would not be harmed by an almost complete exchange of information among the people serving the two competing companies.... I am convinced that the history, make-up, ways of doing business, attitudes of people, operating philosophy and procedures of even directly competing companies are ordinarily so different that information could be exchanged between them with no harm to either.

## Capabilities and Core Competencies

Some capabilities of an individual business are grounded in the core competencies of the parent corporation (Prahalad & Hamel 1990). These require special attention because they are the glue that binds existing businesses, as well as linking functional activities within businesses. A strong argument can be made that successful diversification must be guided more by the ability to deploy these core competencies than by the attractiveness of the market opportunities. Examples of core competencies of a corporation include:

- Casio's ability to harmonize know-how in miniaturization, microprocessor design, material science, and ultrathin precision castings
- 3M's ability to marry a competence with tape and abrasive technologies with intrapreneurial new product development skills to enter such diverse businesses as surgical tape, pressure-sensitive tape, magnetic recording tape, and coated abrasives
- Canon's ability to leverage corporate-wide competencies in sensor technology, digital image processing, precision mechanics, optoelectronics, and fine optics which has led it to become a feared competitor in markets as diverse as optical storage devices, cameras, fax machines, and semiconductor manufacturing equipment

Core competencies are a powerful source of sustainable advantage because they take even longer to develop than business-specific capabilities and require strategic investments and information sharing and coordinating mechanisms that transcend traditional SBU boundaries. At the same time, not all the capabilities of a business need to be linked to the core competencies of the corporation. Indeed, in diversified firms like GE, it is difficult to see what core competencies are shared by plastics, motors, broadcasting, and medical imaging systems. With firms that focus on one market sector—albeit in many geographic areas—the core competence and capability are one and the same.

## Distinctive Capabilities

Every business has acquired many capabilities to enable it to carry out the activities necessary to move the product or service through the value chain.

Some will be done adequately, others poorly, but a few have to be done extremely well if the business is to outperform the competition. These are the distinctive capabilities that support a market position that is valuable and difficult to match. Such capabilities have to be managed with special care through the positive commitment of resources (even if the normal DCF criteria are not satisfied), assignment of dedicated people, and continued efforts at learning, supported by clear goals for improvement.

The main test of distinctiveness of a capability is whether it makes a disproportionate contribution to the provision of superior customer value—as defined from the customer's perspective (Day & Wensley 1988)—or permits the business to deliver value to customers in an appreciably more cost-effective way. Clearly, Honda's prowess with fuel efficient, reliable, and responsive small displacement engines adds a great deal of customer value and sets their cars apart from the competition.

Another attribute of distinctive capabilities is that they are capable of multiple uses, and so can be used to speed the firm's adaption to environmental change. Because of this feature, distinctive capabilities often become core competencies and provide a platform and logic for entry into new markets. Thus Honda has been able to apply their engine and drive train competence to a variety of related markets like generators, outboard marine engines, and lawn mowers. It is less clear whether Honda's distinctive capability in "dealer management" (Stalk, Evans & Shulman 1992), which was used to develop a network of better managed and better financed motorcycle dealers than the part-time dealers of competitors, is also a core competence that guides entry into new markets. On one hand, their skill at managing dealers has been of value in the auto market where Honda dealers consistently receive the highest ratings for customer satisfaction. It is harder to say that the logic of Honda's diversification into related markets was really guided by a desire to exploit this dealer management capability. More likely it is the ability to gain a multiplier effect by integrating both distinctive capabilities that shapes the moves into new markets.

## Classifying Capabilities

It is not possible to enumerate all possible capabilities, because every business has developed a unique configuration of capabilities that is rooted in the realties of their competitive market, past commitments and anticipated requirements. Nonetheless, certain recurring classes of capabilities can be recognized in all businesses, corresponding to the core processes for creating economic value.

Some classes of capabilities are easier to identify than others; usually because they are readily observable within the organization. Thus, the expertise of 3M in applying its core technologies, Wal-Mart's ability to coordinate complex purchasing and logistics systems, and McDonald's achievement of unparalleled consistency of service delivery in dispersed outlets are pointed to as distinctive capabilities that account for durable advantages. The visibility and prevalence of these examples of capabilities that have been successfully deployed from the "inside-out" has lead some observers to argue that firms should be defined by what they are capable of doing, rather than by the needs they seek to satisfy (Grant 1991). This perspective is unbalanced, for it is the ability of the business to use the "inside out" capabilities to exploit external possibilities that matters. Thus, there has to be a matching "outside in" capability to sense these possibilities and decide how best to serve them.

Consider the Corning Incorporated division that manufacturers fiber optic products. Their challenge was to balance demands for increased product customization and faster delivery, while reducing costs to stay ahead of aggressive competition. Originally, their objective was to be the most efficient mass producer of standard fiber optics. As the fiber optic market evolved and customers began to demand more specialized products, it was necessary to convert the process manufacturing capabilities from a rigid, standard-production system to a flexible manufacturing platform capable of building customized fiber products to order. This transition required both an "inside out" capability to produce the low-cost, custom products on a timely basis, and an "outside in" capability for understanding the evolving requirements of customers and energizing the organization to respond to them.

An indicative list of the "inside-out" capabilities would be based on the following internal processes:

- Financial management, control and resource allocation
- Technology development
- Manufacturing and transformation processes
- Purchasing
- Inbound and outbound logistics
- Human resource development, including recruiting, training, and motivating employees
- Environmental, health, and safety

The "outside in" class of capabilities enables the organization to bring the market environment into the organization, and compete by anticipating market requirements ahead of competition and creating durable relationships with customers, channel members, and suppliers. However, there is a third class of capabilities that the organization uses to link the organization to the market, that also calls on the other capabilities (see Figure 2). These "linkage" capabilities are used to develop new products and services, and fulfill customer orders. Taken together the "outside in" and "linkage" capabilities establish how well the business can anticipate and adapt to changing market requirements.

# Building Superior Capabilities for Serving Changing Markets

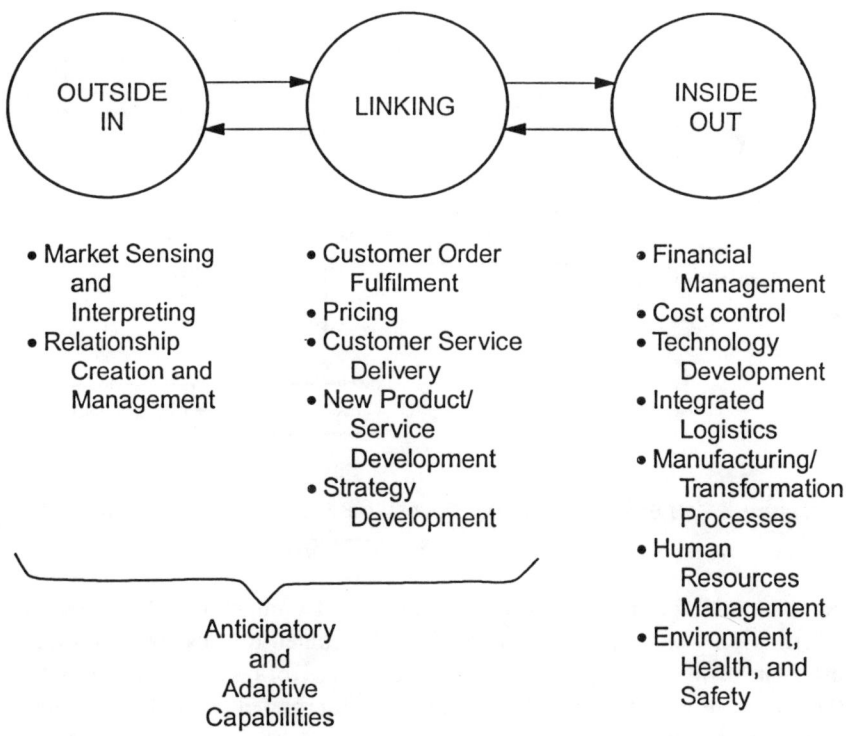

*Figure 2.* Classifying capabilities.

## ANTICIPATORY AND ADAPTIVE CAPABILITIES

Each of the "outside in" and "linkage" capabilities contributes to the overall ability of the firm to anticipate and respond to changing market requirements, and form enduring relationships based on satisfactory fulfillment of orders and availability of innovative products that provide superior customer value. These capabilities come in many guises depending on the market situation. Nonetheless there are common features, shared by successful firms, that provide useful guidance for identifying and enhancing these capabilities.

### Market Sensing and Interpreting

This capability is revealed through the process the business uses to learn about its markets (see Figure 3). These learning processes are initiated by the active acquisition of information about the needs of the market, how it is segmented, how relationships are sustained, the evolving role of channel

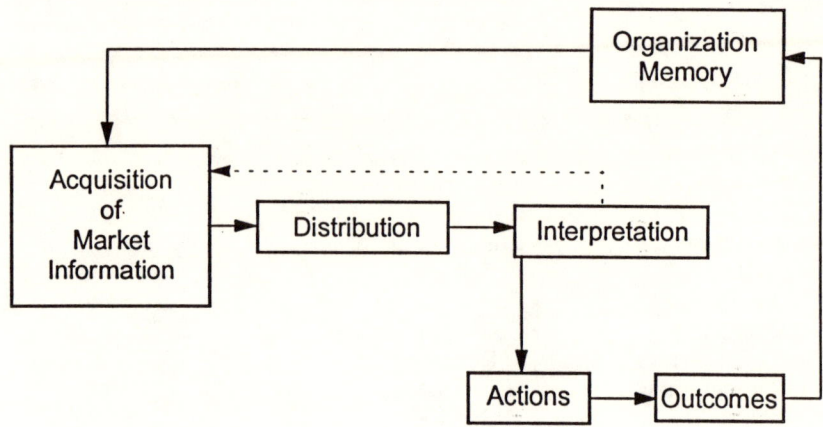

*Figure 3.* The market learning process: Basis of the market sensing and interpretation capability.

partners and the intentions and capabilities of competitors. However, the information won't have value unless it is distributed to those who can make use of it; or placed in readily accessible memory storage for later use. Before the information can be acted on it has to be interpreted through a process of sorting, classification and simplification to reveal coherent patterns. This is the function of the mental models of managers that contain decision rules for filtering information and useful heuristics for deciding how to act on the information in light of the anticipated outcomes.

Market-driven firms are distinguished by an ability to learn accurately about their markets ahead of their competitors and orient themselves to act preemptively on this information. This anticipatory capability is based on superiority in each step of the process, through achieving open-minded inquiry, synergistic information distribution, mutually informed interpretations and accessible memories.

*Open-minded Inquiry*

All organizations acquire information about trends, events, opportunities, and threats in their market environment by scanning, direct experience, imitation, or problem-solving inquiries. Market-driven learning organizations excel by approaching these activities in a more thoughtful and systematic fashion, in the belief that all decisions start with the market. The most distinctive features of their approach to inquiry are the following:

- *Active scanning.* All organizations track key market conditions and activities and try to learn from the departures from what is normal and expected. However, often this is only top-down learning, for there is a blockage of information from the front-line employees. In market-driven organizations, these front-line contacts, who hear complaints or requests for new services, and see the consequences of competitive activity, are motivated to inform management on a systematic basis.
- *Self-critical benchmarking.* Most firms do regular tear-down analysis of competitors' products and occasionally study firms for insights into how better to perform discrete functions and activities. Market-driven firms also study attitudes, values and management processes of nonpareils.
- *Continuous experimentation and improvement.* All organizations tinker with their procedures and practices and take actions aimed at improving productivity and customer satisfaction. However, most are not very serious about systematically planning and observing the outcomes of these on-going changes, so those that improve performance are adopted and others are dropped.
- *Informed imitation.* Market-driven firms study their direct competitors so they can emulate successful moves before the competition gets too far ahead. This requires thoughtful efforts to understand why the competitor succeeded, as well as further probes for problems and shortcomings to identify improvements that would be welcomed by customers.

## Synergistic Information Distribution

Firms often don't know what they know. They may have good systems for storing and locating "hard" routine accounting and sales data, but otherwise have problems finding where a certain piece of information is known within the organization or assembling all the needed pieces in one place. This is especially true of competitor information—where manufacturing may be aware of certain activity through common equipment suppliers, sales hears about initiatives from distributors and collects rumors from customers, and the engineering department may have hired recently from a competitor.

Market-driven firms don't suffer unduly from organizational chimneys, silos or smokestacks that bottle up information vertically within functions. Instead, information is widely distributed, its value is mutually appreciated and those functions with potentially synergistic information know where else it could beneficially be used.

## Mutually Informed Interpretations

The simplifications inherent in the mental models used by managers facilitate learning when they are based on undistorted information about important relationships and widely shared throughout the organization. These mental models can impede learning when they are incomplete, unfounded or seriously distorted—by functioning below the level of awareness, so they are never examined. A market-driven organization avoids these pitfalls by using scenarios and other devices (deGeus 1988) to force managers to articulate, examine, and eventually modify their mental models of how their markets work, how competitors and suppliers will react and the parameters of the response coefficients in their marketing programs.

Further problems arise when the functional managers have very different mental models, and don't appreciate or accept that there are other valid interpretations. Divergent mental models are especially dysfunctional in team activities, such as new product development, where participants may have very different ideas of the performance criteria, target market or positioning. The result is an absence of integrity in the final product (Clark & Fujimoto 1991).

## Accessible Memory

Market-driven inquiry, distribution and interpretation will not have a lasting effect unless what is learned is lodged in the collective memory. Organizations without practical mechanisms to remember what has worked and why will have to repeat their failures and rediscover their success formulas over and over again. Collective recall capabilities are most quickly eroded by turnover through transfers and rapid disbanding of teams. Data banks that are inaccessible to the entire organization also can contribute to amnesia. Here is where information technology can play an especially useful role.

### Establishing and Managing Relationships

This capability is growing in importance as buyer-seller relationships continue their transformation. At one time standard purchasing practices emphasized arms-length adversarial bargaining aimed at achieving the lowest price for each transaction or contract. Not surprisingly the suppliers focused on the individual transactions and gave little attention to the interface with the customer. These arrangements didn't offer much incentive to suppliers to be open with buyers or vice versa. The buyer was unlikely to know a supplier's costs and capabilities and there was little incentive for the supplier to develop superior or dedicated capabilities since they could easily lose the business to a competitor.

Now customers, as well as major channel members such as IKEA and Wal-Mart, are seeking much closer, collaborative relationships based on a high level of coordination, participation in joint programs, and close communication linkages. This suits their better suppliers who confront intense competition that quickly nullifies their product advantages as well as powerful channels that control access to the market. Many markets are mature, so the cost of acquiring new accounts is high relative to the costs of retaining their existing customers. When a secure, trusting relationship has been established, changing customer requirements are communicated more rapidly and the collaborative development of response programs speeds the process of adaption.

Despite the recent emphasis on the establishment, maintenance, and enhancement of collaborative relationships, few firms have mastered this capability and converted it into a competitive advantage. Successful collaboration requires a high level of purposeful cooperation aimed at maintaining a trading relationship over time (Spekman, 1988). The activities to be managed start with the coordination of "inside out" and "linking" capabilities, although these are not the means by which the relationship is managed. Instead, new skills, abilities, and processes have to be mastered to achieve mutually satisfactory collaboration:

## Close Communication and Joint Problem-Solving

Suppliers have to be prepared to develop team-based mechanisms for continuously exchanging information about needs, problems, and emerging requirements, and then be able to take action. In a successful collaborative relationship, joint problem solving displaces negotiations as the communications approach. Suppliers also need to be prepared to participate in the customer's development processes, even before the product specifications are established.

Communications occur at many levels, and across many functions of the customer and the supplier organizations. This demands a high level of internal coordination, and a major shift in the role of the sales function. When the focus is on transactions the sales person is pivotal, and emphasizes persuading the customer through features, price, terms and the maintenance of a presence. The sales function adopts a very different—and possibly subordinate—role in a collaborative relationship. Now the emphasis is on coordinating other functions, anticipating needs, demonstrating responsiveness, and building credibility and trust. Needless to say, there are many barriers to such a transformation of traditional sales forces.

## Coordinating Activities

Instead of coordination being limited to the scheduling of deliveries, new management processes are needed for (a) joint production planning and scheduling, (b) management of information system links so each knows the other's requirements and status, and orders can be communicated electronically, and (c) mutual commitments to the improvement of quality and reliability.

Manufacturer-reseller relations have become a fertile area for the development of collaborative management capabilities, with the major grocery product firms taking the lead. The objective of each party used to be to transfer as much of their cost to the other as possible. This led to dysfunctional practices such as forward buying to take advantage of manufacturer's promotional offers, resulting in excessive warehousing expenses and costly spikes in production levels. Traditionally, contacts between parties were limited to lower-level sales representatives calling on buyers who emphasized prices, quantities, and deals. Increasingly, manufacturers such as Procter & Gamble, and retailers like K-Mart are assigning multi-functional teams to deal with each other at many levels—including harmonizing systems, sharing logistics and product movement information, and jointly planning for promotional activity and product changes. The objectives of this collaborative activity are to cut total systems costs, while helping retailers improve sales.

Firms that have developed a distinctive capability for managing collaborative relationships find they also have more integrated strategies. The integration begins with a broad-based agreement on which customers serve collaboratively. No longer is this choice left to the sales function, without regard to the impact on the manufacturing and service functions. The increased intensity of cross-functional coordination and information sharing required to present a common face to the counterpart functions of the customer, enhances shared understanding of the strategy and the role of other functions. The adaptability of this integral strategy in response to anticipated or actual changes in customer requirements is also improved, for the need for change is more readily apparent to all functions who are better equipped to act in concert. Innovative organizational arrangements based on team formats also speed the rate of adaption.

## LINKAGE CAPABILITIES: THE CASE OF THE ORDER FULFILLMENT PROCESS

Linkage capabilities are exercised through sequences of activities the business has to perform well to actually satisfy the anticipated needs of customers identified by the market sensing and interpretive capability and meet the commitments that have been made to enhance relationships. The order fulfillment, new product development, and service delivery processes serve this linkage role. They also illustrate why the effective management of these horizontal processes—so they become distinctive capabilities that competitors can't readily match—is so different from managing a vertical function in a traditional hierarchical organization.

First, these processes are guided by an integral competitive strategy. All decisions and specific functional actions are shaped by a shared understanding of customer requirements and concerns and a consensus about how to compete and the target markets to emphasize. This guidance is necessary so the setting of priorities and trade-offs can be made as far down in the organization as possible.

Second, process management emphasizes external objectives that are focused on performance with customers (such as their satisfaction with the outcome of the process, whether quality, or delivery time or installation assistance) or are based on competitive performance benchmarks (such as cycle time, or order processing time). This helps ensure that all those involved with the process are focused on providing superior value to external—or internal—customers. These objectives become the basis for a measurement and control system that monitors progress toward the objective and encourages continuous improvement.

Third, for the activities of a complex process to be coordinated, a number of jurisdictional boundaries have to be crossed and horizontal connections made. This is difficult to do when there is no identifiable owner of the process who can isolate sources of delay and take action to eliminate them. When no one has a sense of the total flow of activities in an order-entry process, for example, critical time-consuming steps such as credit checks may be undertaken separately in sequence when they could have been done in parallel to save time. Of course, much of the coordination problem is eliminated if the employees with different skills are grouped as a team to accomplish all the steps in a process. This means having the mortgage loan officer, title searcher and credit checker working together, not in series.

Fourth, information is readily available to all members of the team, unfiltered by a hierarchy. If there is a question of order requirements, delivery status, or parts availability, everyone who is affected by the answer can get the information directly without having to go through an intermediary for processing.

The capabilities needed for effectively managing a process are time consuming to develop, and absorb substantial resources in training, systems development, controls, and organizational redesign. But when the process is *seamless*, the result is time compression, superior value to customers, cost savings and an advantage that is difficult for a competitor to understand and imitate.

The order fulfillment process in Figure 4 illustrates both the problems and benefits of managing a process for competitive advantage, rather than as a sequential series of distinct activities. Often this process is obscured from top management view, because it links activities that take place routinely as sales forecasts are made, orders are received and scheduled, products are shipped and services are provided (Shapiro, Rangan, & Sviokla 1992). Such a process can easily become a disadvantage if unrealistic promises are made to customers, these promises are then not kept and blame is passed around as each function

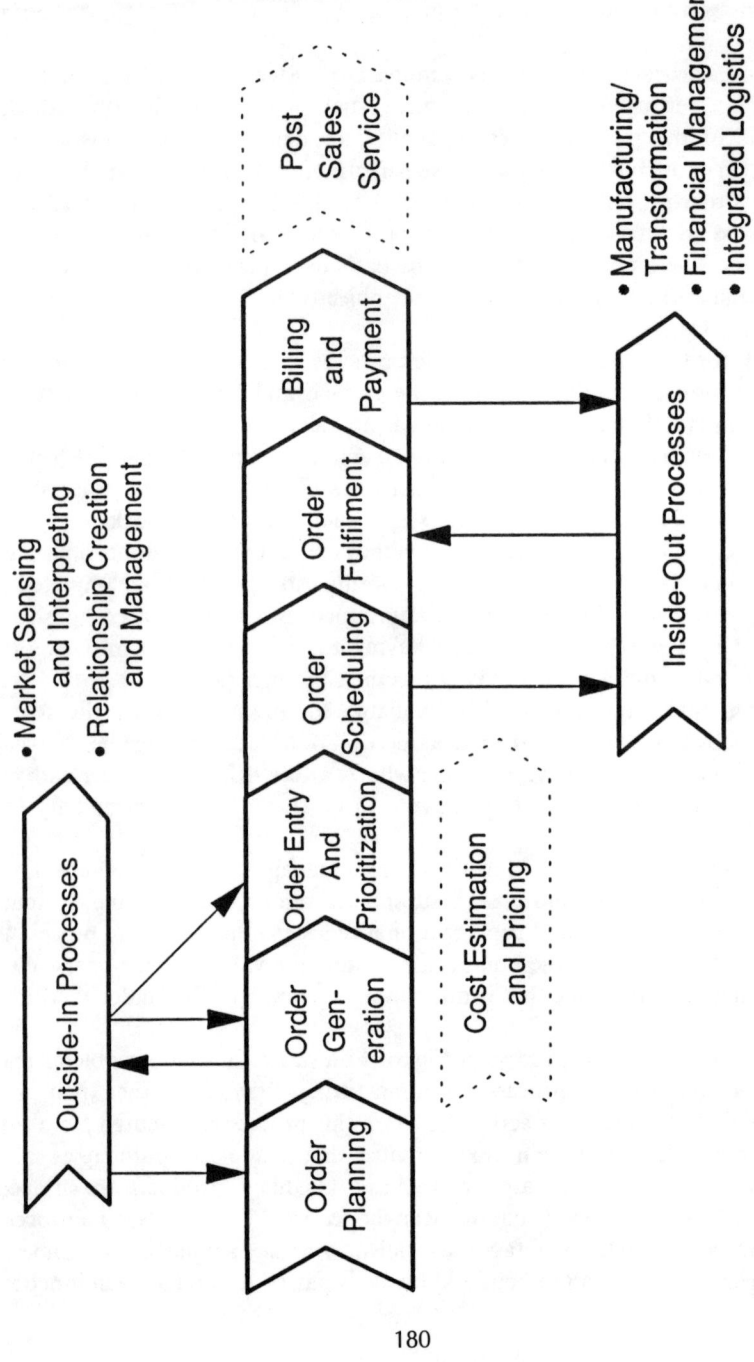

*Figure 4.* Order fulfillment process: Basis of a critical linkage capability.

accuses the other of not meeting their commitments, and inventories expand as each function seeks to protect itself from shortcomings of other functions (in part because no one incurs a cost for holding excess inventories). In addition to horizontal flow problems, there is a significant likelihood that the day-to-day execution of the process will be disconnected from the business strategy. This is where critical choices of which orders to select, customers to emphasize, and products to push are made. Yet the people who make these choices are generally far removed from the dialogue about strategy and how the business intends to gain advantage. Nor are they likely to be held individually accountable for their contributions to the overall strategy.

An additional complexity of the order fulfillment process is the wealth of connections to other processes. It brings together information from the "outside-in" processes, and depends on their ability to forecast, and generate a flow of orders, while being even more dependent on the "inside-out" manufacturing and logistics processes to fulfill the scheduled orders or have capacity in place to service requests and transactions. Finally, there is the allied process of cost estimation and pricing of orders. The management of this activity will significantly improve profitability, if there is clear recognition of the customer value of each order and the costs of filling each order are known. This then permits the kind of individual order pricing to maximize profits that is practiced by the airlines with their yield management programs.

A similar analysis of the other linking processes of new product development, and customer service delivery would reveal equivalent problems of coordination, functional conflicts and lack of strategic direction. The gains in performance from managing them as integrated processes aimed at cutting time-to-market or responsiveness to service requests, are equally persuasive. The question is, how does a business proceed to build a superior capability based on its core processes?

## DEVELOPING SUPERIOR ANTICIPATORY AND ADAPTIVE CAPABILITIES

Firms seeking to enhance their "outside-in" capabilities won't find much direct guidance in the available literature. Until now, most of the emphasis has been on the identification of capabilities and core competencies, and the virtues of competing with capabilities, with less to say about how they are cultivated. A further limitation is most of the attention has been given to "inside-out" capabilities, such as the ability to consolidate corporate-wide technologies and production skills (Prahalad & Hamel 1990).

However, the development of "outside-in" capabilities is not entirely uncharted territory. Useful guidance comes from the closely parallel work on the progress of organizations such as Rubbermaid, Nordstrom's and Frito-Lay that are striving to become market-driven. These firms demonstrate:

- a pervasive commitment to a set of processes, beliefs and values that reflect the philosophy that all decisions start with the customer and anticipated opportunities for advantage, that are:
- guided by a deep and shared understanding of customers' needs and behavior, and competitors' capabilities and intentions, for the purpose of
- achieving superior performance by satisfying customers better than competitors.

The achievement of this orientation—which is at the heart of the anticipatory and adaptive capabilities—requires continuous progress along four interlocking dimensions: (1) the core processes for market learning and relationship management, (2) shared beliefs and values, (3) organization structures and systems, and (4) strategy development and review processes. Each of these dimensions is explored in more depth in Day (1990). For their relationship see Figure 5.

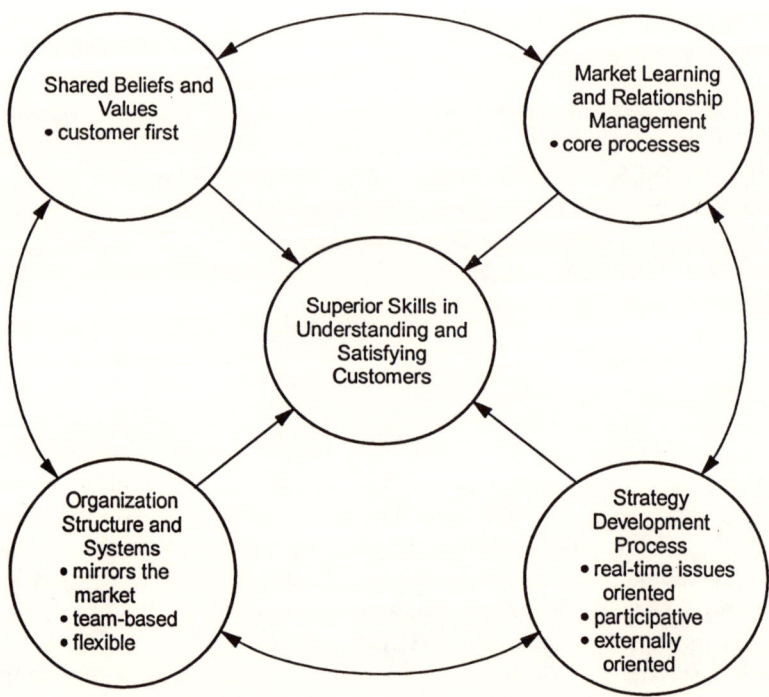

*Figure 5.* Dimensions of market-driven management.

Many firms have aspired to become market-driven, but have failed to instill and sustain this orientation. These aspirants often underestimate how difficult a task it is to shift an organization's focus from internal to external concerns. They act as though marginal changes, a few management workshops, and proclamations of intent will suffice, when they should have been mounting a wide-ranging cultural shift. The degree to which market-driven behavior is embedded in the organizational culture—those shared values and beliefs that give members of an organization meaning and, provide them with rules for behavior—is now well recognized (Deshpande & Webster 1987). Change programs will have to match the magnitude of the cultural shift to have any chance of success. Efforts to develop a market orientation are most likely to succeed with a combination of bottom-up redesign and top-down direction (Dichter 1991). Of course, each firm will have a specific program that is tailored to their specific circumstances and position relative to their competition. Thus a good place to start is by benchmarking the capabilities of both direct competitors, and the best-of-breed in industries facing comparable challenges. This should provide realistic targets for improvement, and yield suggestions for how to proceed. More important, the widespread realization that there is a competitive gap in these capabilities that can hurt long-run performance will help mobilize support and ensure that motivation doesn't flag.

*Bottom-Up Redesign*

The most effective transformations are directed at overcoming the functional balkanization of core processes, and refocusing them toward external objectives. This begins with a comprehensive mapping of these processes to identify disconnects at hand-off points, delays and unnecessary loops, and sequences of activities that can be done in parallel. Careful attention must be given to the openness of the process to external information, and the adequacy of the measurement system. The redesign effort usually requires the formation of teams with responsibility for the process outcome, and an owner of the process. At the same time as the team is given more accountability, senior management have to loosen their control by eliminating tight specifications of procedures and detailed reports. This makes it clear that the team has the responsibility for continuous improvement in the satisfaction of external and internal clients. These changes need to be supported with investments in distributed information systems, incentives for improvement, training so that members of the team know each other's role and can understand and use the information that is available, and forums for discussion of the change process. These bottom-up initiatives won't succeed on their own, because there still has to be linkages between processes (who is going to be responsible for pricing of orders, for example), and boundaries placed on behavior so that energy is not diffused. Also, not every process requires a dedicated team, for that would spread key personnel too thinly. Thus some processes have to be managed by task forces formed to solve particular performance problems and then disbanded. The overall result is that the organization structure tends to be flatter and more flexible, but a clear hierarchy remains. What has to happen at the top of the hierarchy, to guide the bottom-up changes?

*Top-Down Direction*

For an organization to become market-driven, and thus to develop superior anticipatory and adaptive capabilities, top management must make a clear and continuing commitment to putting customers first. This commitment is mainly signaled by deeds and time spent. Words have their place, but the rest of the organization would soon learn the real priorities and behave accordingly.

Senior management leadership is needed to reshape the culture, through such actions as proposing a challenging vision of the future, or setting a major performance improvement target such as cutting time to market in half. Further influence can be exercised through the strategy development process—to ensure broad participation, understanding, and acceptance of the chosen direction—supported by a rigorous strategy review that focuses on pivotal issues and critical assumptions about the ability of the business to compete. All of these moves, and others designed to simplify and focus the work of the organization, should eventually lead to a high degree of integrity of the strategy and enhanced responsiveness to the forces of change.

## TOWARD INTEGRAL STRATEGIES

The overdue shift in emphasis to capabilities does not mean that strategic positioning is any less important (Porter 1991). On the contrary, the choice of which capabilities to nurture, and which investment commitments to make, must be guided by a shared understanding of the industry structure, the needs of the target customer segments, the positional advantages being sought and the trends in the environment.

Two capabilities are especially important in bringing these external realities to the attention of the organization. One is the market sensing and interpretation capability that dictates how well the organization is equipped to continuously learn about its market. The second is derived from the ability to create and manage close customer relationships, so their needs are quickly apparent to all functions and there is a well-defined process for responding. Just how well the organization will respond and adapt over time depends on five linking processes: customer order fulfillment, pricing, new product or service development, and strategy development. The strategy development process plays a special role because it is also a vehicle that senior management can use to ensure adaptability by broadening participation, focusing on capabilities, identifying pressing issues to be resolved, and using the strategy review to force an external orientation. Finally, we come to the question of what is an integraL strategy? The answer proposed here is that the integrity or unity of a strategy derives from a well-defined strategic thrust that aims to continuously adapt the business to the evolving needs of specific customer groups and achieve competitive superiority in satisfying their needs. Integrity comes when this becomes a shared mind-set so there is a common direction, and the capabilities are in place to pursue this direction.

## REFERENCES

Boynton, A.C. & Victor, B. (1991). "Beyond Flexibility: Building and Managing the Dynamically Stable Organization." *California Management Review, 34,* (Fall): 53-66.
Clark, K.B., & Fujimoto, T. (1991). *Product Development Performance.* Boston, MA: Harvard Business School Press.
Day, G.S. (1990). *Market-Driven Strategy: Processes for Creating Value.* New York: Free Press.
Day, G.S., & Wensley, R. (1988). "Assessing Advantage: A framework for Diagnosing Competitive Superiority." *Journal of Marketing, 52,* (April): 1-20.
Deshpandé, R., & Webster, F.E., Jr. (1987). Organizational culture and marketing: Defining the research agenda. Cambridge MA: Marketing Science Institute.
DeGeus, A.P., (1988). "Planning as Learning." *Harvard Business Review, 66,* (March-April): 70-74.
Dichter, S.F. (1991). "The Organization of the '90s." *McKinsey Quarterly, 1,* (Spring): 145-155.
Frazier, G.L., Spekman, R.E., & O'Neal, C.R. (1988). Just-in-time Exchange Relationships in Industrial Markets. *Journal of Marketing, 52,* (October): 52-67.
Ghemawat, P. (1990). *Commitment: The Dynamic of Strategy.* New York: Free Press.
Grant, R.M. (1991). "The Resource-Based Theory of Competitive Advantage: Implications for Strategy Formulation." *California Management Review, 33,* (Spring): 114-135.
Kohli, A.K., & Jaworski, B. (1990). "Market orientation: The Construct, Research Propositions and Managerial Implications." *Journal of Marketing, 54,* (April): 1-18.
Narver, J.C., & Slater, S.F. (1990). "The Effect of a Market Orientation on Business Profitability." *Journal of Marketing, 54,* (October): 20-35.
Peters, T.J. (1984). "Strategy Follows Structure: Developing Distinctive Skills." *California Management Review, 26,* (Spring): 111-125.
Porter, M. (1980). *Competitive Strategies.* New York: Free Press.
Porter, M.E. (1991). Towards a Dynamic Theory of Strategy. *Strategic Management Journal, 12,* (Winter): 95-118.
Prahalad, C.K., & Hamel, G. (1990). "The Core Competence of the Corporation." *Harvard Business Review, 68,* (May-June): 79-91.
Rumelt, R.P., Schendel, D., & Teece, D. (1991). "Strategic Management and Economics." *Strategic Management Journal, 12,* (Winter): 5-30.
Seliznick, P. (1957). *"Leadership in Administration."* New York: Harper & Row.
Senge, Peter M. (1990). *"The Fifth Discipline: The Art and Practice of the Learning Organization."* New York: Doubleday.
Shapiro, Benson P., Rangan, V.K., & Sviokla, J.J. (1992). "Staple Yourself to an Order." *Harvard Business Review, 70,* (July-August): 113-122.

Stalk, G., Evans, P., & Shulman, L.E. (1992). "Competing on Capabilities: The New Rules of Corporate Strategy." *Harvard Business Review 70* (March-April): 57-69.

Teece, D.J., Pisano, G., & Shuen, A. (1991). *"Dynamic Capabilities and Strategic Management."* Unpublished working paper, University of California, Berkeley (November).

# ACHIEVING CONTINUOUS IMPROVEMENT IN BUSINESS STRATEGIES:
## RESPONSE TO GEORGE DAY

Everett Shorey

I am pleased to be here. George Day's paper brought back to me some ideas that we have been working on as strategy professionals for the last few years. And it has driven us to ask questions about the strategy process similar to those George was talking about today. The questions we have been trying to wrestle with are,

- How do you develop strategies in a firm (or, in our case, with our clients)?
- How do you look at strategy development as a business process?
- What things have we learned about that, or think we know?
- What are we reasonably certain of?
- What are we still learning? One of the things we are still learning is that strategy formulation and implementation is, in fact, a process.

One of the most useful changes that has happened in the field of strategy in the last few years has been the emergence of the business process redesign

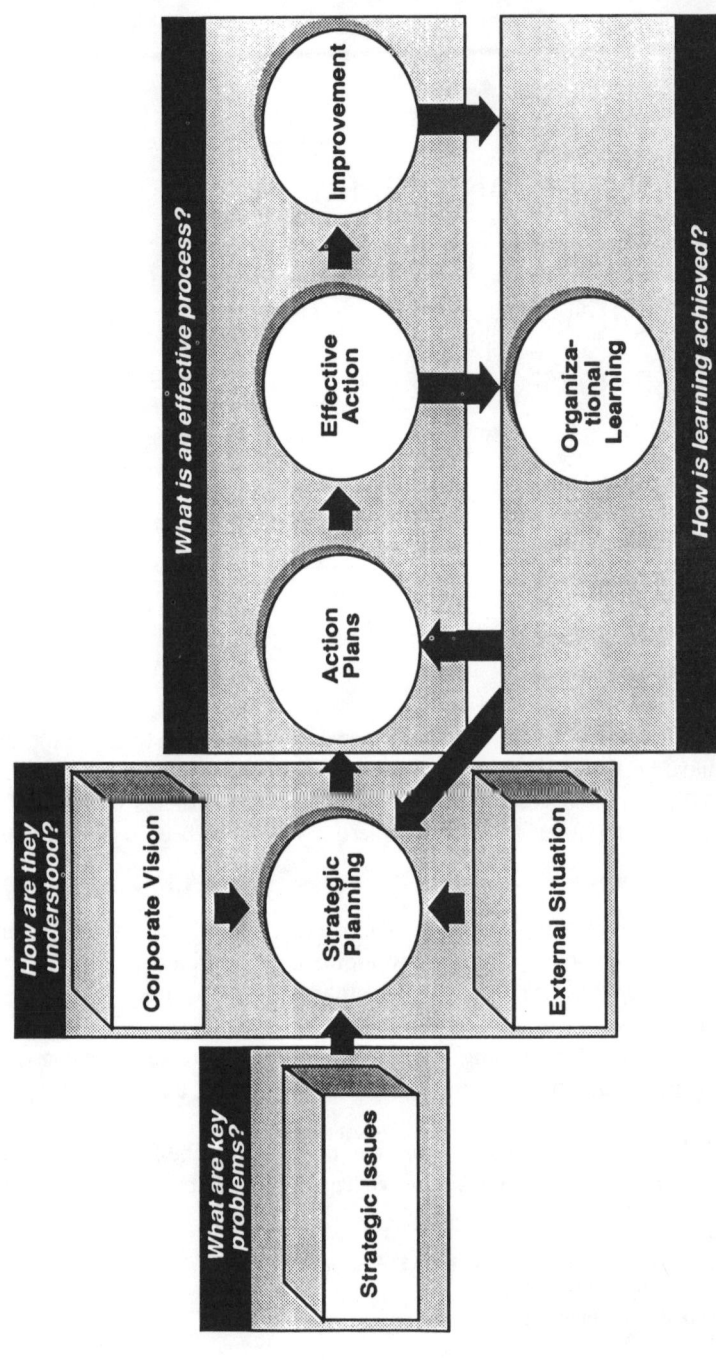

*Figure 1.* Achieving continuous improvement in strategy is a major challenge.

movement. The reason it has been helpful is that it has taught us to think of *strategy as a process*. As strategy professionals, we need to look at how can we use the tools of business process redesign to develop strategies.

Now why do I say that? The strategy business for a long time was very heavily tied to the first two boxes in Figure 1. What sorts of problems, and what sorts of issues are companies trying to resolve? Companies start with a context set by both their corporate vision and the external environment. They then go through the process of strategic planning, try to answer the questions and effect change in their business results. This is the strategy process. One of the things we have learned, as Hans Thorelli stated last night, is that strategy is not just an analytic process. In fact, it is probably only one third an analytic process. *What makes good strategy is that it is a very creative process.*

I unfortunately learned this from one of my former colleagues who was one of the great analysts of all times. He could use a methodology and a set of tools, and he could do elegant situation analyses based on filling out each matrix. Yet he was also the worst strategist I have ever met, because he did not have a creative bone in his body. He would come up with pedestrian strategies that were utterly predictable. As George suggested in his paper, they were basically transparent to the competitors because they were fundamentally drawn out of a rote analysis. So one thing we have learned in working with managers is that a first key element in the strategy process is to instill the ability to think creatively. How can you take all of the analysis you have done and do something creative with it?

One of the next things we have all learned is that if you are going to achieve effective action, you cannot leave strategy to strategists. Strategists do not run companies, managers do, and managers must become integrally connected to strategy. This creates a conundrum; most managers are not instinctively creative strategists. If you are not leaving strategy to strategists—if you are making strategy an integral part of management—you have to *turn strategy into an on-going learning process* because you cannot do strategy every six months, or every two years and have any hope of instilling creativity. As Hans said last night, you've got to do it continuously.

I learned that lesson when I got out of business school, and I decided I was going to learn to play the flute. Now I may not be much of a flutist, but I discovered the importance of continuous learning and practice for what little accomplishment I have achieved. If we are going to require managers to make creative music in strategy, we must expect and allow them practice and teaching. Hopefully, they will become more proficient at strategy than I am with the flute.

While it is easy to prescribe continuous, creative learning linked to strategy development, *implementing* this is a serious challenge. We are challenged with integrating strategy into daily thinking, as if it was our profession, and we need to ask questions such as, How can you take strategy out to managers? How

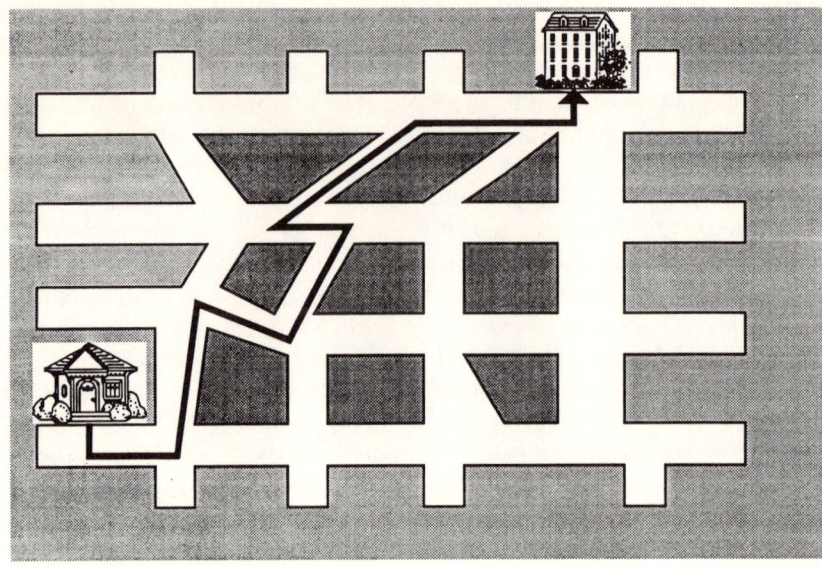

***Figure 2.***   Business strategies are not a road map over a fixed network of roads.

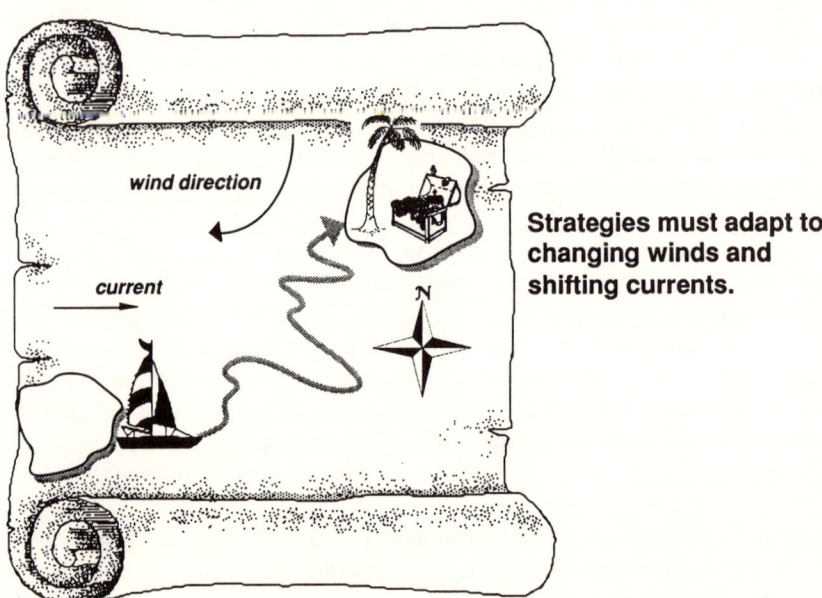

***Figure 3.***   Business strategies are more like a set of sailing directions.

can you get managers intimately involved in the strategy development process? And, How can you get them to do it as second nature?

Until fairly recently, nobody really knew how to integrate strategic management into a continuous process. People did not know how to do that partly because they thought of strategy as a set of fixed road maps. You would develop a strategy and you would say, ah yes, we want to get from A to B, and here is the road map (see Figure 2). In principle, you could write the road map out and then put it away.

The problem is that strategy is not like that at all. Strategy is much more like a set of sailing directions. Consider the reality of sailing in Figure 3. You start at point A and want to get to point B, the wind is coming this way, the current is going that way, and the only thing you know is that if you set out on a northeast compass course you are going to get to the wrong place. If that is the one thing you know for sure, the question is, then, how do you keep sailing?

This is the essence of why integral, continuous strategic management is important—because what you want is the operating manager to continue steering the boat. He or she is faced with different changes in the wind and current, yet the manager needs to keep steering the boat. This metaphor represents the strategy industry today, and it also represents the second main need to *look at strategy as any other business process*: it is a continuous process. George suggested some very important foundations for this process. For example, you have to understand your markets and approach them with "open-minded inquiry," you have to distribute the information in a synergistic manner, and so on.

We have also learned from process reengineering to deal with strategy as a process, as a set of procedures. In order to do this well, we have found there are at least four success factors. First, there has to be absolute commitment by all of the management to develop strategy as a process. You can no longer separate strategy from operations, nor can you separate strategy from *vision*.

Second, when a manager attends a strategic planning seminar and then comes back to work on Monday, he cannot forget the process by next Thursday. Management and strategy must be integrated. There must be broad and very deep management involvement. Both breadth and depth are critical—it has to be done in practice.

Third, we need mechanisms for outside stimulation. One of Fred Steingraber's comments on benchmarking was very insightful: The purpose of benchmarking is not to come up with a wonderful study of what is the "best in class." *The purpose of benchmarking is to stimulate us to think about how we can do our businesses better*, by giving us new and better ideas. Because you cannot simply adapt, you cannot just take the best practice and use it as your process. However, you can take ideas from people's best practices and use them as ways to stimulate you to come up with new processes. So we need

**Figure 4.** Successful strategy requires a clear goal and skilled sailors rather than an infallible map.

mechanisms for outside stimulation, such as benchmarking. Obviously, we think hiring consultants is also an excellent mechanism—it's better than any other that we've ever come across.

Finally, the strategy process has to add real value to managers. It has to be implemented to contribute to operations. Our experience with operating managers is that fully half of them think of the strategy process as an annoyance. It is a thing that they do every six months because it is like castor oil—it is good for them—or because senior management says they have to, but its linkage to actual operations is not obvious. We need a process that ties strategy to operations. Now how can you do that?

What we have noticed is, if you really look at your businesses, there are probably two or three reasonably significant strategic issues at stake at any one time. There are not fifteen; there are probably two or three. You can then put together effective strategy teams which look like process redesign teams that are effectively redesigning our strategies around those few critical issues. These teams ask questions such as, Can we get broad and deep management commitment? How can we use teams as mechanisms which facilitate thinking about strategy as a creative process intimately involving the managers? How can we bring creativity into that process? Are we in fact working on what are true strategic problems?

What do I mean by a strategic problem? For example, we have some clients who are currently going through the kinds of technology transitions people have talked about at this conference. Because of the nature of my practice I would say fully half of my clients at one time or another are going through a technology transition from mechanical to electronic products. It is a very difficult transition, because you essentially have to abandon everything you are good at and move over to something you are not very good at, with a whole new set of manufacturing competitors and usually with a much worse economic situation. It is a transition people hate, but that is the kind of problem that gets managers' attention. You can get a lot of operating management commitment to work on that problem because it is a very scary yet potentially economically rewarding opportunity.

In summary, we are looking at strategy as a *continuous* management process, using process redesign tools and truly trying to integrate creativity and the strategy process with management behavior in a way that we have talked about for many years, but I think are just beginning to get the tools to do. That is the way we as a firm are now seeing strategy, and it is also cropping up in our clients' thinking.

# DISCUSSION

## Kathryn Britney, Chair

*James Rush:*
There appears to be a catch-22 in what you're saying, George. I think I agree with you in that the "integral" might be the mental maps or the shared set of assumptions but the minute you have those it seems to me you close down the inquiry. In fact the "I'll know it when I see it" is backwards; "I'll see it when I know it" is more accurate. So the idea here is that I think once we've got that shared set of assumptions or that mental map, we start really short circuiting our scanning. The learning sort of breaks down. Do you agree with that? If you do, are there ways to break out of that?

*Day:*
I think it entirely depends on what's in that mental model. Let's look at some of the examples I have used. Management's mental models in fact were pretty well shared. They just were not very complete. The notion of sharing I should separate out from the mental model. Sharing means that there is wide agreement within the management team as to what are the important issues and relationships and so forth. This does not necessarily mean that they are complete. Industries are often captives of conventional wisdom, which means that everybody buys in to the same mental model, if you like, and that creates exactly the problem that you are pointing to. So I look at the whole process of developing mental models as a dynamic one, as one of *expanding* them to make sure there isn't that kind of myopia, and then get into sharing a round of very rich sets of understandings, and then bringing the information in to test it. But I take your point: conventional wisdom could be very dangerous. Everybody may be agreeing on the wrong issues, and being myopic about their responsibilities.

*Hans Thorelli:*

Perhaps one might add that the opposite risk is that when the organization is fragmented the information tends to stay with the fragments. It isn't adequately cross-circulated and never becomes integrated, as a matter of fact.

*Day:*

Yes, and then your key people retire, they've walked off with the important information. One manager of a chemical company said, "Well, as of January 1, 120 years of experience walks out the door." He was really unhappy about it!

One participant stated that he thought it is important that we begin to reward information which tends to go against common wisdom.

We are biased in filtering information and we say, well, yeah, that fits our strategy, that fits our assumptions—or we say the opposite, depending upon your perspective. If you reward "contrarian" information, as opposed to sweeping it under the rug, you go a long way toward implementing a learning process, and eliminating some of the problems of this shared model and stroking each other.

*Day:*

And I think outsiders have a role to play, just asking questions, why do you do things this way, what is the rationale for this and that arrangement, and so on.

*Thomas Hustad:*

We are dealing with *organizational learning* now. In the new product context one article surveyed 80 team leaders and basically just asked them, So you have completed your work, and then what happened next? And in almost no cases was there formal organizational learning in terms of leader reassignment, team member reassignment, documentation passed through, or additional inquiry. The most that they came up with really was the occasional plan being written, or someone in desperation calling and saying, "Help," from a next generation team. This organizational learning I think is really a growing problem as we decentralize and have teams. How can we move closer to consistent implementation of your ideas?

*Day:*

There are two issues implied by your question. One is the learning itself, how that happens and gets distributed. The other aspect is something like replications of successful learning experiences. I am just about as concerned about the latter as the former. I will give you an example as to why. Perhaps this is something that resonates with all of you. I have seen a number of companies with extremely successful new product development efforts, where indeed they brought the product to market in half the previous time, deriving major competitive advantage. They were the first movers, but because of what you are pointing to, they didn't actually understand why they were successful. They did not codify it, and they are not able to replicate it. I find increasingly that a success in one area is not followed by successes anywhere else in the company. I think we need to look at that, and that part of the learning process is to figure out what went right. But at times there seems to be a kind of rejection system in place, where other functions and other groups and other parts of the business say, "that may work for them, but we are different." Such behavior, of course, runs counter to the kind of multi-functional learning that you want to have.

As to the broader question of how to *induce learning,* I think re- engineering is an important process, and to have a team or an individual that "owns it" makes sure that the lessons are captured, distributed, acted on and understood. But the learning paradigm clearly is going to be a very helpful one to us, because that is all part of anticipating and adapting quicker. I think you could apply it to any one of the processes which you're managing, so long as you know what the process really is, and can continue to experiment with it.

Often we don't know what happens. As we were talking about this earlier, we have an opportunity in global organizations to try lots of things out in different market environments, try different product approaches, promotional approaches, different organizational designs, whatever it may be. Then learn from that.

*Ronald Stephenson:*

We have talked about learning organizations and *memory* and so forth, but where is the memory? Where should we try to accumulate and repose this knowledge and information? Not only do we lose 120 years of experience because of retirement, we have a constant outflow of people, particularly in larger organizations, via promotions and other attrition processes. So if you want to be an organization in which the organization somehow learns from both successful and unsuccessful sets of experiences, where should we try to repose and organize that information? Because it will leave with people leaving, being transferred to a different division, or what have you.

*Day:*

There are some pretty quick answers I can give you in terms of the obvious system solutions and documentation of management systems, but I think the more interesting approach is to ask, *why do organizations forget?* They forget the important things, the tacit knowledge that holds things together. I think we have the immediate problem when we look at continuity and position; turnover is a major problem that causes amnesia in an organization.

A related problem, which has never been well received by my friends in the consulting industry, is that there is a tendency to rely on your consulting firms, advertising and market research agencies to do the market studies, to do organizational reviews, to do pilot studies for new product or new technology. That knowledge may never be taken into account seriously enough. In fact, it was paid for, but never acted on.

Another thing we do badly, and why we forget, is that when we had a team that really did work, that team is often split apart and sent to a different business unit, to a different country, and we have no way of accessing them. Replication goes out the window! Honda, I think, is able to manage organizational learning through selective promotion of people: they make the people who were successful in the team available to other teams dealing with the same type of issues, say, drive trains. So there's a vertical organization in which people swing in and out of a team and then they take their knowledge to another team that can use it, so they manage the team process, as opposed to splitting the team apart.

A question I was going to ask this morning is, *How do you take advantage of the learning that someone has gained by being resident in Japan for three years?* I know there are plenty of organizations where the people who were abroad acquired an enormous amount of in-depth, on-the-ground information, came back to headquarters to find two things happening. One, their knowledge was not tapped, and, two, they were out of the loop for three years so their promotion prospects were in the wane. This is not a good way to enhance learning. So the approach I would advocate here is, if you want to enhance your memory, you should figure out why you forget, *why* you have to continue to do these studies, and then tackle the root causes.

*Harvey Hegarty:*

The question I have has to do with *creativity*. Both you, George, and Everett Shorey referred to that as being a pivot in launching out and being sensitive to the ever changing environment. To me, that seems fine and good for some of the corporations that we have heard about in this conference. But there is a huge number of companies, especially in the United States right now, that have recently gone through or are continuing to go through downsizing. You referred to the redesign at the bottom before you talked about corporate directions, and I am assuming that you meant that we have to unleash this creativity before top management puts any kind of lid on it. If I am in middle management, and I see what a lot of colleagues are going through, part of me says, yeah, I need to be creative, we need to be creative as a corporation to survive. Another part of me says, I better not get out there on a limb lest that sucker gets sawed off, and I am on the ground with no job. We all know that for every success there are nine failures. If you come up with two or three failures in this kind of environment, how long will most companies be willing to back you before they say maybe you better take your creativity across the street?

*Shorey:*

Obviously, if you're creative and wrong four times in a row you're in trouble. There is some cost to failure. Unfortunately, however, in many organizations being creative and brilliant three times in a row may still bring you a "reward" in the form of punishment for being creative and failing the fourth time. Randy

Tobias touched on what we see from the outside in companies on this whole issue of creativity, and what is the role of middle management. In my interpretation, his basic point was that if you are not of any value, you are in the way. The reality for middle managers now is that if you are not part of the solution you are probably part of the problem. So I would turn this one around. If you're not being creative, you are in trouble. You simply cannot be sitting there occupying a place without clearly adding value.

*Day:*

To Harv's question, I wanted to make clear that by putting bottom-up redesign and top-down direction in that order, I was not implying that the process doesn't require initial leadership and the support of creative efforts. I don't think there is any doubt that if people who have taken good business risks, and were punished for it because there is something that is not viable in the technology (or whatever it may be), and they lose their promotion prospects (or they are sent to corporate Siberia), that that would completely cut off further creativity. So I think the posture I would take is to figure out a way to syndicate risks. Make sure that whenever there is a risk being taken, a new program is launched, a new product is being developed, that you don't isolate the appropriate manager and have that person accountable for all the results. Someone higher up, perhaps several someones higher up, should accept and lay off some of the risk, so that they are also accountable for this business risk. In spreading the risk around a bit, I think you prevent this sense of isolation that would reduce the creativity. You have clearly raised an important question.

# VI INTEGRAL STRATEGY AND CORPORATE CULTURE

# EDITOR'S NOTE

Corporate culture is a subject touched on directly or indirectly in most of our contributions. One session of the collegium was, however, exclusively devoted to current developments in the corporate culture area of special significance to integral strategy. Robert Hershock gave a paper as enthusiastically received as it was delivered, on the topic of cross-functional teams as the driving force to change. Claes Fornell discussed customer satisfaction as the ultimate measure of quality, and, in passing, inveighed against the all too narrow focus which the concept of productivity is ordinarily given in economic analyses and management culture.

Dissatisfied with the slow-motion approach of classical hierarchical organizations to the vital subject of innovation, Hershock was one of the 3M pioneers introducing cross-functional new product development teams into that company, well known for its emphasis on innovation. Named "an expert chimney breaker" by *Fortune* (May 1990), he sees interdisciplinary teams of expertise from all functional areas as the fountainhead of creativity in product development and, no less important, as a key vehicle for dramatically shortening the time from new product conception to introduction. Naturally, such a radical change in the way things are done cannot be introduced overnight. Hershock's narrative of the trials and tribulations involved provides a fascinating guide to what many companies are likely to experience as they are now trying, or will be trying, to do similar things. How are team members and leaders to be selected; what degree of empowerment will/should the team be given; how will its activities—themselves integral in nature—be integrated with the already existing organizations? What training should team leaders and members be given? Last but not least, how can we build the trust and credibility indispensable to such unorthodox organizations? Hershock's answers to these and related questions are those of a practicing expert.

Fornell points out that we tend to measure a few performance indicators at several or all levels of the economy, from SBUs via the firm, industry, sectoral and national levels. These indicators would include production, prices and productivity. These measures have the merit of being relatively simple to quantify, but they all have one major flaw in common: They overlook the quality dimension. This dimension is presumably just as important as the quantitative—the interpretation of the latter is woefully incomplete without being related to the former. Indeed, in this age of growing customer orientation and increasing predominance of the service sector, we may perhaps expect qualitative aspects of performance measurement to take a lead role.

It stands to reason that "quality" will not be measured in a producer-oriented fashion (as is often the case in TQM efforts); customer satisfaction, measured in sophisticated ways outlined by Fornell, will be the order of the day. Although this type of measurement is inherently multi-dimensional, rapid progress has been made in the last decade in causal modeling of the relative importance to customers of an entire array of satisfaction criteria from the level of the SBU or firm to the national economy. Of particular interest is the inherent ability of such measures to signal what investments in "quality" improvements will be of greatest interest to producer as well as consumer from a profitability (utility) and a customer retention (loyalty) point of view.

# CROSS-FUNCTIONAL TEAMS:
## THE DRIVING FORCE TO CHANGE

Robert J. Hershock

### INTRODUCTION

Good afternoon, I am excited about being here and about sharing with you my experience in developing cross-functional teams. I am excited about it because I know after about eight years of experience that they do work and that they work very successfully.

There has been a tremendous amount of change, as we all know, in the marketplace and in corporations today. There is a tremendous amount of market turbulence, where we all have to do more with less. We have major changes in the organization; there is a lot of increasing uncertainty as far as the people are concerned, and there is a personal struggle with change that everybody has. To give you an example, between 1982 and today, 3M has doubled its business, and we have done it with about the same number of employees that we had in 1982. What that means is that employees who are there today really have much broader responsibilities than they ever had before. When we ask these people to take on more responsibility, we really need to train them properly in changing the way that we manage our business.

I want to go back a little bit and talk about some of our history here, because I think it is relevant to why I created the cross-functional teams in 1984. In 1982 I was managing director of 3M Switzerland, a great job. I was enjoying it tremendously over there when I was called back to the States, because a vice president of one of the divisions took early retirement, and I was asked to replace him. The reputation, at that time, of this unit was that it was a hot, division—it was making a lot of money, it was highly profitable, and it was considered one of the premier divisions of 3M company. When I got back here it did not take long to find out that most of the business, and almost all of the profit, was being generated by two older products. When we started looking into our new product area and into the new technology base we found out there was none.

I was able then to successfully take this division from a high-profit, premier division to a crisis within three months (which management wasn't too happy about!). We recognized that we really did have a major crisis because not only did we have competition coming in—because patents had run out on the products—but the government was expanding its role and changing its product certification requirements. There were a lot of issues contributing to the turmoil at that time, and the division was really in a crisis.

We felt that we had to do something and we had to do it fast. The thing that we felt had to change was the way the division was managed, because it was strictly a hierarchial type of a management—top-down management with one person making all the decisions. There was no other decision-making process within the organization. To run an organization like that and to turn it around in a crisis situation is quite difficult.

What I was basically looking for was an organization where we could get more *participation*. We were looking to create an innovative atmosphere to increase risk-taking and push participation down into the organization as low as we possibly could to eliminate all the barriers that had been set up. There were many barriers; whenever you have a hierarchial organization there are barriers. We also wanted to push down the decision-making process to the lowest possible level we had and to transform the organization head from a "boss" to a "leader." Finally, we wanted to cut the time in half that it would take to develop new products. That meant we had to empower the entire organization, and we had to do it very rapidly.

The four main themes I will be speaking about are leadership, planning, training and sponsoring. Although rewards was another element which was linked to our transformation, I had not planned to talk about it today.

In all organizations we have goals. As shown in Figure 1, in order to achieve results from our goals, we work through people, process, and structure. In a functional/differentiated type of an organization as shown in the left-hand part of Figure 1, you have a manager that is controlling; you have specialists that work in very narrow areas and do not go out of those areas; you have a

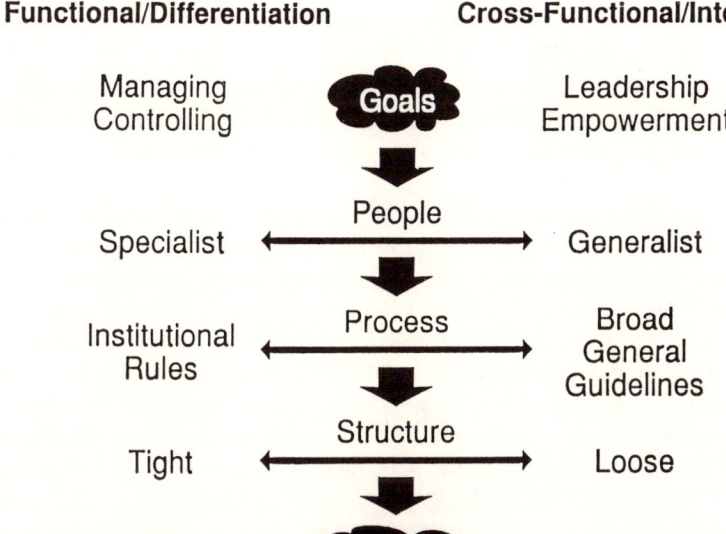

*Source:* ©Douglas Peters and Associates.

*Figure 1.*

great many institutional rules; you have a tight structure and a very *efficient* organization.

This was exactly the organization that we felt we had to change in order to get more creativity into our organization and to get new products out in half the time. As illustrated in the right-hand part of Figure 1, what we wanted to do was develop a cross-functional, integrated organization where the leadership actually empowered everyone in the organization. For "specialists" we wanted generalists who could assume a variety of different responsibilities. We wanted to give them broad, general guidelines rather than the institutional rules that they had in the past. And, rather than having the tight structure that they had before, we were looking for a loose structure—what I was specifically looking for here was not an *efficient* organization but an *effective* organization.

I have to tell you that when you are trying to make this type of a change with people who are accustomed to working in a more traditional, hierarchical organization, it is a very difficult change to make. There were a lot of people who were not comfortable in this kind of atmosphere and they did leave the division; that was fine. They went with other divisions within 3M, so that was not a problem.

What we wanted to do was to really increase the effectiveness of the overall organization by creating these cross-functional teams, by creating a clear charter, and by showing them that they had senior management support. To elect team leaders, we felt that core groups of these cross-functional teams should be no more than eight or ten individuals. We also wanted to have a bridge between the operating committee and each of these cross-functional teams so that we had a director-level sponsor.

When I say that we had broad, general guidelines, I don't mean to imply that we could allow any of these teams to just go out and randomly do what they wanted. There was a lot of planning that went into this entire process. In that planning, some of the things that we tried to do were to create the vision of what the business should look like in the future, to streamline it, to communicate it, and to create the values that we thought were important. We also had other types of broad, general guidelines. For example, we wanted products that were new to the world, we wanted them to be patentable, we wanted certain gross margins on the products, and we wanted products that would have a major impact on sales by the fifth year. These were broad general guidelines.

We were in the respirator business, and we spent a lot of time in planning the types of products we felt that we should have. We did not get down to the specific type of product, however. Planning was done in broad, general terms and detailed issues were left for the teams. That is why we had created the cross-functional teams whose responsibilities were to create the products, to create the charter, to write the mission, and so on. In order to initiate the process, we had to define the role of the general managers and directors, and we had to have buy-in here by everyone. Because if we didn't have buy-in by everyone, the process was not going to work.

Leader selection the first time was also a difficult challenge. This was a radical change, and no one was willing to take the risk of being a leader. So we had to do a little arm bending in order to get these leaders. When I first started our teams, we may have overloaded the system because we started out with 11 teams. We are talking about a lot of people in the process. Some of these people were on more than one team, and to be a team member meant you had to do the team work as well as your present job. We really did overload the system. I think if I did it again I wouldn't overload us again, but obviously this was a learning process for me, as well.

Another major challenge we encountered was in the area of *trust*. When you are trying to empower an organization there is a great deal of mistrust. They hear the words, but they are not sure they want to believe it. They have to see the actions, they are looking to you to see if you are really sincere or if this is just another program, and next year we will switch back if it doesn't work. We had to develop trust in our entire organization, and believe me, they really tested us. They tested the risk-taking and they tested the decision-making all the time. It is easy when you are in management to just give them the answers and let them go, and it was difficult to continue to push the process back down to them and make them get the answers.

One of the changes I made was to eliminate all formal reviews. There was no written correspondence; I didn't want any. I stayed out of their way. I communicated the vision: I talked to every member of the organization about the issues, about the vision, about the value, and about where we wanted to go. My operating committee and I went to our three manufacturing facilities in the United States. We met with every hourly worker. We were there at 11:00 p.m., we were there at 5:00 a.m. We met with every person in the whole organization and related our strategy, our vision, our values, and the issues to every one of them. We told them why this change was important and why we were doing what we did. We had to continue to communicate this message. Rather than having formal written communications between the operating committee and the teams, I had informal progress reviews. Our progress reviews amounted to a lunch once a quarter where we had the team leader and operating committee informally discuss how the team was doing.

## Success Factors

There were three critical success factors for our efforts: Upper management support, team empowerment, and team training.

### Upper Management Support

We tried to be supportive by asking teams questions: What do you need? What can we do to help to move the process along? Are you satisfied? Are you getting enough resources? Again, it took six to eight months to start to create the trust that we had between ourselves and the teams in order to get them to feel comfortable in bringing up problems, because they didn't want you to know what the problems were. That was one reason why I eliminated formal reviews and written reports: there was more time going into the written reports than there was into other efforts, and I did not want that.

We also allowed the action teams to determine the strategies and the timeliness; we did not set them. For example, in one case we totally empowered them to design a new product. One of the major things that we learned was that upper management support is critical. I had one situation at the beginning where the teams weren't doing as well as they should, and I didn't know what the problem was. We had trained all the teams, but I had not trained the operating committee. I thought I had buy-in; but I didn't. One of my directors was stonewalling the whole process. We decided that we should train the operating committee off site, so we went away for three days and went through a training process. We completed the training on a Saturday at noon. On

Monday morning one of my directors came in to me and said that he could not sleep all weekend: he couldn't buy in to this, it was not his style. As a result he left the division and went to another division where he was more comfortable, and we brought someone in who could buy into the process.

The key point I am trying to make here is that unless you have 100 percent buy-in and 100 percent support by the management committee, this process does not work. The management committee was responsible for the planning, and the director-level sponsor played a very critical role because he was the bridge between the team and the operating committee. He was the one that got the team resources, he was the one that got the team whatever they needed, and he was also the one that had to referee a lot of the conflicts that the team had with middle management.

*Team Empowerment*

What does it mean when I say that we tried to totally empower the teams? There is a lot of talk about empowerment today, and everybody has a different opinion about what empowerment is. The best example that I can give you about team empowerment is the following. We had a product that was new to the world. We were going to surround it with seven patents, and we were going to manufacture it in a totally different way than we had ever manufactured anything else before. Our new manufacturing process required a very large turnkey machine, and the one we found was outside the United States and cost a significant amount of money. Any of you who work for a big corporation know what it takes to get a significant purchase approval through the process—25 signatures and many questions. Why do you need it, what color is it, and so forth. What the team did was to visit the manufacturer, and while they were there they placed the order without authorization. The risk and the down side of that action was a 10 percent penalty if we canceled the order. They were comfortable at this time to take that risk so they placed the order. The paperwork went through, but what they didn't tell me was that they had shipped it air freight. As I look back, it was their decision and it was a good decision. Because they shipped it air, they saved six weeks. If you consider that they were trying to cut the time in half to get to the market, then the team saved themselves six months in just those two decisions. These six months paid off at the other end of the process; we made up more than the difference on the freight when we introduced the product.

*Team Training*

I think training is one of the most important factors for successful cross-functional teams. One of the things we found out when we started looking at other companies that were in the process of putting together cross-functional teams, was that many of them put the teams together and walked away saying, "Go invent something." And they didn't do the proper training. We did. We had an outside consultant perform a lot of training. Each team went through three days of training on interpersonal skills, group dynamics, strategies for conflict resolution, and how to conduct meetings. On the last day they wrote their own mission and charter. Then I came in and sat down with each team for several hours and talked about the vision; I talked about the importance of what they were doing, about why their success was important to the division, and why it was important to the company. I got buy-in from each of these teams.

As I mentioned earlier we had 11 teams. Some people were on more than one team, yet they had to go through the training with each of their teams. It was important that the team went through training together because it helped each person understand the differences in the way people approach problems and recognize that there are a variety of different ways to approach those problems. Training also helped the teams understand how we resolved conflict and that the important output is the end result. Training became a very integral part of the process.

## Implementation

There are also three major implementation issues that I want to cover briefly: risk, budget, and middle management.

### Risk

In terms of risk management, we found—and I think this is quite interesting—that teams chose a degree of risk that was appropriate for the best chance of their success. The higher risk strategies tended to decrease team buy-in. But, on the other hand—and this surprised us—the teams' interest was lost when considering lower risk strategies. A lot of people lost interest when the risk wasn't high enough. So it was important that the team decide what the risk level should be.

Externally dictated constraints can affect the risk level. For example, we had one case where I set a time window for a product; I had set the time line rather than having the team do it. This created an enormous amount of problems because it put too much pressure on the team when the risk level went up too high. We were supposed to introduce the product on January 1, and they came to me right before Christmas and said they could do it, but they thought they could make a better product if they had six more months. So I took them off the hook, the risk went back to the right level, and six months later they did come out with the right product. So you cannot force a team, and if you try to force it, you really force the risk level to a point where the team is very uncomfortable. We did learn, however, that the action teams—and we called them "action" teams rather than cross-functional teams—combined "urgency" and "high probability of success" in their own strategies. The teams were willing to take on higher risk projects than they would have taken on as individuals.

## Budget

Budget control, the second implementation issue, is an area that middle managers love. If you are compressing the amount of time to go to market, then you are accelerating the budget by a factor of two or more, so the budgets get way out of whack. If you have "controlling" type people, they get a little uncomfortable when their budget is double what it is supposed to be. Comfort with this situation is important, and we need to make it clear that spending the money up front is okay as long as we are going to see results at the back end of the project. But you need to communicate that clearly to the teams because if you don't, a tremendous amount of friction will result in the total organization.

## Middle Management Concerns

Middle management is by far the biggest challenge of the three issues. In our organization, middle managers had a lot of control over their resources. One result was that the people who were working for them, and who were also on a team, experienced conflict. For example, these people had less control of their individual performance because now a team could say, "You ought to go to Peoria on Thursday," and their manager could say, "Hey, wait a minute, I don't want you in Peoria, I want you here because you have to do your other job." We had a lot of conflicts between middle managers. They were uncertain of their roles, and they were not a part of the decision-making process at the beginning of our whole teaming effort.

During the process an interesting change occurred: the power base shifted away from middle management. We conducted two audits on these teams because we wanted to find out if we were kidding ourselves, or if our plan was really working. We worked with Anne Donnellon from Harvard Business School who was studying the teams as we evolved. In exchange for allowing her access to our teams, I asked her to do an audit. I also had another company do an audit. What we found was an enormous power shift. As shown in Figure 2, there are three kinds of power: personal power, position power, and information power. And prior to cross-functional teams, the power base of each category of personnel looked like the left-hand columns in the figure. As you can see, the supervisors and the managers had a tremendous amount of information power before the shift took place.

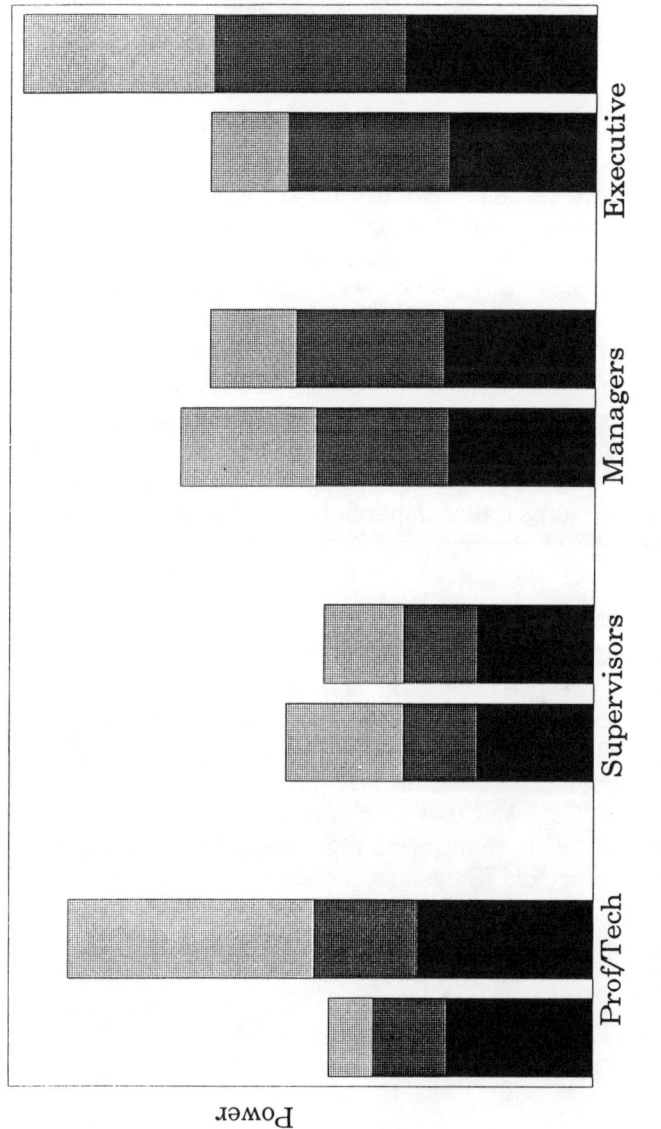

■ Personal Power   ■ Information Power   ▨ Position Power

For each category of personnel, the left-hand column refers to its power position before the shift; the right column to power distribution after the shift.

*Figure 2.* Power shift.

What we found was that 50 percent of the middle manager's job was filtering information up and down the organization. That was what they did, that was where they got their power. When we put the cross-functional teams in place—and we had a sponsor who had a direct bridge from the cross-functional team to the operating committee—the power shifted. As shown in the right-hand columns in Figure 2, the result was that middle management didn't have the power they had before—they were out of the information loop and they didn't know what was going on.

In order to include middle management in the program, we had to go back and train all middle managers in the same areas in which we had trained the team members: the processes, interpersonal skills and group dynamics. Then we had to make them more responsible for results, get them involved in the activities and reward them for the success of the teams and the success of their people on the teams. Finally, we increased their involvement in the *strategic planning process*, so that they felt they were involved. We achieved buy-in from them for both the operating committee and the cross-functional teams.

In the audit we interviewed just about everyone who was on a team. One of the interesting things that was said was this quote, "In a company of this size management is not managing technology, they are managing people. If they manage people correctly, people will manage the technology correctly." I think we sometimes forget this important idea, because we get too concentrated on managing technology, and we forget that, really, what drives our success is people.

*Effective Teams*

In review, then, *an effective team is made from trust, vision, dedication, challenge, expertise, mutual goals, leadership, time and patience*. Teams who were performing well had a great sense of ownership, there was full participation from everyone, the decisions were made by consensus, and there was a win-win climate. The teams took care of their own problems. We had several issues where we had team members who were not performing, so the team threw them off. They did it, they did not come to us, they took them off and got someone else.

Struggling teams had the following characteristics: there was no listening, there was problem avoidance, they couldn't get to the issues, there was majority rule where you had the team leader managing on a hierarchial basis, and there was a win-lose climate. Those teams did not do very well.

Figure 3 shows you what I feel are good team leadership characteristics.

*Action Teams*

The teams were *highly focused* on new products, and each worked on one product only. They had very *specific charters* that they wrote themselves. The

- An equal member of the team
- Highly motivated
- Shares vision
- Excellent facilitator
- Identifies the critical issues and addresses them
- Able to resolve conflict among the team members and among other members of the organization
- Realistic in approaching problems and setting objectives for the team
- Diplomatic

*Figure 3.* "Good" leader characteristics.

teams were *short-term, high-energy* units. That means the team was created to develop a product in a specific time line that it chose and at the end of that time, the team was disbanded. It was not like a traditional business development unit or an on-going team. The teams were *interdisciplinary*, but not functional "representatives." What I mean by that is that we did not choose people because they were a Ph.D. chemist or because they had some specific talent in a given area. We chose people who were good team players. We could bring the other ones in as needed. One of our speakers this morning mentioned one of his outstanding marketing people that nobody could work with. We get some of those guys, too. You don't put them on the teams. You do use their expertise; however, they are never a member of the team, they are brought in as consultants. I indicated that in a lot of these teams there were eight to 10 people but there could have been 40 or 50 people who were involved in the total process. The team members did change as we moved through the process.

The last three action team characteristics which were very important were *top-down support, team leadership* and *sponsorship*. Full top-down support was key. Give them strategy, give them the plans, and get out of the way and stay out of the way. You have to choose a good team leader, someone who is willing to have the characteristics that I showed earlier. Also, the sponsor-director played a very important part as the bridge between the team and the operating committee. The sponsor-director was the one who had the responsibility of getting the resources that the team needed and resolving the conflicts.

# CONCLUSION

In a very short period of time I tried to give you what we did, how it unfolded, and some of the conflicts we encountered. I can tell you we started in 1984, we did in fact introduce new products very rapidly, we did in fact reduce the time by half, and I can tell you that today—in that division—teams are part of the culture. It took about four or five years before we got everyone into the process and achieved a cultural change. That's the way they manage it today, and the business has gone up tremendously. When I took over the business we had 12 percent of sales generated from new products each year. The minimum target with 3M at that time was 25 percent. I just checked last week and they are beating the 3M goal. I have been out of it now for several years, but it is being managed the same way. By now, it would be very difficult to go back to the old way, because the people in the division would not stand for going back to the other type of an organization. It is a very highly effective way to organize and to run your business.

By the way, at the time of this presentation two plants, one in England and one in the United States are shifting totally to self-directed teams.

I will let Figure 4 sum up our experience of what factors make for effective teams.

- Trust
- Vision
- Dedication
- Challenge
- Expertise (Interdisciplinary)
- Mutual goals
- Leadership
- Time and patience

*Figure 4.* What makes for effective teams?

# REFERENCES

Dumaine, B. (1993). "Payoff from the New Management: Thermos Replaced its Bureaucratic Culture with Flexible Interdisciplinary Teams." *Fortune* December 13: 103-104, 108, 110.

Katzenbach, J. R. & Smith, D.K. (1993). *The Wisdom of Teams: Creating the High-Performance Organization.* Boston, MA: Harvard Business School Press.

# PRODUCTIVITY, QUALITY, AND CUSTOMER SATISFACTION AS STRATEGIC SUCCESS INDICATORS AT FIRM AND NATIONAL LEVELS

Claes Fornell

## INTRODUCTION

My concern is with the measurement of economic output—by nations and by firms. That is, the quantity of goods and services produced, their prices, and their quality. National competitiveness and standard of living depend on productivity, as well as the quality of what is produced. Productivity, which has to do with the quantity of output per input (such as the number of hours it takes to build a car), has been measured for many years. Price likewise. Quality has not.

This is about to change—many firms are already assessing quality on a continual basis, including its impact on customer satisfaction. However, for the economy in general and for national competitiveness in particular, there is a need for a more systematic and comprehensive evaluation of quality. There is no good reason for leaving out quality as we track other indicators of the economy, such as prices, production, and productivity. In fact, we cannot accurately interpret price changes or productivity without taking quality into account. Nevertheless, price indices are often compared without any quality adjustment at all.

National Economic Research Associates pose the question, "What does it mean to observe several quarters of rapid price increase if we don't know what has happened to quality?", and suggest that the Federal Reserve is likely to interpret the price increase as evidence of inflation and move to increase interest rates. But is this the appropriate remedy? Conversely, when our economic output declines, there are calls for increased productivity. For example, economist Lester Thurow has stated that America's chances of owning the twenty-first century depends on the answer to a single question: Can we get our productivity growth rate up to the levels of our principal rivals?

## PRODUCTIVITY MEASURES ARE NOT ENOUGH

Poor productivity is usually implicated as the ultimate villain for the weakening of our national competitiveness. Recent improvements notwithstanding, conventional wisdom points to a productivity crisis in the United States, as evidenced in expert testimony before congressional committees, using sagging productivity as an explanation for the stagnating standard of living, as well as for problems in our balance of trade. This reasoning is well founded in economic history; it goes back to scientific management and Frederick W. Taylor. Its relevance in today's economy is never questioned. But it is time to do just that: To what extent do the models of smokestack economics and vintage manufacturing industrial engineering apply in an economy where manufacturing accounts for no more than 20 percent of the total, and where manufacturing itself involves more and more *service* as the final product is marketed? Bizarre as it may sound, it just might be that U.S. productivity is too high rather than too low!

Productivity, as it is measured, reflects *quantity* of output relative to input. If productivity is so critical for economic success, maybe we should benchmark against other industrialized nations that do well and avoid the mistakes of those that do poorly. The Organization for Economic Cooperation and Development (OECD) calculates production per capita. Even though the gap between Japan and the United States has narrowed some, the U.S. lead in 1990 was still very large at about 35 percent—a lead that has grown even larger in 1994. The American economy was founded on principles of mass production. Today it continues to operate from a distinction: *superior delivery of quantity*. The United States produces more output per unit of input than any other nation.

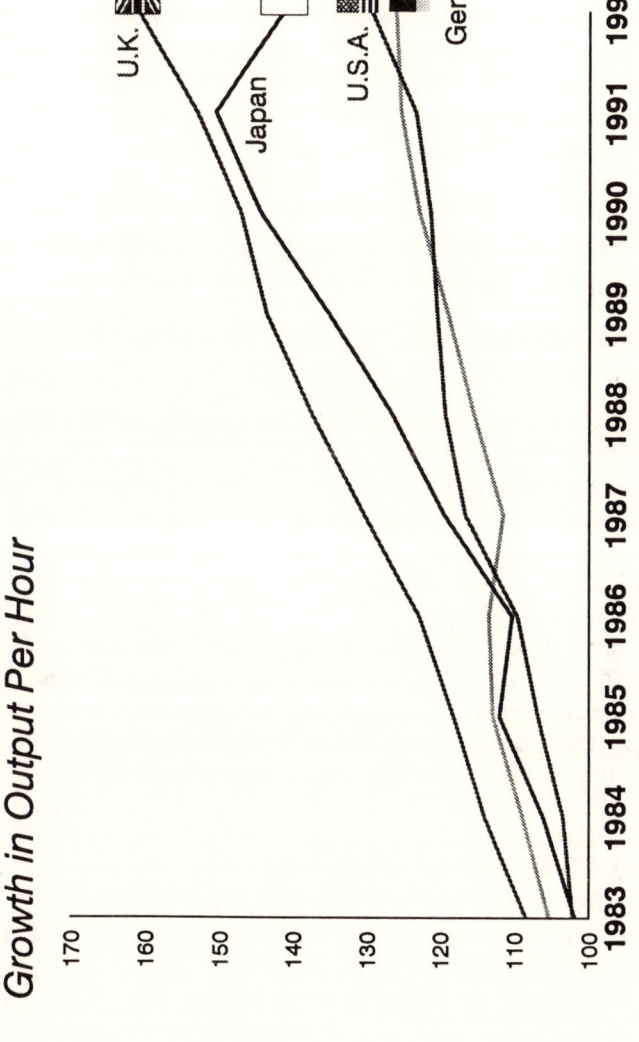

*Figure 1.* Manufacturing productivity: Growth in output per hour for the U.S., Japan, U.K., and Germany.

Let us continue our benchmarking, using Bureau of Labor Statistics data on productivity *growth*. Some readers may be surprised to learn that between 1982 and 1992, the United Kingdom shows 47 percent higher productivity growth compared with Japan. Japan's average annual growth was 4.1 percent; the UK's growth was 6.1 percent.

Is it possible that our 100-year-old obsession with improving productivity now leads us down the wrong track? Standard of living and national competitiveness are not merely determined by efficiency in production. The quality of what is produced matters, too. But, *quality* is not adequately captured in our productivity measures.

We may conclude that increased productivity is a worthy goal, but only to the extent that it does not adversely affect other sources of economic growth. It is also true that increased quality in manufacturing can lead to higher productivity via lower costs (less re-work, fewer complaints, less down- time, repairs, etc.)—*but only up to a point.* As we get closer to six sigma or "zero defects production," where are additional quality increases to come from?

## PRODUCTIVITY-QUALITY TRADEOFFS IN SERVICES

Greater demand for customer service in the manufacturing sector, combined with the fact that the service sector itself by far dominates the economy, makes the suggestion somewhat dubious that "quality is free" (or that costs always decline with better service). A few examples: More children per worker in day care centers increase productivity of day care services, but does it also increase quality? When department stores shift towards more self-service, productivity goes up. But what about quality?

With due respect to total quality management (TQM), economic principles dictate that superior levels of service will, in a majority of situations, cost more than poor or mediocre service. The belief that quality and productivity will *always* go together assumes that the essence of quality is absence of variability as captured by such terms as six sigma or zero defects, consistency, and conformance to specifications. But if quality is to affect not only costs but also *customer satisfaction and revenue*, quality may also mean flexibility, innovation, variability, customizing, and personal service—things that usually have an adverse effect on productivity. Yet these are the very things that are becoming increasingly important in global competition. *The objective is no longer zero defects but zero customer defections.*

So far, the point is simple: According to most statistics, the U.S. has a large lead—relative to the two other major economic powers—in overall productivity. Is this true for quality as well? Is it really plausible that high productivity also means high quality? Those who look to Japan for guidance usually come up with an argument that goes something like this: The Japanese have already demonstrated that quality and productivity are complementary rather than contradictory. Just look at automobiles!

Even in this category, however, it is far from obvious that productivity and quality are congruous. First, it is not really the case that the Japanese are more productive—their assembly operations are, the part suppliers are not. Second, as competing firms approach parity in quality of manufacture, the services associated with the products become the differentiating factors and a main source of competitive advantage. Obviously, there is much more to selling cars than their manufacture. Consider the Lexus cars as a case in point. Widely regarded as one of the best quality autos, they also have, compared with other automobile companies, much lower service productivity. Lexus spends more dollars on dealer training and dealer support than does any other automobile company. *As far as service goes, this has translated into superior quality, but lower productivity*—a typical tradeoff situation.

Consider now what has happened to productivity in the service sector as such. As shown in Figure 2, contrary to manufacturing, there is clear evidence that service productivity has declined and there is great worry over this. In an international comparison, the level of service productivity is still high, but the worry is that other countries will catch up. To the extent that quality in service involves a high degree of personal service, one may just as well worry about the opposite: that productivity is in fact too high and *the decline in service productivity has not gone far enough*! If this is true, the reduction in productivity may be because the service sector is beginning to respond to a demand for improved quality. As it responds further with more personal service, more customization and personnel empowerment, productivity may well continue to go down. Recent trends, however, point more toward traditional thinking: Productivity in services has shown rapid growth in the early 1990s.

## QUALITY AND ITS MEASUREMENT

Let us now address the problems of *quality measurement*. Like productivity, quality can be measured at different levels, from the firm via the industry to the national economy. The focus here is on the firm, although the author directed the development of a National Quality Index (NQI) for Sweden and the American customer satisfaction index (ACSI) for the United States. Over 200 years ago Adam Smith observed that production has but one single purpose: to serve consumption. Any overall measure of quality, therefore, should be taken at the level of demand or consumption—not at the level of supply or production. *It is the customers' subjective evaluation of quality and their subsequent purchase behavior that determine the rate of return on any investments in quality.*

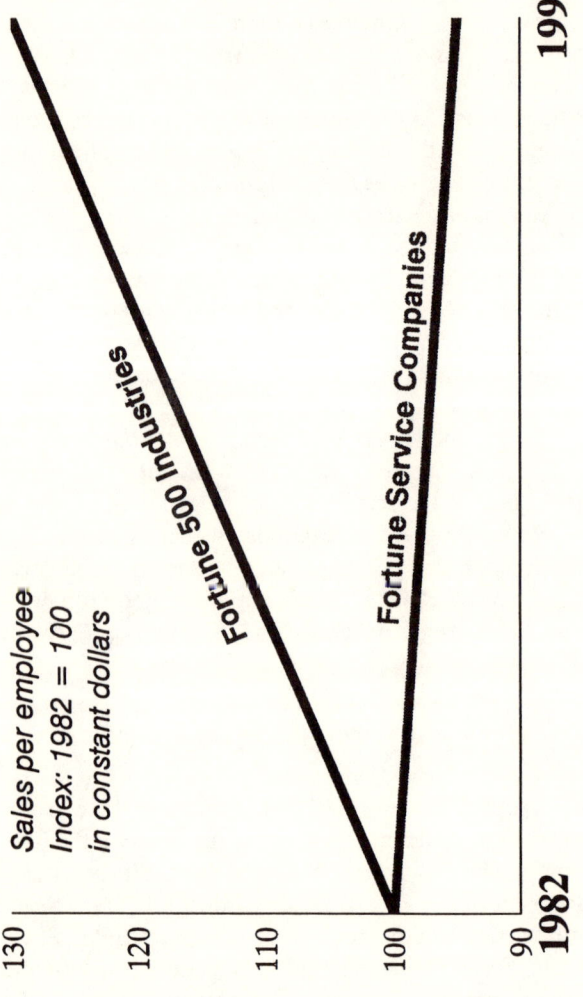

*Figure 2.* Productivity gap.

This means that we have to look beyond current definitions of quality, such as the following:

- Absence of variation
- Conformance to requirements
- Fitness for use
- Six sigma, or even Zero defects
- Exceeding customer expectations
- Customer satisfaction without explicit linkage to behavior
- Even delighting the customer will not do

All those concepts of quality have their uses (TQM and ISO 9000 come to mind, for example), but none of them is as broadly relevant as the definition posted above. Unless quality either shifts the demand curve upwards or substantially reduces costs, investments in quality will not pay off financially. A shift in the demand curve means that the return on the quality investment is captured in higher margins, a higher degree of customer repurchase, or some combination of the two.

Any overall quality indicator will be based on customer satisfaction data and constructed in such a manner that it can be linked to financial returns. The risk of improving quality aspects that the market is not willing to pay for will thereby be reduced. As illustrated by Figure 3, ideally there will be an index at the firm level, at the industry level, at the sector level, and at the national level. As a result, weak (and strong) sectors of the firm as well as the economy can be identified and monitored.

At the national level, aside from helping to bring the balance of productivity and quality into perspective, the quality index should also contribute to a more accurate picture of economic output which, in turn, would be conducive to better economic policy decisions and subsequent improvement in standard of living. At the firm level, the quality (customer satisfaction) index will also be a powerful tool in the planning of integral strategy. At all levels, demand shifting customer satisfaction, as a measure of quality, is both a leading and a lagging indicator. It is lagging in the sense that it reflects how the firm or industry has done; it is leading because customer satisfaction is a strong indicator of future business.

Traditional accounting-based figures may say more about past decisions than they do about tomorrow's performance. In contrast, customer satisfaction is a result of past decisions with strong implications for strategic planning in the firm. It is also possible that a uniform nationwide quality index might promote more economic stability and long term perspective. Disappointing quarterly earnings may have less of a negative impact on Wall Street if accompanied by strong customer satisfaction results. Higher levels of customer satisfaction and loyalty also promote economic stability because they facilitate

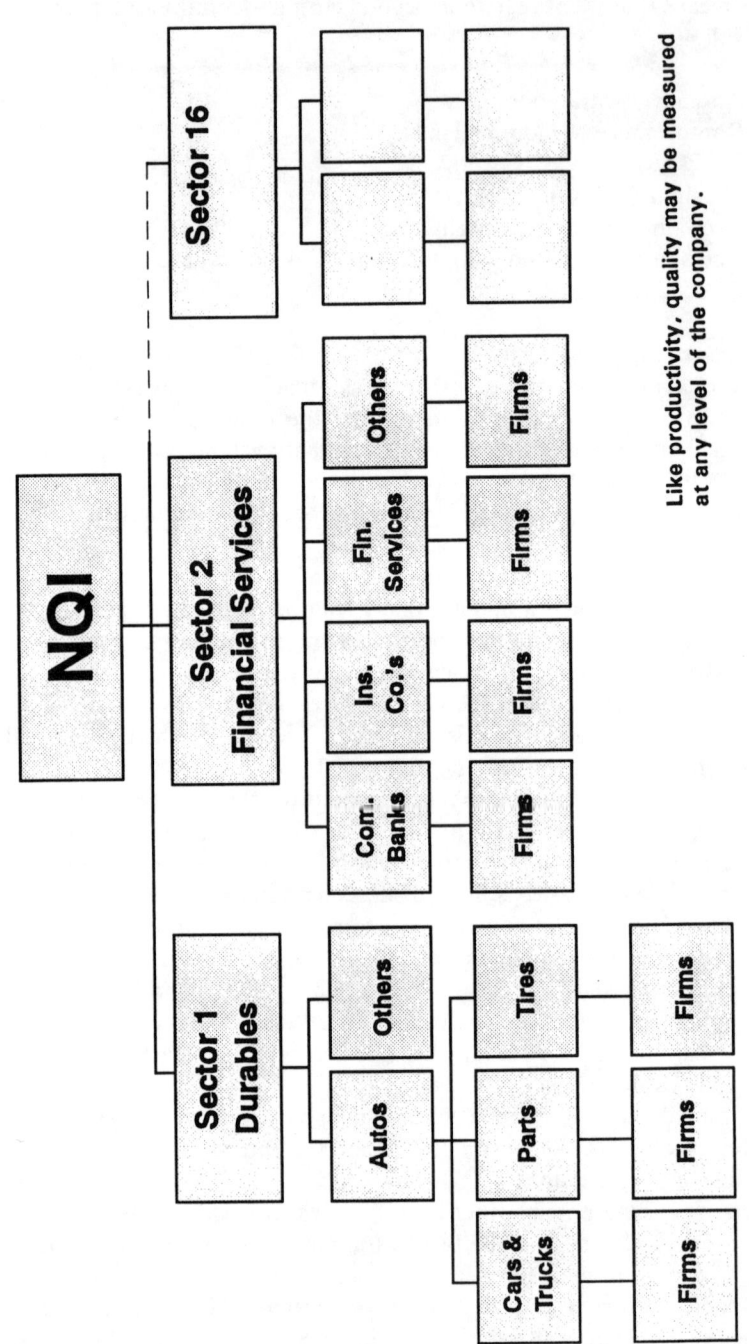

*Figure 3.* Quality indicators at various levels.

business planning and increase the dependability of the buyer-seller relationship.

Quality, as measured by customer satisfaction, is a part of subjective economic welfare. The idea of letting the individual have a voice in the determination of his/her welfare (beyond "voting with their dollars") seems as essential to the concept of a market economy as it is to personal liberty and democracy. The control of productive resources by anyone other than consumers restrains economic freedom and may limit economic growth. The traditional argument against it—that subjective experience is irrelevant to scientific analysis because it is not publicly observable—can now be laid to rest. There have been extraordinary advances in scientific measurement technology in the past 10 to 15 years. Not only can we measure what we cannot see, we can also incorporate these unobservable variables into cause-and-effect systems of equations. The same type of methodology can be used at all levels of the economy, as demonstrated by the Swedish example.

## CUSTOMER ACQUISITION VS. RETENTION STRATEGIES

At the level of the individual company, it is useful to distinguish between two basic strategies shown in Figure 4: The offense and the defense. The offense has to do with customer acquisition; the defense with customer retention.

For most firms, a good defense is critical—it contributes much more to profit than does the offense. This is not to suggest that the offense is not important, but one may wonder if we have paid enough attention to the defense. Consider what has happened to automobiles, cameras, food processors, radial tires, or banking, to mention a few industries with large market share losses to foreig· competition.

There are two basic forms of the defense: switching barriers and customer satisfaction. Switching barriers are things that make it difficult, costly, cumbersome, or even illegal, for a buyer to change supplier. Customer satisfaction is what makes the customer "a willing" repeat purchaser. Most successful firms have a combination of the two.

What is the value of a good defense? Let us look at a very simple example. Take the case of consumer banking. The average bank loses 10 percent of its customers per year. That is, the customer retention rate is 90 percent. What would be the effect of raising this to, say, 92 percent? Let us think in terms of the overall objective of the business firm—the maximization of the present value of future cash flows. What is the value of 90 percent vs. 92 percent retention rate? At 90 percent, there is a ten-year customer turnover—there are, thus, cash flows for ten years. At a retention rate of 92 percent, however, the customers last 12.5 years. That is a 25 percent increase. In other words, a mere two percent increase in retention produces a 25 percent increase in future cash

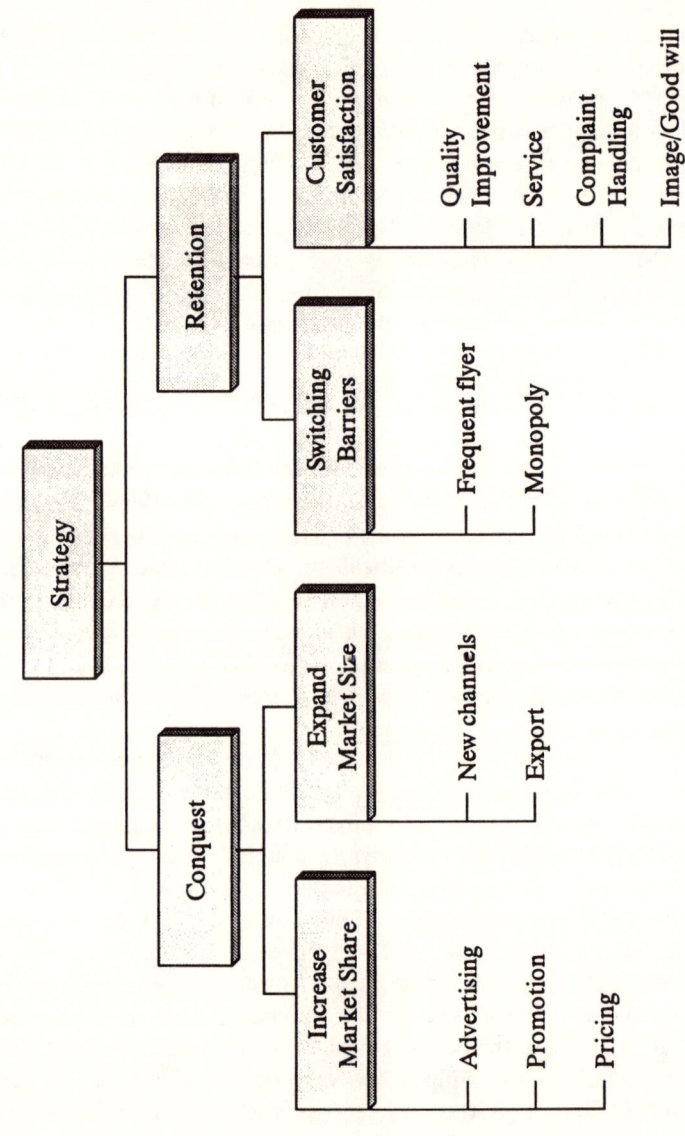

*Figure 4.* Conquest vs. retention strategy.

flows (present value calculations ignored). At lower customer retention rates, the effects will be less spectacular, but often dramatic.

## A QUALITY-SATISFACTION-PERFORMANCE SYSTEM

The question now is, How do we accomplish this? How do we succeed in increasing customer retention? As already implied, the answer does not lie in Total Quality Management. TQM often shows somewhat disappointing results, because it does not address two basic laws of economics: diminishing returns and efficient resource allocation. All quality efforts will, sooner or later, experience diminishing returns—when the cost of quality increases more than the return. Further, most quality improvements will have differential impacts on customer satisfaction and economic returns. The task is to allocate resources in such a way that those quality improvements that have the highest return are achieved. How does one identify those quality aspects? Obviously, one cannot ask the customers what is important. Customers do not know what will give the highest return to the firm. They can't even tell you why they do what they will do, for example, buy more, pay more, be more loyal, and so forth. They can, however, provide valuable information on how well or poorly a supplier performs on a number of quality dimensions. Armed with this data, it is possible to set up detailed cause-and-effect equations, tailor-made to individual firms. Space does not permit details here, but it is certainly possible to devise a system whereby those quality components whose improvement will lead to the greatest effects on economic performance are identified and tracked. Mathematically and statistically this is not straight-forward, but it has been done. In outline form Figure 5 presents a so-called Quality-Satisfaction-Profitability (QSP) System.

From customer survey data, the quality components to the left are rated in terms of what the customers think of the firm. The impact on a customer satisfaction index is estimated. The impact of customer satisfaction on various economic performance measures is also estimated. This enables the firm to allocate resources to those quality components that have the greatest impact on financial performance, and, at the same time, to avoid those quality improvements that the market is unwilling to pay for.

## SUMMARY

The relationships between customer satisfaction and profitability, as well as productivity and customer satisfaction, are positive in general, but there is a point beyond which returns become negative. On the other hand, the relationship between customer retention and revenue has no such diminishing returns, but the cost of keeping the last 1 percent of the customers is likely

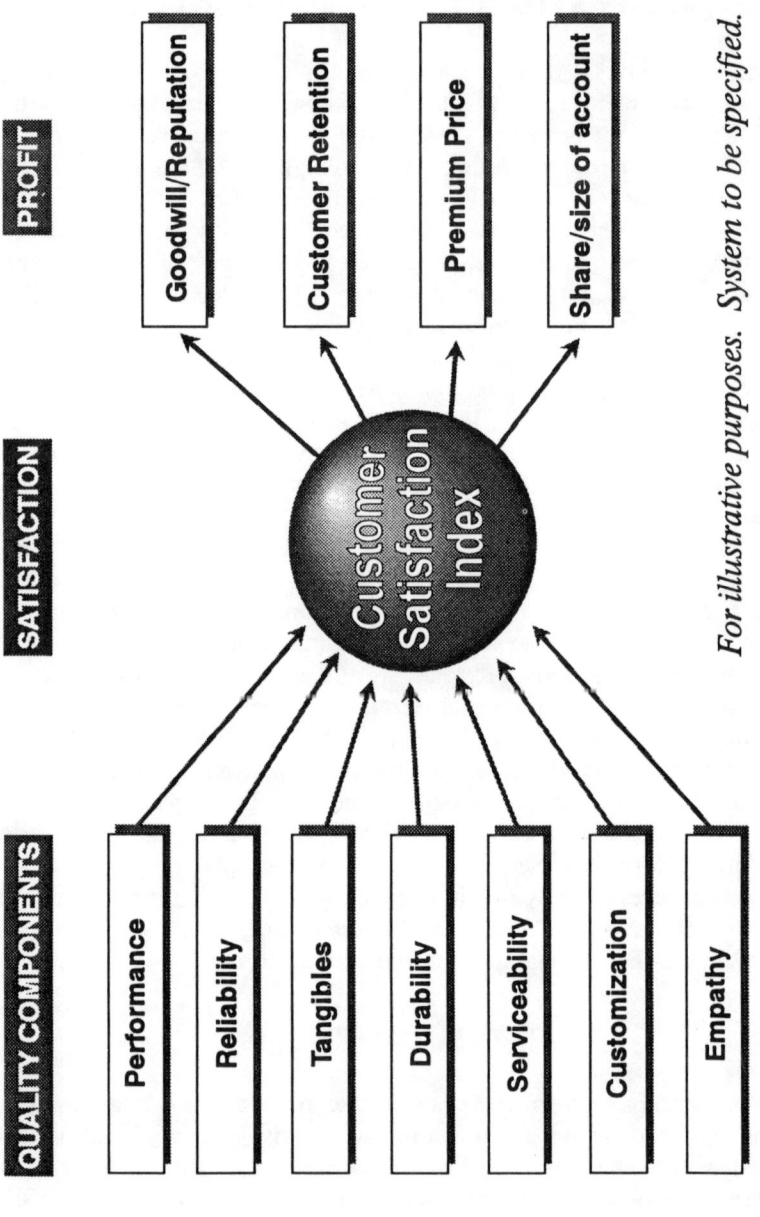

*Figure 5.* A complete quality-satisfaction-profitability system.

to be prohibitive. There are quite a few cases where firms have attempted to find the relationship between profitability and customer satisfaction and failed to find anything but a flat line. This is due to either inappropriate measures of profitability or poor measures of customer satisfaction. We know that customer satisfaction and long-term company financial performance tend to go together (Anderson, Fornell, & Lehmann, 1994), just as we know that intelligence and scholastic performance go together. We also know that both satisfaction and intelligence are not only matters of degree, but also multidimensional in nature. This requires advanced measurement techniques. Fortunately, such techniques are now available, and constantly being improved upon. If we were to measure intelligence in the same simplistic manner that satisfaction all too often is measured, we might have people indicate, on a 5-point scale from very dumb to very smart, how intelligent they are. The result is not likely to be very informative—nor is it going to be predictive of scholastic performance. Therefore, it is not surprising that many firms fail to find a relationship between their customer satisfaction measures and economic returns. The relationship is there, but it is not detected by simplistic measurement devices. We know this because the ultimate judgment of quality is in the eyes of the beholder: the customer.

## REFERENCES

Anderson, E.W., Fornell, C., & Lehmann, D.R. (1994). "Customer Satisfaction, Market Share, and Profitability: Findings from Sweden." *Journal of Marketing*.

Fornell, C. (1992). A National Customer Satisfaction Barometer: The Swedish Experience." *Journal of Marketing, 56*,(1): 6-21.

Fornell, C. & Robinson, W.T. (1983). "Industrial Organization and Consumer Satisfaction/Dissatisfaction." *Journal of Consumer Research, 9*, (4): 403-412.

Fornell, C. & Wernerfelt, B. (1987). "Defensive Marketing Strategy by Customer Complaint Management: A Theoretical Analysis." *Journal of Marketing Research, 24*, (4): 337-346.

Fornell, C. & Wernerfelt, B. (1988). "A Model for Customer Complaint Management." *Marketing Science, 7*, (3): 287-298.

Fornell, C. & Westbrook, R.A. (1984). "The Vicious Circle of Consumer Complaints." *Journal of Marketing, 48*, (3): 68-78.

# DISCUSSION

## Allen Paison, Chair

*Kathryn Britney:*
Are there separate training programs for the team leaders, or is there a support system for the leaders to help them think through some of their questions and issues? From my point of view, and some of the organizations I have worked in, I would be hard pressed to find people within the organization to serve in that role without consultants or someone to help them think through some of the issues.

*Hershock:*
The leaders went through the same process with their teams. The second time around the leaders were all volunteers. We did put leaders through some training then, but that was an afterthought. As I said, this was an interim process, and there was not much written about it. But, yes, we did go back and put them through some leadership training. At the beginning we did not, they just went through the same training as the rest of the team.

*Hans Thorelli:*
To what extent does this "sourdough" spread throughout the 3M company?

*Hershock:*
We started with 11 teams. Two of the 11 teams canceled their product. They felt the product was not right, and they came to us and we dropped it. From the new product area of that division, the teams have now spread into the manufacturing area and into all the other areas of the organization. I do not know the total number of teams. We have been using this process now at 3M with some fairly good success. But it really comes down to the issues of

leadership and buy-in. They have also had some failures where we didn't get the buy-in, or the leadership was not there to drive the process through. A lot of people are very uncomfortable with this. For example, controller type people are not going to be very comfortable with the process of letting go. So we have had some great successes, but we have also had some failures. But we are moving ahead and each division now has a responsibility of going through the whole process of putting in at least one cross-functional team.

# Research in Global Strategic Management

Edited by **Alan M. Rugman**, *Faculty of Management, University of Toronto*

REVIEW: "The book is good and definitely worth reading for those interested in the effects of EC development."
—*RCSA/CJAS*

**Volume 5, Beyond the Diamond**
1995, 294 pp. $73.25
ISBN 1-55938-434-4

**CONTENTS:** Introduction, *Alan M. Rugman, Julien van den Broeck, and Alain Verbeke*. PART I. STRATEGIC MANAGEMENT AND INSTITUTIONAL DYNAMICS: A GLOBAL PERSPECTIVE. Transnational Networks and Global Competition: An Organizing Framework, *Alan M. Rugman and Alain Verbeke*. The Strategic Management of Multinationals in a Triad-Based World Economy, *Daniel van den Bulcke*. PART II. THE DYNAMICS OF NATIONAL COMPETITIVE ADVANTAGE: METHODOLOGICAL PERSPECTIVES. A Critical Analysis of Porters Framework on the Competitive Advantage of Nations, *Leonard Waverman*. The Generalized Double Diamond Approach to International Competitiveness, *Chang Moon, Alan M. Rugman and Alain Verbeke*. Are Diamonds Forever? An Industrial-Economics Perspective, *Marc Jegers*. PART III. STRATEGIC MANAGEMENT AND INSTITUTIONAL DYNAMICS: THE ROLE OF GOVERNMENT. Government, Institutional Dynamics and Competitive Advantage, *Frans van Widen*. International Strategic Management and the Dynamics of Government Policy, *Rudy Martens and Koen Vandenbempt*. PART IV. STRATEGIC MANAGEMENT AND INSTITUTIONAL DYNAMICS: THE EU AFTER 1992. Institutional Dynamics in the EU, *Marc de Clercq*. Competition, Strategic Management and Industrial Restructuring of Europe After 1992, *Leo Sleuwaegen*. Author Index. Subject Index.

Also Available:
**Volumes 1-4** (1990-1994) $73.25 each

**JAI PRESS INC.**
55 Old Post Road # 2 - P.O. Box 1678
Greenwich, Connecticut 06836-1678
Tel: (203) 661- 7602   Fax: (203) 661-0792

# J A I P R E S S

## Research in Strategic Management and Information Technology

Edited by **N. Venkatraman** and **John Henderson,**
*School of Management, Boston University*

**Volume 1,** 1994, 184 pp.     $73.25
ISBN 1-55938-782-3

**CONTENTS:** Editors Introduction to the Series, *N. Venkatramana nd John Henderson.* Organizational Fit and Flexibility: It Design Principles for a Globaly Competing Firm, *Sirkka L. Jarvenpaa and Blake Ives.* A Model for the Investigation of Linkage Between Business and Information Technology Objectives, *Blaize Horner Reich and Izak Benbasat.* The Determinants of Business Unit Reliance on Information Technologies, *V. Sambamurthy, Robert Zmud, and Andrew C. Boynton.* Integrating External and Internal Perspectives of Strategic Information Technology Decisions, *Rajiv Sabherwal and John H. Grant.* The Develpment of Instruments to Assess Information Systems and Business Unit Strategy and Performance, *Uolande E. Chan and Sid L. Huff.*

> **FACULTY/PROFESSIONAL** discounts are available in the U.S. and Canada at a rate of 40% off the list price when prepaid by personal check or credit card and ordered directly from the publisher.

**JAI PRESS INC.**
55 Old Post Road # 2 - P.O. Box 1678
Greenwich, Connecticut 06836-1678
Tel: (203) 661- 7602     Fax: (203) 661-0792

# Advances in Strategic Management

Edited by **Paul Shrivastava**, *Department of Management, Bucknell University,* **Anne Huff**, *College of Business and Commerce, University of Illinois* and **Jane Dutton**, *Graduate School of Business Administration, University of Michigan*

The *Advances in Strategic Management* series is a vehicle for communication of new research in the field of Strategic Management. The scope of the field is defined broadly. It includes, but is not limited to, work on traditional topics, such as, goal formulation, environmental analysis, strategy formulation, strategic decision processes, strategy implementation, strategy evaluation and control, top management teams, corporate and business unit strategies, international strategic management, mergers and joint ventures, etc.

The series is also committed to expanding theory and analysis of Strategic Management beyond these traditional topics. It welcomes papers that examine non-traditional topics, report exploratory but highly significant ideas, use innovative methods, provide critique of existing ideas, and build bridges between Strategic Management and other business and Social Science disciplines.

Papers presenting theoretical and/or empirical analysis of strategic problems, comparative and analytical case studies of strategic issues, and application of concepts, models, and techniques to strategic problems are welcome.

Papers of any length conforming to any standard style format (APA, ASA, etc.) should be sent to the editors. Papers will be reviewed by the editors and external reviewers where necessary.

**Volume 12,** 1995   (2 Part Set)                          $146.50
ISBN 1-55938-269-4

Volume Editors: **Paul Shrivastava,** *Department of Management, Bucknell University and* **Charles Stubbart,** *Center for International Business and Culture, Southern Illinois University at Carbondale*

**Volume 12 - Part A - Challenges From Outside the Mainstream**
1995, 305 pp.                                               $73.25
ISBN 1-55938-981-8

**CONTENTS:** Introduction, *Charles Stubbart and Paul Shrivastava.* CHALLENGES FROM OUTSIDE THE MAINSTREAM. Journal Ranking Naciraema Ritual: The Case of

I.C. MacMillans Publishing Forums, *Alex Stewart.* Commentary, *Alan Meyer and David Preston.* Commentary, *William B. Gartner.* The Thrill of Victory and the Agony of Hainv to Compete: An Ethical Critique of a Myth About Competition, *Daniel R. Gilbert, Jr.* Commentary, *William D. Roering and Lawrence J. Lad.* Strategic Management as Domination and Emancipation: From Planning and Process to Communication and Praxis, *Hugh Wilmott and Mats Alvesson.* Progress and Its Discontents: Data Scarcity and the Limits of Falsification in Strategic Management, *Joseph Lampel and Zur Shapira.* Commentary, *Joseph T. Mahoney.* Mainstream and Radical Theories of the Multinational Enterprise: A Critical Review and Sysnthesis, *Marc T. Jones.* Commentary, *Jean J. Boddewynn.* Towards a Reconcilliation of the Theory-Pluralism in Strategic Management - Incommensurability and the Constructivist Approach of the Erlangen School, *Andreas Georg Scherer and Michael J. Dowling.* Commentary, *William McKinsley.* Interactionism and Systemic View in the Strategic Approach, *Lucia Zan.* Commentary, *Tony Simons.*

**Volume 12 - Part B - Challenges Within the Mainstream**
1955, 208 pp. $73.25
ISBN 1-55938-982-6

**CONTENTS:** Introduction, *Charles Stubbart and Paul Shrivastava.* CHALLENGES WITHIN THE MAINSTREAM. Managing Strategic Change: Power, Paralysis and Perceptive, *Cynthia Hardy.* Commentary, *Peter J. Frost and Vivien Clark.* Next Steps for Corporate Strategy, *E.H. Bowman.* Core Principles: A Blackl Hole of and for Strategy Theory Building and Buildoro, *Coral R. Snodgraoo and Lawronoo R. Jauoh.* Commentary, *R. Duane Ireland and Gary R. Carini.* A Comment on the Relevance of Strategy Research, *C. Gopnath and Richard C. Hoffman.* Commentary, *Marjorie A. Lyles.* The Diffusion of Strategic Management Frameworks, *Alfred A. Marcus, Robert S. Goodman and David N. Grazman.* Commentary, Eric Abrahamson. Organizations are Activity Systems, Not Merely Systems of Thought, *J.C. Spender.* Commentary, *Dennis A. Gioia and Ajay Mehra.* Toward a Non-Economic Centered Resource Baseview of the Firm: Continuing the Conversation, *Alan L. Brumagim.*

Also Available:
**Volumes 1-9** (1983-1993)        $73.25 each
**Volumes 10, 11** (2 Part Set)    $146.50 each